Women of the Way

Women of the Way

Discovering 2,500 Years of Buddhist Wisdom

SALLIE TISDALE

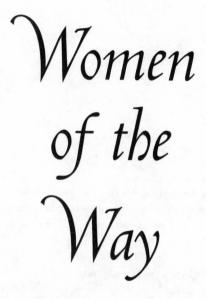

HarperSanFrancisco
A Division of HarperCollins*Publishers*

HarperCollins books may be purchased for educational, business, or sales promotional use. For information please write: Special Markets Department, HarperCollins Publishers, 10 East 53rd Street, New York, NY 10022.

HarperCollins Web site: http://www.harpercollins.com
HarperCollins®, ®, and HarperSanFrancisco™ are trademarks of HarperCollins Publishers.

FIRST EDITION
Designed by Joseph Rutt

Library of Congress Cataloging-in-Publication Data

Tisdale, Sallie.
Women of the way : discovering 2,500 years of Buddhist wisdom / Sallie Tisdale.—1st ed.
p. cm.
Includes bibliographical references.
ISBN-13: 978-0-06-059816-7
ISBN-10: 0-06-059816-6
1. Buddhist women—Biography. 2. Buddhist nuns—Biography. I. Title.
BQ850.T57 2005
294.3092'2—dc22
[B]

06 07 08 09 10 RRD(H) 10 9 8 7 6 5 4 3 2 1

Dedicated to all the old women, refreshment sellers, little girls, rice cake vendors, laywomen, princesses, wandering nuns, courtesans, and goddesses who endlessly preach the Dharma in countless stories and are never named.

CONTENTS

INDIAN ANCESTORS

AFTERWORD: THE NEW ANCESTORS

Acknowledgments

I want to especially acknowledge my sangha at Dharma Rain Zen Center, for making room for these names in our daily services and listening to me talk about them these many years. I would also like to thank my many other friends in the Dharma who have helped with this project, including the community of Great Vow Zen Monastery; Blanche Zenkei Hartman, Roko Chayat, Dai'en Bennage, Abbess Aoyama Shundo, and Zuiko Redding for important leads and information; Alison Yuko Krieger, who brought me warmth when I was cold and lots of chocolate; Fathai Fasue of the Miao-Fa temple; John Wong; Jan Chozen Bays and Laren Hogen Bays for hospitality; Tomoe Katagiri; and Katherine Thanas, Wendy Egyoku Nakao, Mitra Bishop, and Grace Jill Schireson for support and encouragement early in the project.

Many scholars and librarians have contributed to this book. I wish I could name them all, but as is often the case, many helped me graciously and anonymously. I am especially grateful to Patricia Fister, Miriam Levering, Tom Kirchner, William Bodiford, Ding-hwa Evelyn Hsieh, Amy Ching-fen Tsiang and the research librarians at the University of California at Los Angeles; Yongping Guan and the research librarians of Lewis and Clark College; Linda Walton and the librarians of Portland State University; Willow Zheng; Rosario Aglario; and especially Judith Boltz, for her selfless offer of time and experience in translation.

In Japan, one is always treated with courtesy, but I offer my humble thanks to Goda Tetsuzō at Yōkōji; Yashki Chijō of Sōsenji Temple, who showed me where the Enzūin had stood; Kensho Miyamae and his whole family for hospitality and guidance; Maeda Naomi at the Institute for Zen Studies; Tadahiro Kondo for guidance in Kamakura; and Hiroko Takada of the Nara National Museum for spending many hours doing what I couldn't do, and for a new friendship.

I was aided in my nascent study of Japanese and Japan by Mikio Daicho Ohgushi, who also helped with the translation. Friends who read and commented on this manuscript include Sylvan Genko Rainwater, Jeffrey Kenryu Binns, David Kakumyo Lowe, and Dawn Domyo Sater. Domyo has been instrumental in shaping the final form of the dedication chant. David Choten Robinson read between the lines.

Portions of the essay, in substantially different form, originally appeared in *Tricycle* magazine and *Buddhist Women on the Edge* (North Atlantic Books, Berkeley, 1996). My editors at HarperSanFrancisco were Anne Connolly and Gideon Weil, and, as always, Kim Witherspoon was my agent and knight in armor.

I owe a debt to the many nameless guides, security guards, taxi drivers, temple attendants, train conductors and bus drivers who steered me in the right direction—sometimes by sending me in the opposite direction than I had intended to go.

Lastly, I cannot say the words to thank my teacher, Kyogen Carlson, for all the ways he has thwarted me these many years.

INTRODUCTION

Bright Grass

Some years ago I visited Eiheiji, the Zen temple established by Dōgen in 1243 in the mountains of rural Japan. I was traveling from temple to temple with my Zen teacher and several fellow students, stopping only briefly in each place.

We accidentally arrived at Eiheiji on a festival day, and there was no one ready to receive us. The guestmaster hurried off and eventually returned with a young man named Taiken, an awkward fellow with thick glasses and somewhat limited English skills. He gave us a short tour of the public part of the temple, then showed us the English-language tourist video.

"Do you have any questions?" he asked carefully when it was finished. The video had been full of beautiful pictures of monks walking in the snow and chanting by candlelight.

"Are women allowed to practice here?" I asked, knowing the answer.

Dōgen was a medieval man who brought a radical element of equality to Japanese Buddhism. He was by no means the first to state unequivocally that enlightenment and Buddhist accomplishment was possible for everyone. Many male Chinese teachers had women students, including laywomen, who were recognized as teachers and masters. But Dōgen is emblematic to Zen Buddhism; he is one of the great poets of our inner experience, a person of supreme intellect and rigorous practice. Eiheiji was Dōgen's attempt to create a perfect monastic world at a time of upheaval in both Japan and Buddhism. He moved to these isolated mountains with only a small community of students. At Eiheiji he hoped the "pure standards" of Zen monastic life could be taught and perfected, and when he came, he brought with him both men and women.

Today Eiheiji is a training temple almost entirely limited to young Japanese men who serve in neighborhood temples. Guests can stay for a few days in a separate building. Officially, there is no rule against women practicing in the training temples, but women don't practice here. Few Western men do either. On the great mountain gate at Eiheiji's entrance are inscribed two quotes by Dōgen. On the right side is written, "To practice here is very difficult. Even a person of high rank cannot enter the gate easily." On the left side are the words, "Anyone with a sincere desire to practice Buddhism can enter this gate freely."

"Umm, well, umm, . . ." Taiken began, seeking an answer to my rude question. Japanese people will go to some lengths to avoid saying no directly, and it cost our host some discomfort simply to answer. Many of the original buildings of Eiheiji were burned down long ago. The temple today is large and elaborate and beautifully constructed; its many buildings, each with a specific purpose, are connected by covered walkways and paths winding among tall trees and across a tumbling stream. There is a lot of room there. "Officially, yes," answered Taiken. "But we have no facilities."

Pursuing more information was at least as impolite as asking in the first place. But I had come to a place inside myself where I really needed to ask, and needed to hear the answer, even knowing it. I have loved Dōgen since I first read his words, long before I began to understand them. Eiheiji is a symbol of intensive practice—what is meant to be Dōgen's "pure" practice—and many Zen students harbor the occasional fantasy of life lived this way, and of living for a time at Eiheiji specifically. Few people actually fulfill it, in part because Eiheiji today is designed to serve a small and distinct demographic. I didn't really want to practice at Eiheiji—not at my age, not at this point in my life or training—but I had had the fantasy. More importantly, what was represented by the difference between the open heart of Dōgen and the closed doors of Eiheiji had become deeply troubling to me.

"Why not?" I asked. Why, in this big complex of buildings, at a temple more than eight hundred years old, did he say they had no facilities?

"We have not had time to build bathrooms," he said. "Someday . . ."

And to my own surprise, I began to cry. I felt a grief much deeper and more potent than I had suspected. I felt a kind of outrage at this official explanation, at the casual dismissal of half of us from this particular world.

This book is a collection of stories about women throughout Buddhist history who are crucial to our history as Buddhists, and as Zen students in particular. Many became masters in their own right. These names form a line roughly from the time of the Buddha to the late twentieth century, and at my home temple they are chanted every other day as those of ancestors deserving our attention and respect.

When I began practicing Zen almost twenty-five years ago, I knew little of Buddhist history, and nothing of its treatment of women. I realize now what a remarkable introduction I was given. I received the precepts from Jiyu Kennett, the first Western woman—and one of the only women ever—to train at Sojiji, the other national Sōtō Zen training temple in Japan. My teacher, Kyogen Carlson, was one of her chief disciples for many years in the monastery she founded, where men and women live side by side. In a variety of settings I've seen male and female monks and lay students practicing and living together, men and women holding equal rank, men and women taking turns in each ceremonial and administrative role. This is the normal Zen world to me, to my teacher, and to many American Zen Buddhists.

As a feminist, I was sensitive to sexism in other arenas, but I practiced for years before I saw it in my religion. I gradually came to see that equality is not the norm for most Buddhists. I saw this, but I didn't believe it. I heard stories about the inequitable treatment and sometimes outright abuse of women by Buddhist authorities, and I found a way to dismiss them—for a while.

On a sunny afternoon, browsing the shelves at my temple library; on a rainy evening, pulling out book after book at the university library; late at night, perusing my own shelves; year after year, reading histories, anthologies, diaries, commentaries, scriptures, collections of poetry and art—I realized at last that most of the huge body of literature is all about men, written by men, and addressed to men. I don't think it is necessarily intended to be this way, and I firmly believe the Dharma is not about this. But many commentaries and histories of Buddhism do not discuss the experience of women at all—literally, not at all. It is as though being a man is what being a Buddhist means. Women are a different matter; they exist in footnotes and parenthetical asides, where they exist at all.

In some ways this is the worst thing. This is the slippery part. Instead of insults, there is a closed door; instead of blunt refusal, there is only a gentle denial, or no answer at all, as though the one asking were a child who didn't merit an explanation. The worst thing is not having to walk out the gate at night in the cold, but having to walk out the gate at night in the cold to go to separate quarters while the men sleep in the meditation hall. It is this polite assumption of the default position, the feeling of being forgotten, the amnesia.

Such invisibility extends in all directions. Though there are many examples in both ancient and more modern Dharma, even explicit instructions about equality and nonseparation, the institutions of Buddhism are deeply segregated. In Shingon Buddhism and Rinzai Zen, there are no women holding the highest rank in Japan. Tibetan Buddhism excludes women from the highest ranks. Theravadan Buddhism holds all women perpetually below men, regardless of seniority. Men and women do train together at several small Sōtō temples in Japan, but these are unconventional places largely catering to foreigners. The institutional hierarchy generally forbids women from practicing in the main training temples, although since 1986 the Sōtō Shu regulations permit this. (I am told that a woman could sue for admission to Eiheiji and other training temples if her request to enter was denied.) A number of Western women have found their way into various temples in Japan, but they remain the exception to an informal but potent rule. Jiyu Kennett's groundbreaking time at Sojiji did not actually break much ground.

I could understand the roots of institutional sexism easily enough. As Buddhism traveled from country to country (and era to era), it absorbed and blended with each culture it encountered. Buddhist practice can transform a person, but it doesn't remove deeply embedded beliefs easily—Buddhism doesn't cure people of their culture, and sometimes Buddhist rhetoric reveals more of a cultural agenda than a spiritual one. The separation of men and women has become so deeply embedded in most cultures that it seems natural to many people, and so it seemed reasonable in a religious context.

The historian Patricia Ebry notes that in China people routinely wrote family histories describing property and parentage without mentioning any women at all—every mother, every daughter, every wife, left out of the lists. Should we be surprised that the names of accomplished Buddhist women weren't always kept in the official records? In ancient India women were expected to be dependent first on a father, then a husband, then a son. They were thought to be like children with ferocious libidos and were carefully controlled for this reason. Is it any wonder that nuns were too?

The historian Miriam Levering, who has translated records listing a number of female Dharma heirs of Chinese masters, believes not only that there were many transmitted women with heirs of their own in China, but that this history was lost through centuries of selective record-keeping and cultural suppression. In Japan, Keizan and his immediate disciples, writes the Buddhist historian William Bodiford, "certified a number of women as Zen masters, fully authorized to administer ordinations and to lead monastic funerals and other ceremonies.... [Some] founded their own lineages within the Sōtō order.... There must have been many more nuns at medieval Sōtō monasteries than current records indicate." Why do we know so little about them? "[Because] most Sōtō nuns conducted their training in small hermitages located outside the monastery gate. They were always under the supervision of the male Zen teacher and monks of the monastery, unable to assume any positions of monastic authority."

For these disparities to continue now has to mean one of two things: either women are being denied the same access to training and authority as men, or women aren't as capable of understanding the Dharma as men. Either possibility is unacceptable to me—and, I think, to the Dharma. Unequal treatment is so clearly at odds with basic Buddhist principles that I found it difficult at first to understand how it could be policy. A foundational belief of Buddhism is that the attributes of the self are without essence—all that makes a person a unique individual changes continually and eventually dissolves. We are each of us becoming something new, ceasing to be what we were, all the time, and those things we tend to think of as "self" are impermanent and fleeting. We are taught in our first lesson as Buddhists that to grasp at something as permanent is the very source of suffering. For the rest of our lives as Buddhists we contemplate this tendency and all it implies and generates. To treat men and women unequally is to act as though gender *were* permanent, eternal, with intrinsic self-identity—exactly the opposite of all other phenomena. It is to contradict the teaching.

In most cultures, in most countries, in most periods of time, a woman's life is difficult by virtue of being a woman. Some sects of Buddhism eventually taught that a woman suffers from inevitable evils or "obstructions," such as having to leave home to be married, having to give birth, being neglected when she is old. Since no one wants to live with such things, no one would want to be born as a woman.

The *Sutra of the Past Vows of Earth Store Bodhisattva* describes the bodhisattva Kshitigarbha, commonly known as Jizo. The sutra states: "If there are women who detest the body of a woman, and who full-heartedly make offerings to Earth Store Bodhisattva's image ... they will never again be born in worlds where there are women, much less be one.... From the power of the meritorious virtues resulting from these offerings to Earth Store Bodhisattva, they will not receive the bodies of women throughout hundreds of thousands of tens of thousands of aeons." By the time Buddhism came to Japan, the existence of things like these evils of a female birth were not a symptom but the explanation for the problem. If women were creatures of neutral value, their conditions would be neutral—like men's. Since their conditions are negative, women must be negative, must have "moral and ontological inferiority," in the religious historian Bernard Faure's words. Buddhist men, "unable or unwilling to distinguish between biological constraints and the arbitrary constraints imposed by society," perpetuated these constraints in the spiritual realm.

What Faure calls "the Buddhist 'rhetoric of equality' " has a long history, but that equality has "remained general and abstract." Instead, marbled throughout the enormous Buddhist canon are many kinds of comments and stories, both old and new, describing women as less compassionate than men, limited in wisdom, and jealous and obstructive by nature.

The *Udayanavatsaraja-parivartah*—*The Tale of King Udayana of Castasa*—in the *Maharatnakuta* says, "Women can destroy pure precepts. They retreat from doing merits and honor. Preventing others from rebirth in heaven, they are the source of hell. . . . The dead snake and dog are detestable, but women are even more detestable than they are."

John Stevens cites two old Chinese Buddhist sayings. The first says, "If there were no women, every man would be a bodhisattva." The second adds, "The best thing about Buddhist heaven is that it has no women."

We may be willing to see Jizo's vow to help a woman be born as a man as an acknowledgment of the desperation and suffering many women are condemned to by their gender. Personally, I would prefer a vow to free all beings from such damaging prejudices as misogyny—for what are we to make of this twentieth-century commentary on Jizo's vow, written by Tripiṭaka master Hsüan Hua?

> First we will discuss the Five Obstructions. The first is that women are not able to become the Great Brahmā Lord because that position is accomplished through purity, and the body of a

> woman has a great many impurities. Second, women cannot become Śakra [a kind of god] . . . upon reaching the heavens their bodies become male, because only males can be lords of the heavens. Although Śakra has some desire remaining, that desire is quite light; women, on the other hand, are extremely libidinous. . . . Third, women cannot become demon kings. This is not too bad. They cannot attain this position because demons are extremely hard, solid, and firm, while women are extremely soft and weak. As soon as anything unusual comes up they are at a loss and have to seek help. . . . Wise kings have hearts of great compassion and kindness; they teach people to maintain the Five Precepts and the Ten Good Deeds. Whenever women see something good occur to others, they become jealous, and this keeps them from having great compassion. . . . Fifth, they cannot become Buddhas. Buddhas have ten thousand virtues; women have many evils. They are jealous and obstructive, and their hearts are about the size of a sesame seed.

There is a lot more where this came from.

"When sex is conceived as an important factor for attaining Buddhahood, the perfect sex is always masculine," says the translator Diana Paul. Because maleness is seen as neutral, the ideal state, the natural state, only women have gender—"gender" becomes a lack of maleness. So it is not the difference *between* women and men but the difference of women *from* this ideal state that is the problem. Femaleness, not gender, is the real problem.

A Japanese nun named Eshun was famous for her ability to turn such beliefs around, gently getting the best of every man who harassed or obstructed her. Her story may be partly apocryphal; records are scarce. What interests me in the comments I find in modern writing on Eshun is the urge to insist that she *must* be apocryphal—not so much because of a lack of evidence but because she is so brilliant. Barbara Ruch notes that one modern Japanese scholar believes she "must be a fabrication comprised of the best of many people, thereby allowing her to excel men." Too wise and steady and clever, too mature and undistracted by sex, to be a real woman.

Women are often seen as lacking some vital quality for the deep levels of the practice. Many of the men who followed the Buddha as monks left their families in poverty and disarray. A few were told to return and take care of business, but over time the willingness to turn one's back on parents, spouse, and children was seen as evidence of one's determination to seek the truth.

Women historically have had an altogether different relationship to monastic practice than men. Since they haven't been free agents, they couldn't leave their families without permission. Others weren't willing to abandon aging parents or young children. Denied permission or constrained by duty, many women studied and practiced in private for decades. Some adopted the appearance and behavior of monks—not eating after noon, shaving their heads, and so on. In certain cases, a woman who waited until she was old to be ordained was treated as proof that women lack the great determination needed for real understanding.

The strict division between the life of an ordained person and the life of the layperson is as old as Buddhism. I believe there should be significant differences in lifestyle, as they are parallel but different paths. However, we might ask whether the traditional differences are still the most appropriate ones. The religion scholar Rita Gross makes the point that most domestic acts are revered in Zen monasteries. The ordinary is made a point of reverence and attention—cooking and doing the dishes, sweeping and sewing, washing one's face and teeth, weeding the garden. Such acts are imbued with spiritual meaning in one's Zen training and used as metaphors for internal experiences; discovering wholeheartedness in doing itself, no matter what one is doing, is crucial. There is nothing sacred about sweeping the walk of a monastery, and nothing profane about sweeping the kitchen at home. But in a vast literature and endless works of art, the monk sweeping the stone walk is emblematic of a high pursuit, cast in an entirely different light than the woman sweeping the kitchen while her toddler eats breakfast. Which act is more difficult to do well, to do with mindfulness and selfless attention? What exactly makes them seem so different?

Monastic practice reveres domestic acts with one exception: monks don't do child care. Again, I am indebted to Rita Gross for making the blunt suggestion that day care would in fact be a sensible business for a Zen monastery. Responsibility for child care keeps many committed Buddhist women out of monasteries, even for brief retreats. Imagine if a woman could go to the cloistered temple and be free for eight hours of the day to do her zazen, her silent work, her study and her contemplation, while a monk cared for her baby. Cleaning toilets is considered excellent Buddhist practice. Why not diapers? Why not envision our community in these new ways? In fact, a few monasteries now have limited daycare programs

Some of the most damaging stories told about women claim we are promiscuous, lustful, and seductive by nature. In the *Aṅguttara Nikāya,* one of the earliest sources of Buddhist writings, is the line, "I see no other single form so enticing, so desirable, so intoxicating, so binding, so distracting, such a hindrance to winning the unsurpassed peace from effort . . . as a woman's form." The almost irresistible power of desire can be thwarted most readily by two things—separation and disgust. Rationalization of sexual desire is not unique to Buddhism, but a recurring story in all the major religions, and in the history of power between men and women. Men feel desire in a woman's presence; thus, desire is a woman's fault. It is something women do *to* men.

The set of traditional monastic rules of conduct called the Vinaya is much longer for women than for men. One at a time, rules were added for both men and women in response to problematic behavior, including quite specific rules about sexual gratification and the use of animals, knotholes, vegetables, and other items as substitutes for human partners. Rules prohibiting women from practices like sleeping alone at the base of trees or bathing alone in rivers were added to prevent rapes and assaults. A lot of the rules for women address lascivious and suggestive behaviors like rubbing against a monk or carving a squash into the shape of a penis for use in masturbation.

Susan Burcott, who translated the poems of the first Buddhist nuns, wonders if this obsession with a woman's lustful behavior is a way of saying "one must pass through the world of samsara, of birth and rebirth, of seduction by women, in order to reach the holy place where desire and temptation no longer exist." A monk obsesses about an idealized woman because "she is the necessary foil to his purity." Without temptation, the ability to transcend temptation doesn't exist.

Part of the concept of monastery is the creation of a place free of everyday responsibilities and choices. This doesn't mean a place free of desires, obstacles, and preferences—quite the opposite, in fact. With the usual noise of daily life removed, the objects and opinions in our mind become blindingly apparent. In the mirror formed by a blank wall, in hour after hour of zazen, every preoccupation is examined. Why don't women and men practice together in places like Eiheiji today? I have asked a number of people in positions of authority in Japanese monasteries, and the reasons I hear come down to distraction. Women are powerfully distracting to men, I am told. A few people note that men are also distracting to women. (I have yet to hear anyone mention the dilemma of gay and bisexual people.) In any case, I think both lust and romantic love are more likely problems in mixed communities.

No one seems to question why this particular preoccupation, this one opinion, this desire, is not open for examination like all the rest.

I was startled to hear from an American woman in Japan that she didn't mind the fact that she wasn't allowed to stay at her teacher's temple, because she understood how distracting women could be to the monks.

"It should be a place free of distractions," she said, "except the ones in your mind."

"Isn't lust and sexual desire something in our minds?" I asked her.

"Yes," she admitted readily. "But the monks are young, and it's a big distraction."

Japanese men have told me, quite humbly, that they enforce separation because men are weak. (One priest told me there had been a nun practicing for a time with the monks at his training temple. It was "a difficulty," he said. Why? I asked. "Because she wasn't as strong," he said. "She couldn't work as hard." "What about the old monks?" I asked. "Aren't they weaker too?" He had no answer.)

One monk told me that if men and women practiced together in the training temples, the women would still have to live separately, owing to male sexual frustration. Separating people like this, he pointed out, would be wrong, because the Dharma teaches us not to separate ourselves from each other. His solution? Leave things as they are.

There are times I can laugh about this. I am distracted by hunger, cold, lack of sleep, and physical discomfort. I am attracted to some people, annoyed by others. If I complained about such things in a monastery, I would be told to get over it—quite properly so, as one reason for such practice is to clarify our attachments and discover how we identify the self with externals. All that we are talking about here is that lust is a particularly painful sensation. Is it so much more painful than all the rest? Is equanimity so fragile? Monks who are expected to manage icy winters, sultry summers, swarming insects, hard labor, and many other difficulties in pursuit of enlightenment are unable to cope with the presence of women. Women are the one insurmountable obstacle to their practice, more than a man can bear.

I leave for last the story which is most troubling to many Western Buddhists—a story which, I suspect, has driven women away from Buddhism—that the Buddha didn't want women to be ordained and declared they should be under special discipline.

"Admission of Women to the Order," collected in the *Culla-vagga* section of the *Vinaya-pitaka,* the monastic rules of discipline and records of the early Buddhist councils, is a document that has long generated controversy. There are multiple versions of it in several languages, and its historical provenance is unproven. It presents a variety of interpretative challenges, not least of which is its date of origin. Some historians think it had to be written hundreds of years after the Buddha's death because it refers specifically to "ages of Dharmic decline," a phrase that wasn't in use for at least two hundred years after his death.

Alan Sponberg, a Chinese literature scholar, offers the fascinating theory that the "Admission" is an archetypal description of the controversy over the place of women that took place for centuries in the Buddhist community. The existence of an independent women's community was unprecedented in that culture, and to many it was unthinkable. Sponberg suggests that, as occurs in many sutras, individuals in the "Admission of Women" take various stands to represent different opinions and that the negotiations over the status of women in the story represent actual negotiations going on between various philosophical divisions of the time.

In the "Admission," the Buddha predicts that the Dharma will decline in five hundred years instead of a thousand because women become ordained and leave home. He doesn't, however, say that women cause the decline. Perhaps it is the weakness of men in women's presence that is the problem. Perhaps it is the centuries of conflict and confusion between us over this.

When I wrote the stories of the first Buddhist women, my inclination was to ignore the "Admission," but I saw that it had to be addressed. This document represents something significant in our history—no matter who wrote it and recorded it. We are challenged to understand our roots in a realistic and not an idealized way, to see the Buddha as a person and an individual, to understand the social and cultural world in which Buddhism appeared. I've come to see that the "Admission of Women" remains a comment on problems between men and women in Buddhism today.

My early disbelief did become anger after a time, partly as I realized that my apparently harmonious community wasn't as strife-free as I had thought. Years ago, my community softened the masculine references in the scriptures, and I found myself wanting to harden them a new way. I wanted to change every "he" and "him" to "she" and "her" for a time. I wanted the men to feel lost the way I felt lost sometimes—unseen, unacknowledged. I imagined chanting an ancestral line of women instead of men every day. I wanted women teachers with whom to identify, but I also wanted the men with whom I studied to catch on to the isolation that women felt. I was a bit righteous and a little bitter at times; I was plagued with petty thoughts, and I wasn't alone. Other women in my sangha felt similar distress; many of the men didn't seem to understand that distress and became distressed in their own ways. The tension in my sangha was the same tension that has rippled through most American sanghas at times—tension about gender and power and roles, about what we take from each other and what we should give.

The worst thing wasn't my hash of mild discontent. (My discontent can always find a home—that's the nature of discontent.) The worst thing was that people in my sangha, my religious community, my heart's home, felt torn and separated by the questions we couldn't avoid. We grappled with this problem as a group and as individuals for years, until we found ways to talk to each other about this struggle.

The anger faded and disappeared. I see more clearly than before how we all are marked by the past. Each of us inherits cultural beliefs without intending to do so; we are all colored by historical circumstances. I have to know my history because I *am* my history; I have to know what is true today because I *am* today.

Part of the American character is the urge to push at boundaries. We are used to differences, and most Americans are fairly tolerant, I think. We are open enough as a culture to question our own cultural conditioning—not only about gender but about race, ethnicity, nation, age, class, and sexual orientation. It also happens that Buddhist practice requires us to question our assumptions—all the dear and deeply held beliefs by which we conduct our lives. One of the privileges of being an American Buddhist is the opportunity we have to speak openly about such things and try new things. American Buddhism can justly claim to have given women a far more equal share than that given in any other culture. We have to be careful not to think that talking about it means we are free from cultural conditioning.

Only in the West do men and women routinely practice together. What seems strange to do in Japan seems strange not to do in the United States, and it is hard for many Americans to imagine not practicing together. I know of a prominent abbot in Japan who believes that a mistake was made decades ago when married priests went to America and gave us the "wrong idea" about men and women practicing together.

A number of sanghas have been shaken by revelations of inappropriate sexual relationships in their communities—almost always between male teachers and female students. Such relationships unavoidably reflect a larger social structure of disparate power. There are also many practice communities here, including communities of monastics, who have had no more problems due to gender than any other group, who have had no scandals, no extraordinary conflicts, who are able to practice together in celibacy, with respect, and who develop relationships with each other in faith.

The problems that do occur, whether they are sexual issues or power issues or just discomfort, are, to me, one more reason why we should practice together, why we should not quit, why we should try harder, in every way we can, to see past the smokescreen of our pasts. We will be able to see through gender and sexual desire only when we can see it clearly in the first place. Avoiding the problem doesn't cure anything.

Know me by my delusions; this is one of the best ways we can know each other. Let me know you by yours. We are sacks of karma. If I know your karma, I can know you. How else can we find each other? How else can we, a community of human beings, find our way?

This is part of the fine and troubling line central to Buddhist practice, the endlessly subtle lesson of bowing to our past conditioning, our habits and flaws, even as we learn to dance with and forgive them. But it is a little too easy to accept such things as discrimination and separation as simply cultural artifacts or the inevitable result of human ignorance. "We have no bath" is a kind of shorthand for avoiding an uncomfortable and quite complicated discussion that raises profound questions about culture and Zen. (As an example of that complexity, note that many public and temple bathrooms in Japan are unisex. What does the lack of a toilet mean in that context?) Discrimination—by gender, race, class, in any way—is contrary to Buddhadharma. To accept that women are equal to men—to really accept it, not just say it—is quite a radical notion; it requires action. Partial equality is not possible.

We are all haunted; the ghosts of our families and our past experiences are the dreams we make of each other. Gender is key to how we approach intimate human relationship. Whatever the reasons, we give it extraordinary power—it is a part of love and loss, pain and pleasure. It can be an obstacle, and it can be a doorway. As a woman, I sit a little differently from the men who have for thousands of years written the texts on how to sit. My center of gravity is different, my back aches with menses, I burn with menopause. The body teaches, and this is part of that lesson—we are different each from the other even as we are the same.

Women are marked by the tiny, pulsing tides of the body. We are bound peculiarly by our bodies. Women have to take care at night, even in zendos—women learn to take care all the time, to withhold something, to keep their bodies a little tense. Women learn to watch out for empty elevators and stairwells and parking garages and to drive with the car doors locked. I hear the lamentations of women, their long ululations of loss amid oceans of tears—losses unique to women and so often compelled by men. I see massive historical patterns that are not coincidental, not imagined. Yet everything about our forms, our bodies, our minds, thoughts, and feelings, is empty—that is, without intrinsic value, bound to dissolve. Gender, like bodies, comes and goes, conditioned by many things. At the same time, as with other physical characteristics like skin color, it is a kind of destiny.

Form or emptiness? Both.

In the *Vimalakīrti Sutra,* an unnamed goddess appears and lectures Śāriputra on his attachment to discrimination and differences. She says he is afraid, still bound by habitual thoughts and desires. In response, he asks, "Why don't you change your female sex?" This, to him, is still the problem. Gender is form.

The goddess answers, "I've been here for twelve years and have looked for the innate characteristics of femaleness but have not been able to find them. How can I change them?" Gender is emptiness.

When Śāriputra makes it clear that he doesn't accept her argument, she does something quite startling. Gender is form? Here it is, she answers, and in the blink of an eye turns *him* into a woman. Then she asks, "Why don't you change your female sex?"

"I can't," he answers, suddenly wishing, it seems, that gender was actually emptiness after all. "I don't know how I got this form," he goes on, and there is something plaintive there, because he is so uncertain, concerned that there is some *thing* there. Then the goddess points out that if he can become a woman, then any woman could become a man, and there is nothing essential about gender at all. Then she changes him back—and remains a woman herself, while Vimalakīrti praises her high attainment.

It is easy to be deafened by the shrillness of some of the misogyny—easy to forget how much else there is in the Dharma. In commentaries on the *Lotus Sutra* and on the *Sutra of Queen Śhrīmālā,* gender is mentioned only as a passing and unimportant quality. In the collection called the *Karuṇā-puṇdarīka-sutta,* Shakyamuni himself makes this vow: "After I attain perfect enlightenment in the future, if there is a woman who decides to become a renunciant but is prevented from receiving the great precepts and attaining her purpose, then I will not attain true enlightenment."[1]

If one sutra or commentary contradicts another, which do we believe? The sutras are supposed to be Buddha's words, but they say different things. How do we know which sutra to trust? Can we pick and choose what we like? We know as we know everything else—by feeling our way to the truth of these complex and textured words through our experience, a process of time, effort, and humility.

How to practice with this recognition is an open question. My own answer has been to turn to the ancient practice of honoring the lineage. The history of every religion is embodied in real people; in Buddhism we call that "lineage," and it is vitally important to Buddhist practitioners of all kinds. In temples and shrines, the entire line of names, from the origin of Buddhism to the present, is chanted regularly. It represents authority, teaching, connection to our past, the inheritance of religious truth. We honor our ancestors, who gave their lives to this practice, by reciting their names, investigating their lives, studying and revering their experiences—by remembering them.

While there are many lineages cited throughout Buddhism, they form a tree. The trunk is our ancient history, the earliest ancestral teachers we all share. Then a branch splits off, and another, separating from a common teacher into schools, and then into sects, splitting into finer lines as the lineage climbs toward the present. The official lineages are entirely male without exception; a few have women only in the last generation.

The conventional wisdom about Buddhist lineage is that it traces an unbroken line of teacher-disciple relationships from the time of the Buddha. The people named received their training in an intimate relationship with a teacher who recognized their mastery of it and authorized them to teach in turn. Because of these recited lines of single names, some people have assumed that each teacher would have only one Dharma heir, when in fact this is rare. Many teachers have had multiple heirs, and some have had none. The lineages are continually branching trees, looking very similar in their breadth and becoming more and more individual as the new growth is added.

The idea that each teacher has only one heir helps feed the belief that the list of names we recite goes hand to hand back to the historical Buddha without gap.

This isn't true, of course, not in a phenomenal sense. Many of the people whose names we recite were real and their lives were clearly documented. Others are shadowy figures, and some entirely apocryphal. Two of the most significant ancestral teachers, Nagarjuna and Bodhidharma, do not appear as clear historical figures at all; biographical details are sketchy at best, and mythical to some degree. Only after the Sixth Patriarch of Zen, Hui Neng, appeared in China in the seventh century does reliable historical documentation exist, and there are gaps long after that. In turn, this documentation itself—transmission records, anecdotes and koans, and so on—was based on oral traditions and only written down generations after a person died.

"These fictions were very useful to heirs of these lineages in the Sung dynasty," writes the historian Miriam Levering. "They had more authority as sons of the Buddha and as transmitters of the Buddha's awakening than members of other schools.... Perhaps Dharma transmission was always to some degree political." The lines that have come to us today are the names of those who survived political and cultural wars that destroyed or silenced equally accomplished masters. Religious lineage has a lot in common with the more ordinary form of genealogy; both are imperfect descriptions of the past. Precisely for this reason, the ancestral lineage is also a perfect description of a specific past.

Lineage is important to me personally, not just because it is part of my practice. It matters in a way that my family genealogy does not. Both represent a part of my past; the Buddhist lineage also represents my present and my future. The ancestors have, over many years of study and practice, become real and alive to me. They are models, guides, and parents as well as teachers. They are imperfect, flawed, and struggling people who were not that different from me; their awakening and transformation makes mine possible. Given that an unbroken male line is a fiction, how can there be a women's lineage at all? There can't be an official one—throughout history, very few women masters and teachers have been able to create lasting lines of students. Many have had Dharma heirs, but their lines typically last only a generation or two, through both institutional and cultural resistance. But there has always been a women's line, of a kind.

Myths express the hidden—they provide words for what is hard to describe, images for the unseen. Myths evolve through the telling of them, and in telling them to each other and to ourselves, they become other, broader myths. Telling, retelling, shaping, and reshaping, we turn the stories of our long history into a story about you and me, and in so doing we change ourselves and each other. We've known for a long time how to do this with the patriarchs; I am learning how to do this with the matriarchs as well.

In this sense, the inevitable gaps do not concern me. The story of women in the world and women in the Dharma is a story partly about fragments and gaps, invisibility, broken connections, and separation. According to the ancient Japanese history called *Nihon Shoki*, the first ordained Japanese person was Zenshin, a teenage girl who traveled to Korea for two years. Today she is largely forgotten by museums, history books, and chronologies of Japanese Buddhism. Few Japanese seem to know her name, even in the old temples. I know no more than the few comments in a very old history, but it is enough to recognize the persistence and courage of her life, her insistence on discipline and training, her willingness to risk everything for the truth. I need stories like that.

In the extensive record of the famous Layman Pang, who lived in the eighth century in China, his daughter Lingzhao appears many times. They travel together and often spar on points of Dharma. She always wins, as in this example:

Pang decided to test his daughter again. "What does this old saying mean, 'Bright, bright are the grasses in the meadow. Bright, bright is the ancient teaching'?"

"Such a wise man, and you talk like that," Lingzhao answered.

He grunted. "So how would *you* say it?"

"Bright, bright are the grasses in the meadow. Bright, bright is the ancient teaching."

Pang had no answer. Lingzhao is throwing Pang's teaching back at him, renewed and alive. To him, it is an old saying; to her, it is this living moment. All her considerable wisdom is contained under her father's name. Lingzhao is one of a thousand thousand bright pieces of grass, growing in all directions, anonymous and free. I need stories like this too.

I believe in an unobstructed, living transmission, all the way back to the Buddha—beyond the known names, the shared stories. Shakyamuni's awakening radiates freely throughout space and time, crossing all barriers of form—if it can't cross barriers, it isn't truly awakening. Lineage really represents eternity. Whether we know all the names and dates, despite wars and purges, regardless of human error, we know an unbroken transmission of truth simply because we meet the truth today. Transmission is partly a realization that there is something that is the same in another, something that the other has also seen. If we recognize something that is the same in a story, this is good. Working toward clarity, we find a place where human accidents and perfect Dharma come together and feed each other. My teacher, Kyogen Carlson, wrote the dedication, which we recite after chanting the women's lineage. It says in part that "we honor all those beings, women and men, known and unknown, who gave their lives to the Dharma for our present benefit." We have recently added the name of Nyogen Senzaki to this dedication. Senzaki was an important influence in the early years of American Zen, and he strongly supported women's practice. He had no Dharma heirs of his own. We are continuing to explore the broader meaning of this chant as a way to honor all those teachers whose lineages did not survive. Honoring those whose names are both *known* and *unknown,* those who are famous and those who struggled in obscurity—finding respect for both is essential.

Obstacles often become doorways: what we struggle with frees us. My bitterness made me long for a women's lineage, and finding a lineage has been the anodyne for my bitterness. When I began casually collecting the names of women in Buddhist history, it was for my own edification, my own reassurance. I expected to find only a few names, but to my surprise there was a bounty; our history is rich with stories. Some years ago I suddenly realized that there were enough names from enough times and places to form a metaphorical ancestral line representing many different kinds of women—old and young, lay and monastic, rich and poor. I realized that it was possible to chant the names of women who had held the Dharma, for my present benefit, from the beginning of Buddhism until today. Engaging with the stories of these women, I have been so humbled by their patient perseverance, their courage, their very lack of bitterness in circumstances much more difficult than those most Buddhist women face today, that my own difficulties are paltry indeed—and my effort to move past them even more important.

The desire to recognize the women in our Buddhist past is spreading among American Zen centers. Several centers now recite the names of the first Buddhist nuns of ancient India, either occasionally or after the traditional line. I know that such a recitation is unconventional and, to some people, inappropriate. I think we do well to remember that the greatest teachers of our history are people who moved against the stream, sometimes at huge personal cost. We recite their names, we remember them, *because* they were reformers. If we codify the lineage in such a way as to forbid more reformation when it is needed, we've lost something key in what they gave us.

Nevertheless, a line of women must always be artificially constructed. Too much history is lost for a series of names to arise naturally from the 2,500-year history of Buddhism. Only the names of the most exceptional women are remembered now—extraordinary women who were particularly adept, powerful, articulate, fearless, and persistent. In this selection are some, but not all, of the nuns known to have practiced in the Buddha's time; some, but not all, of Dahui's female heirs; some, but not all, of Tōkeiji's abbots; and so on. It is deliberately constructed to include a variety of examples and stories, because the many thousands of ordinary Buddhist women who also found their way to a great awakening, as we all can do, are lost.

This bounty of stories and names is partly due to recent scholarship by several remarkably dedicated historians and translators. I feel deep gratitude to the many scholars who have labored to bring these stories to us today. But the finest scholarship cannot rescue what does not exist. So many records have been lost and destroyed, leaving tantalizing clues. In China, for example, there are many recorded references to the poetry of educated nuns, but very little of the poetry has survived. I've found multiple versions of the same story, and sometimes the same story is told about two different women. Crucial details are missing. There are troublesome gaps in time, with few or no stories of women, especially during the centuries-long history of Buddhism in India after the Buddha's death. Scholars are likely to find points with which to quibble here, and for any mistakes of fact I apologize.

This is not a work of scholarship itself, but a narrative history, using known facts in historical context to tell the story of a life—of many lives. I have used what facts I can find to place the life of each woman in a proper context of time and culture, using her words and her teachers' words, the events of their time, wherever it is known. But I have had to use my imagination to find the lives of these women. For the imagining, I don't apologize.

I think we have the right to reimagine our past. After all, it has been told to us for a long time, through the imaginations of the men who kept the records. Partly this reimagination is a way that we change our relationship to it—we learn to see the past in a different way, a broader way, from different perspectives, and that helps us to understand what happened. As women, so long and in some cases so utterly denied access to our factual history, we have no choice but to imagine the past—with the best of intentions, with clear eyes. And lastly, being able to place ourselves in the position of another teaches us to engage with the people right in front of us in a new way. We can only guess at another's experience from inside our own, but the effort to do so can be powerful.

In the case of the specific women in this book, the known facts vary a great deal. For some women, we may know only her father's name, her birthplace, her teacher, and some small comment on her accomplishment. Even with relatively well-documented women like Miaodao, there are gaps. We know her parents, some details of her childhood, when she was ordained, and, in remarkable detail, what happened twenty years later when she met her true teacher. But what happened in those twenty years? The records of Layman Pang say that he and his daughter Lingzhao wandered for fifteen years, crisscrossing China. Where did they go? For almost all the women in these pages we have a brief record of their enlightenment—a poem, a teacher's comment, or a sermon—but nothing of their long journey toward it. How to know the shattering breakthrough, the slow transformation, the remaking of a person into one of mature awakening, except from inside our own effort?

There are practical problems not easily resolved. In bringing forth women's history, one always faces the problem of terminology. My inclination has long been to avoid using diminutive or gender-specific words like *bhikkuni, nun, abbess,* and so on. I believe that as long as there are *priests,* on the one hand, and *female priests,* on the other, women will never have a truly equal place. At the same time, I want to remember the struggles that are specific to women.

For a long time, I disliked the word *nun* for female Buddhist monastics. (My community uses the words *monk* and *priest* for men and women both.) At the same time, I now experience *nun* as a women's word for a women's world; it is semantically precise and connects to other places and times. My resistance is not to the image of a nun but to the limited equation that says "monk = priest" but "nun ≠ priest."

Until this century, the Japanese term *daiosho*, "great priest," was only applied to men. In Japan today many nuns use *daiosho* for deceased women priests, and others add the Japanese suffix *ni*, which specifies female, for *ni-daiosho*. Some Buddhist women favor such terms as *bhikkuni* and the use of *ni* because such markers help us save this history for the future. In 1986 the Sōtō-shū Administration, the rule-making body for the Sōtō Zen church, decided to abolish *ni* from the titles of female priests, the same year they ended the regulations preventing women from entering the traditional training temples. They did this without consulting any of the women concerned, and were surely surprised by their resistance to this change.

"The common opinion of the monastic women," writes Paula Arai in her important book about the lives of modern Japanese nuns, "is that removing the character *ni* also removes any recognition of them. Rather than removing the *ni*, monastic women think it would be clearer and less discriminatory to add the character *nan* [*dan*] (male) to male monastic titles." She adds that distinguishing men from women in this area is less discriminatory than not making the distinction, because "it does not allow inequities to remain hidden in vague statistics."

Historically, priests have many names—names given at ordination or transmission or by second teachers, names of the place they taught, names honoring them after death. Many women in Buddhist history are known only by a single name. Sometimes women retained their family names after taking vows, unlike men. Some may never have been given a second name; others are lost or not yet found. Many of the women's names as we know them are not "proper" names for chanting—family names and so on. But this lack of propriety in official eyes is a reflection of their history. Their names can be awkward to chant because of the varied lengths and rhythm. This too reflects a history so often awkward. The line is evolving; we are trying to create a new tradition, and by their nature traditions can't be hurried.

In my community of Dharma Rain Zen Center, we now chant our traditional lineage—entirely men, except for the last name, Jiyu Kennett, my teacher's teacher—and these women's names, alternating day by day. Saying the women's names out loud like this instead of the traditional names was uncomfortable at first. A number of women felt a wave of suppressed resentment suddenly demanding release. A number of men felt suddenly thrust into exclusion and hiddenness. Gradually our way of doing this has become just our way. It feels ordinary now, and for newcomers it is the normal way, part of what Buddhist practice means. We can move toward solving a problem sometimes by creating a space bigger than the space that gave birth to it—a bigger world.

In meditation, we place ourselves on the Buddha's seat. I believe that there we can recite any lineage in gratitude—with awe, bewilderment, humility, and love. As long as we practice, none of our ancestors are dead—our fathers are alive, our mothers are alive. The breadth and depth of teaching is seen when we expand our ancestry this way. Every line is our line, all ancestors are our ancestors.

The story is told that the great *Lotus Sutra* was spoken by the Buddha but he knew that people weren't ready to understand it. Much maturing was required, and so the Nāgas, the beautiful dragon people who live beneath the sea, took the *Lotus* and other great sutras under their protection until it was time. Then Nagarjuna was given these sutras, and they spread throughout the world like a fire, to become Mahayana Buddhism. This is called the third turning of the wheel. Perhaps there is a fourth turning still to come—the one that contains the teaching that frees us from prejudice at last. Perhaps this teaching is buried under the ocean still, in the hands of the caring Nāgas, who are saving it for us until we can understand.

Sometimes the whole construct of gender and difference, history and change, falls away for me entirely. Then *we* are truly not *many,* we are truly one, no *he* and no *she,* and we sit beside each other in intimate silence. My teacher and my students and my friends and I sit together, and when I breathe in, I breathe in their outward-flowing breath, and when I let my breath go, we sigh together. We are unstirred by the relative, by the moving, evanescent world.

Then we stir again.

As I write this in the spring of 2005, my discouragement and grief about these issues seems to belong to a time long ago. I have lived with these women for quite a while and have taken great nourishment from the depth of their persistence and understanding. They humble and inspire, the way good teachers always do, and I recite their names regularly, bringing to mind a picture of their lives when I do—their solitary steps, their devotion and strength, their upward gaze past the smallness of the places in which they sometimes lived.

I have another memory now, attached to my sorrow, balancing it. A year after visiting Eiheiji, I was staying at San Francisco Zen Center's city residence, and by coincidence so were two of the people with whom I'd been to Japan. One afternoon a Japanese monk walked into the dining room.

"He looks familiar," said one of my friends, and suddenly we realized it was Taiken, our guide at Eiheiji whose words had made me cry. He looked at us and turned around abruptly and left. A while later he returned and bowed deeply. He was ashamed, he said. He remembered us, and he was ashamed. He had done such a bad job.

"I am here now to study American Zen," he said, "and speak better English."

That evening we took him out to dinner—the three of us who had met him in Japan, and another Japanese priest and his wife. Taiken had to leave for home soon enough, to do what he was expected to do—take over his father's temple, marry and have sons. Men are bound by their bodies too.

What did he want to do before then? "See America!"

We walked out into the soft San Francisco twilight to do just that.

We ate platters of good food, went window-shopping, and then found a funny café, a kind of combination dessert shop and tavern. Standing in front of the glass case filled with tall layer cakes and cream pies, staring at the bar behind, Taiken announced, "I want to drink alcohol!" So we did that too: beer after beer, talking and laughing in a curious amalgam of Japanese, English, and dramatic gesture.

"I do not want to go home and get married," he said, beginning to slide politely sideways in his chair. "I want to stay in America."

"I want to stay where men and women practice together. Everyone mixed up together." It was a good night.

MYTHICAL ANCESTORS

The Buddhist canon in its entirety fills hundreds of volumes. Much of this is taken up by sutras, which traditionally means the words of a buddha, a fully enlightened being. Many of the sutras are short, simple stories or lectures, often called discourses, told by the historical buddha to his followers. They arose from an oral tradition and were used to expound and explain the teaching. Sutras are intended to invoke awe and faith as well as understanding, to comfort and instruct, to affirm and inspire. Buddhist belief includes the existence of uncountable buddhas in uncountable buddha realms, both before and after this particular world and its buddha, and some of the great sutras take place in this universe. An extraordinary ease with unbounded space and time marks many of these sutras, which may be the most blissful and miraculous of all religious literature.

Sutras are marked by particular qualities, though within those qualities they vary a great deal. The language of the sutras is formal. Some are funny, and most are filled with deliberate (and sometimes mind-boggling) repetition. The central concern is always the nature of enlightenment itself. Most include lessons or lists, some are oral histories of debates and events, and some use archetypal and mythical imagery, including the kind of everyday miracles common to religious myth. Certain characters appear again and again, fulfilling particular roles. Śāriputra is often presented as a dull fellow who needs to be instructed repeatedly in order to understand the teaching. Mañjuśrī represents wisdom. Ananda sometimes speaks for the Buddha, in his role as living memory.

The blurred boundaries of concrete reality and the world of the formless fill and define the great Mahayana sutras, which describe a universe of flexible time and space. The Buddha easily appears in multiple worlds, in many places and times, sometimes in many worlds at once. He walks in the air, levitates his audience, builds temples in the sky, or transforms the environment in order to make a point. Flowers rain from the heavens; music fills the world. There is little or no barrier between the human world and the worlds occupied by other beings, such as dragons, demons, gods, and bodhisattvas. The characters in sutras move readily from form to form, life to life, world to world, appearing in each other's places and times effortlessly. Their names evoke great qualities—Energetic Power, Lion's Foot, Diamond Matrix, Forest of Virtues. Prophecies are made, predictions fulfilled, and the merit of many lifetimes comes to fruit.

In such a malleable literature, Māyā, whose story is told in several places, including the very long *Avatamsaka Sutra,* is able to die in the human world and later appear elsewhere, in the world of the gods. (The *Avatamsaka Sutra* is so long and repetitious that its main stories are collected in a separate appended chapter, the "Entry into the Realm of Reality," for ease of reading. It is from this section that I've taken the latter part of Māyā's story, as well as that of Prabhūtā, found elsewhere in the world of the gods.)

The dragon people, or Nāgas, appear in many stories throughout the Buddhist canon. The Buddha preached a very brief sutra to them, in which he says that theirs is a rebirth of extraordinary beauty. The Nāga princess, who has no name but whose story is famously told in the *Lotus Sutra,* demonstrates the ease with which a wise being can transform from shape to shape. Her story has been interpreted in more than one way over the years. My own interpretation is based in a careful reading not only of the short section in which she appears but of the *Lotus Sutra* itself, which is devoted to the universality of enlightenment.

Another woman of the Nāga realms appears in the *Sutra of Sāgara, the Nāga King,* also called the *Ocean Dragon King Sutra.* (The sutras are deeply interrelated, and so are their characters. King Sāgara is the father of the nameless princess.) Another dragon woman, known by the name Silk Brocade and other titles, meets the Buddha in this sutra when he travels to the dragon's kingdom beneath the sea.

Queen Śhrīmālā is a figure we know little of these days, but whose lectures and miraculous meeting with the Buddha were well known in historical Buddhist China and Japan. Her story, the *Śrīmālādevīsimhanādasūtram,* or the *Lion's Roar of Queen Śrīmālā,* at last available in English (from Tibetan and Chinese translations), was widely read and lectured upon historically, but today it is little studied. I think this is unfortunate, and not only because in her short but challenging tale the Buddha insists that the story be kept alive. It begins, like many sutras, with Ananda's memory: "Thus have I heard," says Ananda. "The Buddha commanded that Kausika and I keep this story alive, telling it again and again, sharing it with all the gods and people of all forms."

The following stories are taken directly from the sutras but are cast in my own words. Those familiar with these sutras will notice that some of the repetition, especially the repetition of cosmic and miraculous images, is missing, as a concession to the storytelling and the modern reader. The context of time and place is added in some cases. There is no substitute for the original, of course.

the mother
Mahā Māyā

Māyā's name meant "free from deceit." She was raised with her sister Gotami in the Kolyan clan. They lived in the town of Devadaha in the foothills of the Himalayas, where the high fields filled with larkspur and poppies in the spring. Houses perched on steep hills below white peaks. Brooks tumbled past spruce trees with orchids growing in their roots; the wild tea was a dozen feet high, and the sun strong and white when it crossed the peaks. In summer the meadows bloomed with rhododendrons, and in winter the cedar and fir trees were draped with snow, and mountain sheep broke slowly through the drifts below their home.

Māyā grew up cheerful, fearless, and full of fun. Her more serious sister sometimes despaired of Māyā, but she also delighted in her. When the sisters were of age, they married Śuddhodhana, the tribal chief of the Śākyas.

Not long after their marriage, Māyā had a strange dream about an elephant with six long, perfect tusks. The elephant was white as milk, white as the mountains where she had been born, and it shot out of heaven and entered her right side. She saw an enlightening being in the sky above her emanating light from his entire body, and the light entered her body from the head down, filling every pore. Each ray had the names and magical properties of enlightening beings, and in Māyā's dream they became spheres, filling her. What a wonderful feeling, this being full was—spheres drifting through spheres without obstruction, everything in harmony. She saw a Great Buddha on his lion's throne, the congregation of beings attending him, the wheel of the teaching, turning. Then her body became the size of the world, and her belly expanded until it was as big as space, so big that innumerable beings could enter it.

The next morning she told Śuddhodhana about the dream, and the beings who had entered her. "They walked around taking steps as big as the universe," she recalled. "I know it sounds strange, but you know what dreams are like—it seemed perfectly normal. In the dream I knew that I had done this before, countless times. What do you think it means?"

Śuddhodhana called for a seer who specialized in reading dreams, a bent old man who smelled faintly of cardamom. The seer thought it was a very good dream—profound, mysterious, important. Together they looked at Māyā, who was sitting on her cushion, serenely, with a little secret smile. For a moment the king felt a bit lost, as though they were separated by oceans, by a great and new difference between them.

"I suspect she is pregnant," said the old seer. "And if I'm right—and you know I'm usually right—the baby is going to be something special indeed. A great ruler of some kind, but what kind? We will see," he murmured, already turning to go. "We will see, we will see."

Māyā was more comfortable, healthy, and strong being pregnant than she had ever been in her life. She felt as light as air, walking through the cool hallways of the palace with her feet barely touching the stone floor. She had no complaints, no distress—she thought it was lovely to be pregnant. Meanwhile, Gotami became pregnant as well, and together the sisters strolled the palace grounds, arm in arm.

One day Māyā was seized with the desire to go to the garden of Lumbinī, and Śuddhodhana sent her off in a palanquin with all she could want: attendants, midwives, musicians and garland-makers, healers and cooks.

Walking by the stream, Māyā felt weak all of a sudden and lay down under a natural ceiling of mahua trees, heavy with sweet flowers. The trees woke up and bent down to spread a bower over her, the first of many strange things that day. The crowd of servants surrounded her in a hushed circle. Perfume gradually filled the air, and unseen bells began tinkling. On the bank of a crystalline stream she spread her legs and the baby slipped free. His body was shining gold, his eyes were blue and clear, and a lock of hair fell between his eyebrows. His toes were webbed. On the sole of each of his feet there was the sign of a thousand-spoked wheel.

Then everyone gasped, because the baby stood and walked for seven steps. Behind him, in each footprint, a white lotus bloomed. Then he stopped, raised a finger to the sky, and spoke: "This is my last birth," said the infant, who did not seem young at all. "I am born for the welfare of the entire world." Water the color of moonlight rained down on him.

Māyā saw all this through a veil; she was slipping away already, sliding into sleep, hot and satisfied with the slow pulse of fierce, almost unbearable love, like all new mothers.

She was carried back to the palace, the baby lying beside her, solemn and silent. Who would believe he had ever spoken? But he rarely closed his eyes. Māyā was feverish by the time they arrived and never left her bed. Gotami rushed to her, Śuddhodhana sent for the doctors, but Māyā was done with this life. Birth and death are just moments, mere breaths, and when the time comes to slide from one to the other, there is no point in resistance. She had grown past the suffering that cannot be avoided by even the luckiest of creatures. She slipped away without struggle into the inexhaustible light of abundance, the sublime, the omnipresent, the unspeakable, the inexpressible—that is, into love.

Māyā was able to do something most of us cannot: she retained her consciousness after death and chose a rebirth in which she remained herself, fulfilled. In another realm, a realm of gods and bodhisattvas, she met Sudhana, a student of the Way who was on a great quest and seeking guidance. He knew what he wanted to do, but like the rest of us, he didn't know how to start, how to go about things, and so he wandered from teacher to teacher, asking a lot of questions and getting a lot of answers—some confusing, some not.

When he met Māyā, she was sitting on a throne built like a great jewel lotus. Bells sounded, and their chimes turned into the names of all the buddhas. Jewels hanging in the air reflected all their forms.

Māyā was magically able to look at all beings at the same time. To each person she appeared as that person wanted to see her. Not surprisingly, they all wanted her to look just like themselves. So to this one, she looked like this one, but more beautiful, and to that one, like that one, only in its most perfected form. Because she could see all the eras of time rising and falling about her, she knew what each being needed and how to provide it. She was, in other words, filled with enlightening beings, exactly as she had dreamed.

Sudhana, on his long quest, came to see her. He thought she looked a little bit like himself, and this was wonderful. He bowed, and then asked, "Please tell me, noble woman—how does an enlightening being achieve omniscience?"

"My own liberation," she told him, "is one of knowing great vows. I was the wife of Śuddhodhana and the mother of Siddhārtha, who was born miraculously. But he was only one of many miraculously conceived children of mine, each of them an enlightening being. It began in a world called Elevated, in a land known as Supreme Lionlike Majesty, in a city known as Possessed of the Best of Banners, under a king called Great Energetic Power, at a temple known as Conspicuous Rays of Light, dedicated to the god Radiant Eyes—but then, it's a long story. You don't need to hear all of it.

"Anyway, it turns out that I have been this lotus-pond goddess for an untold time. How fine the world is! How precious our lives. It has been my privilege and delight to deliver to many worlds many buddhas by many names. The time will come when I am the mother of Maitreya, the buddha of the future. And others too."

Sudhana was silent, amazed, and full of wonder.

"It's hard to understand, isn't it?" she said kindly.

Sudhana nodded, gazing at her with joy.

"And yet, I think you do understand this, Sudhana. I think everyone does."

Eventually he left her marvelous presence, taking with him the vision of her charitable womb, a womb that crosses time and space and is always with us.

radiance
Ratnavati

The Buddha was friends with the Dragon King, leader of the Nāgas who lived beneath the sea. Nāgas were widely admired for their power and wisdom. They were a little seductive, a little intimidating, these creatures made of equal parts youthful human beauty and serpentine grace. Their watery kingdom was a flowing world filled with jewels. The Buddha went down there to preach one day, taking several monks with him.

Many dragon people came to question the Buddha, and he patiently explained the paramitas, the Buddhist virtues, and the importance of keeping the Precepts, the guidelines for ethical behavior. "Keep constant gladness," he said, and the young Nāga woman sometimes called Ratnavati and sometimes known as Precious Silk and sometimes called Jewel Brocade laughed. Ratnavati laughed easily and often. Her clothes were simply splendid all the time, and she was greatly respected for her sweetness and calm.

The dragons had a lot of lovely jewels, quite a lot, but each one was unique and worth a great deal. Jewel Brocade, followed by ten thousand of the dragon women, stepped forward. Each gave the Buddha the rare jewel from the palm of her right hand. Speaking together in a tinkling chorus that left a strange and tantalizing sensation, they said, "We have done excellent contemplation and awakened today to the incomparable thought of enlightenment. In the future, we too will attain this perfect enlightenment, thanks to you. We will teach and care for the Dharma forever."

Mahākāśyapa, the Buddha's foremost disciple, was sitting beside him. His brown robes were a little dusty, and one shoulder was bare. At the time of this meeting Mahākāśyapa was past middle age. He was born with thirty of the thirty-two marks of a buddha and had been a disciple for many years. Among the monks he was most renowned for his discipline, moral strictness, and ascetic practice. Mahākāśyapa's mind often wandered to lofty places, and now and then he would be distracted by things, like the way a single flower turned lightly in the breeze. It was in the small moments, the ordinary moments between people, that he faltered. When Ratnavati and the chorus of women made this simple statement, he couldn't help but protest.

"Excuse me," he said, with that unmistakable tone of a man explaining something to a child. He was sitting—naturally—in full lotus, and he chose not to stand up, which would have been the respectful thing to do. "Supreme Enlightenment is rather difficult to obtain." He said this a bit sardonically. "Perhaps you don't realize what is involved. And besides, why do you think you can do it? You're female. You must not know that Supreme Enlightenment can't be realized in a female body."

Ratnavati laughed at this absurd notion, and her voice was like birds, like bells, like wind chimes and ice. "Why, it's easy!" she exclaimed. Maybe this dour fellow was trying to make a joke. "Easy as turning over your hand!" She flipped her delicate hand back and forth in illustration. "All you need is a pure mind and a pure intent." She looked at him more closely and realized he wasn't joking at all. So she took a deep breath and tried again. "If women can't do it, then neither can men. To be a buddha is perfectly natural! It's a matter of body and mind, that's all. I already *am* the path."

Mahākāśyapa was hooked.

"Why, are you saying you already *are* enlightened?" You see, he thought he had *her* hooked.

Ratnavati was deft and well spoken, and while she was never looking for a fight, she was perfectly able to stand her ground. If this fellow needed a lecture, she was the one to give it to him.

"You still think there's a difference between pure and impure, between emptiness and form," she said to the Buddha's foremost disciple. Then she rapidly gave a long discourse on the nature of emptiness and phenomena. She talked about the emptiness of delusion and enlightenment, the emptiness of grasping and attainment, the emptiness of bodhisattvas, and finally, the emptiness of the Buddha himself.

The Buddha was watching this exchange cheerfully. He had known Mahākāśyapa a long time and had recognized him from the first moment as a true disciple; he knew Mahākāśyapa was capable of great humility and effort. And he knew that even his first disciple wasn't free from human foibles. He needed sympathy to temper his discipline.

For some time the princess continued to explain the nature of things to Mahākāśyapa, who had less and less to say as time went on and finally gave up trying to interrupt her words.

"Both one's body and mind realize the path, at the same time, without effort," she patiently continued. "Without effort, you see—if I am on the path, it isn't because the path is what I am getting. Do you understand?" She peered at him hopefully.

Still lost in his own ideas, not really hearing her words, he saw this as a chance to make a point. "If you're on the path, then turn the Dharma wheel!" he cried.

She sighed at last. Why was this fellow so obtuse? "This is the Dharma wheel right before you!" she said, gesturing toward herself, her lovely brocade gown. "This. I turn it without effort, I turn it with my own non-attachment to turning, I turn it with emptiness, with non-obstruction. It turns as cleanly as the sea. How else would I turn it?"

And still, he was a dull fellow. One more time he protested, "But a woman can't turn the Dharma—women aren't on the path to Supreme Enlightenment!" He was down to tautologies now.

"I will attain Supreme Enlightenment," she finally answered him, "when you do." This, of course, was the crux of the matter, what she had been saying in various ways. Supreme Enlightenment cannot be attained—that is, it can't be grasped, or won. It isn't outside anyone, it isn't *there* instead of *here.* Either one *is* Supreme Enlightenment, entirely, or one is far away from knowing that one is.

"But I never will attain it!" he exclaimed. "It cannot be attained."

"Exactly!" she answered. At last—it certainly had taken him a while to get the point. Behind her, five hundred bodhisattvas reached the state of total patience, understood the emptiness of things, and sighed with pleasure, their breath a breeze of sweetness.

"Very good, very good!" said the Buddha. All the dragons, warriors, gods, demons, ghosts, and other beings in the audience thought the young Jewel Brocade would surely attain the path of enlightenment that cannot be attained.

"Without a doubt," chuckled the Buddha, having thoroughly enjoyed himself at this debate, "without a doubt, in a few hundred eons, you will be an all-pervading buddha, Ratnavati. We shall call you Universal World, the Completely Enlightened One in a world known as Radiance."

She clapped her hands in delight—a world called Radiance sounded great. The chorus of dragon women sang like stars and tumbling brooks. Meanwhile, Mahākāśyapa was staring at the ground, lost in his own thoughts, seeing through his last few obstructions. The Buddha leaned over and carefully put a handful of jewels in his lap. The disciple would find them eventually. Then he bowed to Ratnavati and began to speak to the crowd again.

the buddha of universal light

Śrīmālā

Śrīmālā was the daughter of King Prasenajit and Queen Mallikā of the Kingdom of Kosala, at the time the Buddha lived among us. When she was a young woman, Śrīmālā married King Yasomitra of the great city of Ayodhya in the Ganges Plain. She lived with him in the palace in great luxury, spending her days in the whitewashed rooms, on the rooftop terraces, in the gardens, and on the balconies screened by lattices for her privacy.

One day, Prasenajit heard the Buddha speak, and his universe crumbled apart; without anything changing at all, everything changed. All he had held dear turned to dust, and at the same time he was seized with the intense desire to treat each thing he encountered as though it were a rare gem. He invited the Buddha to court, where many heard him and were converted to his ineffable teaching, including the queen. Their only sorrow was that their daughter was not there to listen too. They knew her for an intelligent, compassionate woman capable of great subtlety and were sure she would understand.

They wrote Śrīmālā a letter, describing what they'd learned.

She was lounging on pillows when the letter arrived, while one attendant oiled her long, black hair and another painted the soles of her feet with lac dye. Her lips, the tips of her fingers and toes, and her palms were already crimson. A third attendant massaged her neck and breasts with sandalwood perfume.

A courtier entered the room, bowing deeply. "A letter from Kosala, Queen," he said.

She reached for the letter eagerly; she missed her parents. Turning to the window for light, she leaned on the stone casement. Below her, she saw the gardens of the kingdom, the bathing pools and lakes, a set of swings under tall palm trees. Far away, past the city walls, the jungles of the Ganges spread like a carpet.

When Śrīmālā read her parents' letter explaining their newfound love of the Buddha's way, she understood it in its entirety. Instantly her mind was filled with bodhicitta, the tender wound of compassionate love for all beings.

She gazed out the window and felt her heart fill with a great longing to meet the Buddha. Her wish was so profound and powerful, so pure, that in that moment the Buddha appeared in the air before her, his body inconceivably radiant and yet near and safe.

Śrīmālā bowed deeply with her hands folded in front of her face and then knelt on the stone floor in front of him. Her tears splashed across the floor.

"Yours is the most beautiful form in the universe," she said. "You have no match, not in form or glory. Your wisdom is greater than any obstacle." Her voice was filled with wonder and confidence, the way one sounds speaking a newly discovered fact. Amazing! "You have comprehended everything. Please protect me as I am today. Help me to raise this seed of enlightenment."

He smiled, a lovely smile. "I've helped you for many lives, Śrīmālā," he said. "I've already helped you in this life. I will always be here to help you. But all you need to do is go on as you have been. Nourish the kindness in your heart and the wisdom you've already gained in many lives."

This was great news to Śrīmālā, who had not realized her previous births until then. But when he spoke, she remembered all of them, and her gratitude and reverence for the Buddha increased greatly.

"Yes, you have been praising the Tathāgata for a long time, or you wouldn't be able to see me now. This merit, this long work, means that you will be a buddha as well. You will be Tathāgata-Arhat-Samyaksambuddha Samantaprabha, the Buddha of Universal Light. The world where you will rule will be free of evil. Its inhabitants will never be sick or grow old, and every person born there will be glorious—they will look splendid, smell of perfume, pass their days in ecstasy, and lead long, strong, happy lives. All will be Buddhists and only follow the Great Vehicle."

Naturally (as is the way of these things), innumerable gods, arhats, bodhisattvas, devas, demons, and Dharma kings were eavesdropping on this conversation. When they heard the Buddha's description of this land, they all immediately vowed to be born there someday.

Śrīmālā stood, looking the Buddha in the eye without fear.

"I vow—" she began, and the palace's walls fell away as she spoke. She and all other beings were bathed in the honey light of a summer morning, when the air is still cool and fresh. Cushioned thrones floated in the air, and the Buddha sat on the central one, cross-legged, listening carefully.

"I vow," she began again, speaking slowly, quite amazed, "to be moral, to be respectful, to seek equanimity, to practice generosity, and to feel joy for the happiness of others. I vow to share all my wealth, but never to try to convert others for my own gain. And I vow to be a friend to friendless people, always remembering their pain."

She stood up a little straighter. "But I won't hesitate to stop what should be stopped, to destroy what needs destroying, even as I fix what must be fixed. In all these ways, I vow never to forget the Dharma, the Doctrine of the Great Vehicle."

She raised her arms to the sky, her face to the sun. "If these vows are true, may flowers rain down on us, making a beautiful sound!"

And flowers fell, garlands of kadamba and sirīsa blossoms in scarlet and orange, and the music of bow harps and flutes played in the sky. Everyone present—that is, everyone in the world—vowed to stay with Queen Śrīmālā forever. And the Buddha smiled again. His smile before had been astonishingly lovely and fine, but now, because of her vows, his smile glittered with rainbows of light—blue and yellow, crystal and crimson and gold, red and white and silver light in concentric rings expanding through all the worlds of form and the heavenly worlds as well.

After a time, the Buddha rose from his seat and offered it to Śrīmālā, who sat comfortably in the center of the crowd, pulling her skirt neatly around her bare feet. While the Buddha listened respectfully, she uttered her own great Lion's Roar, a lecture of potent, round wisdom. She had comprehended the entire teaching from the words of a single letter, and since that moment this understanding had exploded within her.

When a flower is ready to open, it simply opens, all at once; when a fruit is on the edge of ripening, it needs only the faintest kiss of sunlight to finish the work. Śrīmālā was like this—utterly ready. For a long time—for a long, long time without growing tired, and without tiring those who listened—she discussed the nature of bodhisattvas, who might be monks or laypeople, men or women. She described the Womb of the Buddhas, the Great Mother Matrix, the very source of Truth, the Tathāgatagarbha. She described emptiness, thusness, nonduality, and many other profound and difficult things. Most of the people listening understood some things she said. A few understood most of what she said. When she talked about the embryo of the Illustrious Dharmadhātu, the embryo of the Dharmakāya and supramundane Dharma, and the intrinsically pure embryo, hardly anyone understood a word. But they liked listening anyway.

"Lord," she said quietly, looking over her audience, "to accept the Dharma is identical with the Dharma; the acceptance of the Dharma is not different from the Dharma. She who accepts the Truth is herself the Truth. She who practices the Perfections is herself the Perfections."

And still she spoke for a long time more.

When she finished, the Buddha stood up, smiling happily, and said, "Excellent! That was simply excellent. You are standing very close to a hundred billion buddhas! Clearly, you can explain this subtle Dharma very well."

With those words, his radiant body exploded with light, bathing everyone in the audience, and then he floated up into the sky above them and walked through it toward the city of Śrvāstī.

Queen Śrīmālā and her attendants bowed in his direction. The palace walls returned, and she called a great gathering of the people to her. When they arrived, she spoke calmly of all she had understood. First, the women and girls over the age of seven years converted to the Great Vehicle. Then her husband, King Yasomitra, converted. Finally, the men and boys over the age of seven years agreed to its Truth and converted too. Ananda told her story many times, just like the Buddha asked.

the supernatural one
Nāga Deva

During the Buddha's years of teaching, he met many bodhisattvas. Such teachers and guides are wise, compassionate, and powerful, but they aren't fully enlightened. Remaining in flawed forms in the world of duality and suffering so they can help others, they are themselves lost in duality and suffering and marked by it. Enlightenment is never a single act but an ongoing event, a newly made thing.

Mañjuśrī, the Bodhisattva of Wisdom, had just returned from the Nāga kingdom, where he had converted an uncountable number of beings to the Truth. He had been especially impressed with the Nāga princesses, who were quite adept at the Dharma.

That day the sun was hot, and the monks and laypeople gathered in a grove of fig trees near a cool stream to rest. Many other bodhisattvas were there too, and also Śāriputra, one of the ten great disciples of the Buddha. The bodhisattva known as Wisdom Accumulated asked Mañjuśrī whether he knew of anyone who could comprehend the entire teaching at once.

"I certainly know of one," Mañjuśrī answered. "The daughter of the Nāga king is really something—loving, kind, and so smart! She can understand the most difficult, subtle, and obscure teachings immediately and explain them eloquently. And she is still the sweetest creature, full of compassion for all kinds of beings."

Wisdom Accumulated stood up at these words. "Now, wait a minute," he said, smiling kindly. "I appreciate your point, but a bodhisattva must spend immeasurable kalpas in ascetic practices, accumulate great merit, practice the paramitas for a very long time, throw away body and mind again and again, before even being born as a male human being. How could a young girl do it in a moment? I don't believe it." Śāriputra was nodding in agreement. Truly, this was a difficult thing, and not for girls.

Before Mañjuśrī could explain, the Nāga princess herself appeared. She was eight years old and had a face as delicate and pure as a lotus. Her eyes were black and radiant. Like all Nāgas, she was beautiful, with a long, sinuous body covered with iridescent scales reflecting every color, and she moved as smoothly as water. She bowed gracefully before the Buddha, her long, muscular body bending down, and recited a poem of praise to him, his beauty, and his teachings. Everyone listening had to admit she was quite eloquent, at that. Then she repeated a vow she had made many times: to teach the Dharma wherever she could. This was her ritual, repeated every time she came to visit her friend the Buddha in his sacred grove.

When she was done, the Buddha scooted over on his patch of fragrant grass, patting the place beside him so she could curl up nearby and share his bowl. But Wisdom Accumulated and the disciple Śāriputra couldn't contain themselves. They had to challenge this intimidating creature.

Together, they slowly approached the pair, who sat laughing quietly together. Śāriputra, perfectly correct and making a small bow, addressed the girl. "Daughter of Sāgara, princess of the Nāgas, I've heard so much about you. Your vow is a good one, and I congratulate you. But I don't believe the story we've been told."

She looked at him for a long moment, then quietly said, "Oh?"

He shook his head, and Wisdom Accumulated shook his head too. They stood, towering in height above her.

"Bodhisattvas practice for innumerable kalpas and train diligently to perfect the practice before achieving their rebirth," he went on. "To be a bodhisattva is a matter of great effort. A woman's body is soiled by its nature. If a woman practices for eons and never falters and completely fulfills the perfections, she still can't be a buddha. She can never do this because she is subject to the Five Obstacles. Surely you know this—you know a woman can't ever be Brahma, or a Śakra king, or a devil king, or a wheel-turning king, or a buddha. So how could you, a simple girl, do it?"

Here we go with the Five Obstacles again, she thought. The Nāga princess watched Śāriputra as he spoke; she saw the tension in his body, the faint traces of anger and jealousy in all his gestures. He was suffering just at the sight of her.

For eons men had plagued women with such things, coming up with this list and that one to prove—what? Better than most, Nāgas understand that superior beings have no need to prove their superiority. When people hold others down to make themselves bigger, it proves only their own weakness. Besides, the Five Obstacles weren't even sensible: the teaching claimed that women can't be Brahmas, heavenly kings, Śakra kings, devil kings, wheel-turning kings, or buddhas because they are women, and because they are women, they can't be Brahmas, heavenly kings, Śakra kings, devil kings, wheel-turning kings, or buddhas. And because they can't be Brahmas—so on and so on. It was silly, and it was much worse than that. People who believed in the Five Obstacles believed half of all the beings in the world couldn't be enlightened.

"So," said Śāriputra again, "what makes you think *you* can do it?"

Now, Śāriputra was sometimes known as a great teacher, the foremost in wisdom of the Buddha's disciples, but that day he wasn't. We all have our days. Confronting a quiet girl with the body of a snake, the great disciple Śāriputra lost himself in self-regard. He was showing off to his teacher, currying praise, and doing this by pushing down another. He was acting, in other words, like a bit of a bully. The Nāga princess saw all this. She saw a blind man, a man who could not see his own fingertips, let alone buddhahood, in front of him, and she took pity.

Nāgas have precious jewels in their foreheads; hers was worth more than three-thousand-million systems of worlds. She removed it and gave it to the Buddha, without a word. He took it with a smile, this little jewel, this wholehearted offering worth more than worlds. Then the princess turned to Śāriputra and said, "Well, I gave a precious jewel to the World-Honored One, and he accepted it. Wasn't that quick?"

All the monks, nuns, laypeople, and others gathered nearby agreed, and so did Śāriputra, who had no choice. "It was quick," he admitted, "but this isn't the same as comprehending the entire teaching."

He would insist, she thought. So she glided toward an open space of grass between the trees and rose up on her coils before him, glimmering in the dappled light beneath the leaves, her long tongue flickering briefly between white teeth. With only a hint of challenge, she said, "Employ your supernatural powers and watch me attain buddhahood."

With these words, in the space of just a moment, she turned her body into that of a man with the thirty-two marks and eighty properties of a buddha. We think such a thing must be very hard to do, but it isn't. There are beings like this everywhere we turn, their marks hidden under the skin, under clothes or hair, behind language and custom. Most eyes can't see through these things—appearance, difference, otherness. That's where the magic lies. Nothing special in assuming the form of a man with the thirty-two marks and eighty properties of a buddha—but wondrously supernatural to see one. What magic is greater than the one that opens our eyes? What spell is more powerful than the one that casts off the prejudice and hope, the fears and desires, that blind us? The Nāga princess could see a buddha in Śāriputra; perhaps, in time, he could learn to see a buddha in her.

In this beautiful form, she carried out all the practices of a bodhisattva, proceeded to the Pure Land, sat on the jeweled lotus, and attained correct, perfect, complete enlightenment. She lectured on the Wonderful Law to all beings in all directions—to women and men, devils and gods, animals and dragons, to boys and girls, to bodhisattvas, buddhas, bullies, and blind louts equally. She did this in the space of an instant, in the silence between words. And in that space, that instant, Śāriputra understood the profound subtlety of the Law of the Universal Nature of Buddhahood appearing in all beings, in all forms.

Finally, with a sigh of relief, the little girl took off the skin of a man and set it aside. Śāriputra slipped into the trees to sit in silence for a while, examining his new understanding, while she slithered back along the grass and slid into place again beside the Buddha with a sweet, small smile, and they began to speak together again.

the generous woman
Prabhūtā

In the realm of bodhisattvas, Sudhana wandered. His mind was refreshed and nourished by the teachings of various spiritual benefactors, and he was opening like a blooming lotus into someone powerful and strong. He gradually made his way to Samudrapratishthana, to find the lay disciple known as Prabhūtā. Everyone he met knew of her and directed him to her house, which was in the exact center of the town.

The house was very large and adorned with jewels. There was a door on each side, and the doors were also adorned with precious jewels. He stood at the main door for a moment, hands joined, head bowed, before entering with hope and joy.

In the center of the house sat Prabhūtā, a young and beautiful woman, in a jeweled chair. She was watching him as though she had been waiting for him a long time. Her thick black hair was loose and long across her back, and her dark skin was smooth and fresh. She wore only a white robe and nothing else—no decoration or makeup, no combs or bracelets or tattoos. Sudhana was overwhelmed by her radiant appearance and could only think of her as a transcendent teacher from the moment he saw her face.

Prabhūtā sat in the center of the room, and around her were ten million other chairs, each perfect in proportion and craft, each decorated with precious gems. Ten thousand women attended her, and their voices were like the melodies of a mountain stream, their bodies fragrant as spring. Sudhana felt himself release a lifetime of anger, jealousy, deceit, and sorrow on simply seeing them. The scent of their hands and feet was like medicine, and when they spoke, the sound of their voices filled him with joy and humility.

The attendants turned always to Prabhūtā, listened to her, saluted her with their joined hands, bowed, watched her, ready to wait on her every need. There were only the women and the chairs, and in front of Prabhūtā, a single vessel, and nothing more.

"Noblest one," said Sudhana, when he could finally speak, "I am searching for perfect enlightenment. I want nothing less. But I don't know how to live as an enlightened being lives. I don't know how to do what enlightened beings do. I have heard that you teach enlightened beings. Please tell me how to live and act as enlightened beings do."

Prabhūtā smiled, and it was like the sun of the first mild sunny day in the alpine meadows of the mountains.

"Mine is the liberation of an unending treasury of good." She pointed to the vessel in front of her. "This is all I need. From this one vessel I give all sentient beings the food they desire, variously flavored. From this one vessel I give a hundred, a thousand, a hundred thousand, a million, a billion beings whatever they wish, satisfying them, making them happy. It never runs out. I could feed a billion worlds, no matter what food they wanted to eat. I can give thirsty people whatever they wish to drink, and let them rest on any kind of bed or couch they desire, and dress them in the clothes they long for, and bathe them with the lotions and perfumes they love, and carry them through the wide streets in palanquins, under banners and flags, however they would like."

She smiled encouragingly at Sudhana. "I don't decide what food to give, you know. I give the food *they* want. And that is all that sentient beings really need, and that is what enlightened beings do. Give people what they want."

Sudhana couldn't speak. How could it be so easy?

Prabhūtā turned slowly around the room, inviting him to see the women who attended her. "Do you see them?" she asked. "There are tens of hundreds of thousands of women just like me, whose practice is the same, who are pure and mindful, understanding and powerful, all devoted to taking the form that pleases people, giving hungry people the food they desire. In a single instant these women pervade the universe. They go everywhere. They feed the gods and demons and the hungry ghosts.

"And what do they feed them? They feed the gods a god's food. They feed dragon food to dragons and bird food to birds. This is the only way."

"Look."

Sudhana turned and saw a stream of beings coming through the four doors—dragons, demons, ghosts, titans, centaurs and snakes, saints and children. They came to Prabhūtā, and she invited each one to take a seat of jewels, brought delicacies and drinks to each one, clothed them, scattered flowers about, hung banners and pennants above their heads, placed crowns and necklaces on their bodies, and fed them the foods they wanted to eat. And the vessel never ran out.

Prabhūtā turned to Sudhana. "This is what I know—the inexhaustible treasury of good manifestations. But there are many other kinds of good. There is good like the ocean and good like the sky, and good like mountains and rain. You need to learn about those kinds of good too. So go now, and learn more."

Sudhana was in no hurry to leave her. He stood and looked at her for a long time, never tiring of the sight of her, never tiring, until finally he backed slowly out of her house and journeyed on. She remained, and remains, giving each person who passes whatever that person wants, without begrudging or judging, freely, with joy.

INDIAN ANCESTORS

In its early days in northern India, Buddhism seemed to be just another of many cults of the time, each of them rising from the same deep Vedic roots. It was firmly built on a Brāhmanistic tradition, though its leader disdained the brāhman lifestyle and teaching of the priests themselves. As Siddhārtha's teaching spread, its ability to completely uproot and transform lives became obvious to many established leaders.

Buddhism was the leading edge of a wave that would rise and travel for a long time before breaking—a wave of reform that would change many of the religious and cultural beliefs of the time. It questioned the fundamental assumption that a person is born with innate qualities determined by class, race, and family. It taught moderation in an immoderate world, universal charity and equality in a world of conflict and injustice. Buddhism rejected asceticism and luxury both at a time when there was little in between. Most of all, Siddhārtha taught that there is a way out of suffering; he taught about salvation at a time when fatalism was the religious foundation. The end result was a philosophy that brought radical social and political change.

The stories of the first nuns are all from the time of the historical Buddha. Only a few sources exist describing their lives, and the main source is the writing of the nuns themselves. They tell their stories almost entirely in verse in a collection called the *Therīgāthā,* or *Poems of the Elder Nuns,* included in the sutta-pitika, a collection of sermons, sayings, and stories from the time of the historical Buddha. There are several translations of this work in English. A few women, such as Khema, are mentioned in the Buddha's Discourses, and a few others, like Pajāpatī, are mentioned in a variety of historical and religious writings. This book contains only some of the stories of the early nuns; there are several other women represented in the complete work. Some of these women are represented by little more than a poem; in other cases there are brief anecdotes and sketchy biographical details, and in a few cases lengthy stories and dialogues.

Certain versions of the *Therīgāthā* contain detailed descriptions of the women's previous lives, their rebirths. It is natural that early Buddhist literature relies on the lessons of previous lives to explain the behavior of a current one. The world of early Buddhism was based in a philosophy of rebirth and the endless wheel of existence. The writing of the time rises out of an oral tradition steeped in myth and a culture bathed in the elaborate and cosmic verses of the *Bhagavad Gita* and other Vedic writing. I've included brief versions of these previous lives here, in deference to how these women might naturally have seen themselves, and to how such stories were told at the time.

The women's community of the Buddha's time was vital and expansive. After the Buddha's death, both the monks and the nuns began to congregate in more permanent communities and to build residences both outside and inside villages and cities. Then women faded gradually from the records of Indian Buddhism, first into the margins and then disappearing altogether. Whether this reflects an actual extinction of the Indian nuns or simply a lack of historical record is unknown.

The "Admission of Women to the Order" is a document first recorded several hundred years after the Buddha's death. The historicity of the document is uncertain and vague. It tells a version of the story of the first nun, Pajāpatī, and the Buddha's reaction and predictions regarding a women's order. I leave it to readers to decide the meaning of this story for themselves.

the leader

Mahā Pajāpatī

The great rivers of India, glacial and cold, fall from the vast wall of snow-covered, rugged mountains. First in waterfalls and small icy pools, then in rapids, through canyons and gorges, the swift water grows dark with silt and smashed rock until it plunges into the plains. The land slowly flattens out, and the rivers spread and warm, widening, leaving behind the fertile silt. Their waters are endlessly broken by canoes and rough sailing boats, and endlessly renewed.

The mother of the Buddha, the great Māyā who died soon after his birth, had a sister named Gotami. They came down from the mountains like the rivers to live with the king in Kapilavastu, a hot, whitewashed town on the plain with balconies on every side and gardens in every view. They were privileged and well nourished. They wore fine clothing and many ornaments and walked past flocks of peacocks in the lotus gardens.

Māyā gave birth on a day marked by miracles and died a few days later. Gotami took the infant, holding him while people cheered his birth, and later that day she cried in the mourning ceremonies for the dead queen. Then Gotami delivered her own son and nursed the two boys herself, each to a breast, instead of letting the wet nurses do it. She and the king waited through the dangerous first days, nameless days when babies often die. But both boys were strong. Gotami held her nephew for the naming ceremony when her husband Śuddhodhana whispered "Siddhārtha," which means "All Prospering," into his ear several times, and then she held her son while he whispered, "Nanda."

Gotami fed the two babies their first solid food—rice gruel and ghee to ensure glory, ram's meat for strength—saw them through colicky nights, oversaw the piercing of their ears, and smeared them with yellow oil after baths. Most of all, she loved them.

The boys grew up together. When they were three years old and ready to begin school, Gotami gave birth to Sundari-nanda, a daughter. Sundari stayed with her, and the boys spent more and more time away—studying history, economic theory, and the epics, playing games, learning to hunt, learning to be men. They painted small black tattoos near their eyes and dyed their lips with red powder, shaved their chests, and smeared their skin with sandalwood paste. When they were old enough, they grew neat beards and put on turbans, admiring each other's fine appearance in embroidered pants and girdles of gold.

They grew into young men with their own harems. When Siddhārtha was twenty-nine years old, he married Yaśodharā.

Gotami knew all this time that her nephew was unhappy. Nothing seemed to please him or distract him from his brooding ways. When he disappeared in the night, sending his charioteer to carry back his hair and clothes, she cried herself to sleep for many weeks, thinking she would never see him again.

Shortly after he had gone, Yaśodharā discovered she was pregnant. Gotami had to laugh a little—what a development this was, what a strange circle was being circled. And then something even stranger happened—Yaśodharā felt well, and the pregnancy developed, but she never gave birth. Not for a year, not for two years. For six years she remained comfortably with child and didn't deliver.[1]

Then Siddhārtha returned, a new person altogether. Many of the tribespeople were cool to the young man who had walked away from them. But Śuddhodhana and Gotami welcomed him joyfully. Yaśodharā bowed to him, went to her rooms, and immediately gave birth to a son she called Rāhula. With her in-laws, she listened to her husband explain where he had been and why, and what he had learned. They were converted to his new religion at once. So were Nanda and Sundari-Nanda and many of the men and women of the court.

After that, Gotami was always called Pajāpatī, which means "Mother of a Great Child."

When Siddhārtha took his leave for the second time, gently turning away from protests, he took Nanda and his cousin, Ananda, with him. Pajāpatī cried herself to sleep again for a time; she was getting older and felt a little lonely. When Śuddhodhana died a short while later, she and Sundari-Nanda were truly alone.

One by one, then by dozens, women found their way to her, begging for help and support since their own sons and husbands had gone with Siddhārtha. It was said that Siddhārtha stole sons and widowed women wherever he went. Then the Kolyans and the Śākyas went to war with each other, and many more men died. Their widows came too, until five hundred women surrounded Pajāpatī, and all of them were alone, except for each other.

In the autumn, when the cooler season began and the plateau started to dry out from the hard summer rains, Siddhārtha came near Kapilavastu again. This time he met Rāhula, who was then six years old. The child was enchanted with his famous, evasive father and asked his mother to let him go live with the monks. As Siddhārtha was preparing to leave, Pajāpatī begged for an audience with him, and when he held out his hand to her, to his beloved aunt and stepmother, she began to cry.

"I love you," she said. "I believe in you, and I want to come with you. Let us come with you." She cried. "Let us join you."

He looked upon her, benignly but from a great distance. He was beyond loneliness, but he also knew that his was a terribly lonely life at times. So many changes, so much new in the world, nothing to hold. He was an enlightened being, and a human being too. Even buddhas are subject to the conditions in which they appear, and enlightenment is not a fixed state that we can hold on to. It must be renewed, rediscovered, as we ourselves are renewed and rediscovered. The Siddhārtha who was Shakyamuni, the Tathāgata, the Great Honored One, knew with vivid clarity that all things are equal and empty. The Siddhārtha who was a young Indian prince reared in luxury lived in a world where men and women lived different lives. Men sought and struggled; women took care of things. What would happen to the world if women started seeking too? He was trying to spread a new teaching, create something altogether new, and already he had heard complaints from kings and ministers and priests, rumors of trouble. He'd already made a lot of changes, and too many for some.

Besides, he thought, *she's my* mother. *She's an old woman. This really isn't proper.*

"Give this up, my mother," he said, not unkindly. "Do not ask."

But she asked again. "Do you know?" she said. "Do you have any idea what you've done? What has been left behind?"

"No," he said again. "You should be home. What would become of the world if women didn't take care of the home?"

She asked again, and he refused again. Then he left for Vesālī, with his monks, and she was left behind.

Pajāpatī had gathered merit in many Buddha realms in the past. As the head of the water-carrying slaves, she had cared for five Pratyekabuddhas, Self-Enlightened Ones. As the Chief Weaver, she had fed five hundred Pratyekabuddhas. She had resources—she had ekacitta, single-mindedness, her own deep well of it. Pajāpatī sat down on the ground, cut off her hair, and put on yellow rags. So did Yaśodharā, who was now also without a husband or a son, and Sundari-nanda, several women from the harem, and the five hundred others, and they set out together for Vesālī.

Villages then were stockades, walled to keep out tigers, elephants, and other beasts, some of which were human. They stopped now and then in travelers' rest houses, this vast crowd of women, and the village people gathered to visit with them. They crossed canals, walked around reservoirs, and stumbled through muddy irrigation ditches in the rice fields. They slept under eucalyptus and birch trees or in groves of bamboo, and sometimes, washing out their clothes, they saw a crocodile or hippopotamus break the water of the river. They walked, day by day, for 150 miles.

When they reached Vesālī, the women stood outside the gate, crying all together, making a terrible noise. Pajāpatī was dirty, and her bare feet were covered with sores, and she stood right at the front of the crowd.

Ananda appeared at the gate.

"Why are you here, Mother?" he asked respectfully.

"Because he said no!" she cried. "Help us!" At this point all the women behind her started calling out too. "Help us!" they shouted.

"Help us, Ananda!" It was quite a scene. The city began to notice and came to see.

"We have no place to go," said Pajāpatī. "How can we take care of our homes if no one is home? We have no families to raise, no husbands to care for. We long for the truth of this life, the same way you do. We are the same as you are now."

Ananda wasn't sure what to do. It was more than unseemly—it was unprecedented, this mob of women making demands, these aristocratic ladies wrapped in rags, without hair. And at the same time he was struck with awe at the depth of their cries, at the raw hunger in their request. He went to tell Siddhārtha about the women outside the gate.

"Why don't you let them join?" he asked. But Siddhārtha just repeated the reasons he'd given his stepmother. Ananda asked again, and again, and Siddhārtha continued to refuse.

Finally Ananda asked, "Aren't women competent, Siddhārtha? Can't they understand the same as men?"

"Yes, of course," Siddhārtha answered. That had never been the question, he wanted to say. For a moment the great teacher was a little confused by his own thoughts. What exactly was the problem? He couldn't quite explain. He feared problems, not for himself, but for the future of what he was trying to do.

Ananda interrupted his musing. "And Pajāpatī, my friend—she is your aunt, your stepmother, she nursed you! How can you turn her down if she is as capable as a man?"

Then Siddhārtha had no answer.

Finally, reluctantly, inevitably, he went outside and looked at the courtly lady who had reared him, now a disheveled woman among other disheveled women, a scene to be recorded and gossiped about for ages. Then he looked at her, really looked at her. She stood before him exactly as he had stood when he stepped out of his world, his family, his rank. Without being wife, mother, queen, what was she?

Even buddhas must practice eternally. Even the greatest of us can only remember our past enlightenment, and we don't always see our present delusion. Wishing he could, he was no longer able to refuse. Perhaps he realized that this new way of life he had invented for men meant that women had to find a new way of life too. With a sigh, he said, "All right. Women may enter, but they have to follow special rules."

When he had first accepted disciples, he had required that they follow four guidelines: to live only by begging, to wear only rags, to sleep under a tree, and to use cow urine, considered the best of medicines, when sick. Day by day he had added specific rules, each in response to an error one of the disciples had made—usually something he had never imagined needing a rule to forbid. Now he declared that women were to follow all the rules the men followed, and several more. No matter how senior, every woman would be required to bow to every monk. Their individual ordinations had to be approved by the men, and the punishment for women breaking rules would be greater than that of men. Monks could criticize and correct the nuns, but the nuns could never do so to a monk.

For lifetimes, Pajāpatī had vowed to become an arhat, a person whose passions and delusions are stilled, who is free of desire and ignorance. So when she heard this, she wasn't swayed. Her stepson was a very young Buddha still. If he demanded that she follow a few extra rules so that the world he was changing so radically would not change in one particular way—well, so be it. Perhaps she remembered his diapers and rolled her eyes.

"Yes," she said out loud. "I'll pick up and carry these rules like a garland of blue lotuses on my head."

So began the great experiment. There had always been a few female ascetics wandering the countryside. But there had never been so many women, living in pairs or small groups near villages, sharing small shacks made of mud and reeds. Some even lived in the forest alone, sleeping under trees like the men. They became a common sight, their heads shaved and wearing plain saffron robes. They carried only a water filter, a razor, a belt, and a bowl. When they menstruated, they were allowed to wear a hip-string.

There was no daily schedule, no particular rites. The women bathed twice a month and each day begged for alms in the villages. They could accept rice, fruit, beans, nuts, grains, and roots. Now and then they had a bit of brown sugar or salt. Unless they were sick, the nuns weren't allowed to eat honey, fish or meat, ghee, oil, or curds. If there was not enough food for everyone, they drew lots to see who ate.

Normally in India women shaved their pubic hair and allowed their head hair to grow; only prostitutes allowed their pubic hair to grow. And then nuns did too and shaved their heads instead. They were so strange—they left home, didn't marry, had no children, and debated in public. Eventually there was a rule that women could not be accepted for ordination unless it was proven that they had a healthy uterus. Too many people had begun to say that these strange women must be barren or flawed to take this life.

By then the monks had 227 rules instead of four, each new one the result of a monk's error or misbehavior. Eventually the women were required to follow 84 more rules than the men. They did so, without much complaint, and they did it very well.

Siddhārtha taught Pajāpatī as she had once taught him, and she quickly came to a deep understanding. "I have reached the place where everything is still," she told him one day. Then she stood up and recited a verse:

For a long time I've wandered
through lives, being mother, father, brother, son, grandparent,
never understanding things or finding what I need.
But that is done. Shattered is the round of rebirth. This is the last body.
No more Pajāpatī shall come to be!

Some years later she sat down under a tree with Siddhārtha and asked that he revoke the rule requiring nuns to be subject to monks no matter who was the senior. It was time, she thought, for the women's community to be given more power. He refused. Such a thing had never been seen before, he said. Never in the history of this world had there been a community of people with power divided equally between men and women.

"Accept it for now as it is," he said. "It won't always be this way."

Pajāpatī lived to be 120 years old. One day she suddenly remembered all her past lives, reviewed this one, and realized it was coming to an end. At that moment there was an earthquake and a pounding rain. The wind sounded like people crying. When she asked her stepson for permission to die, all the people began to cry.

"Show us a miracle," Siddhārtha said, "for any fool who still thinks women can't attain enlightenment like men."

So she split into many bodies, became invisible, walked through a tree, levitated, and made great heat. Then she lay down, ready to die. Sundari-nanda put her head on her mother's lap, while Pajāpatī entered a succession of samadhi states until she was gone.

Flowers fell, mountains shook, and at her funeral the sun, moon, and stars were all visible in the sky. After her body was burned, Ananda found relics in the ashes and gave them to Siddhārtha, who said, "Pajāpatī has been the great trunk of the women's tree."

Eventually she was called the greatest in experience of all the women. Some of the later record-keepers claimed that the Buddha told Ananda privately that the Dharma would last only five hundred years instead of a thousand, just because she and the other women renounced their homes and took up the robes. But the Dharma is still here, after all.

wisdom body

Khema

At the time of the Buddha, about 2,500 years ago, a person was born into a clan and into a caste and never left them. They were permanent marks, one's essence, and together they determined almost everything about a person's life. Even objects had caste—timber, gems, clothing, and food were all divided and ranked and used in ritual ways to preserve the crucial distinctions.

Three classes, the brāhman, ksatriya, and vaiśya—priests, warriors, and farmers—were expected to study the Vedas and do the ritual sacrifices. The brāhman taught religion; the ksatriya protected the people, and the vaiśya bred cattle, traded, farmed, and lent money. The *Bhagavad Gita* taught, "It is better to do one's own duty badly than another's well." Of course, this meant a lot of people did their jobs badly. But now and then someone was born into exactly the right place.

King Bimbisāra, the ruler of Magadha, was one. Like Siddhārtha himself, Bimbisāra was born a warrior. He studied the Vedas, kept the borders safe, and tried to improve education and take care of the farmers during famine and drought. He was strict with his men, energetic with his harem, and tireless in working to improve roads and irrigation throughout the kingdom.

Bimbisāra's chief consort was named Khema, which means "peace." She was from an aristocratic family in Sagala. Khema was beautiful in a rare, lush, unforgettable way; her skin was the color of gold, and her eyes like a slice of twilight sky.

Khema was in love with beauty, especially her own. She wore splendid skirts—long muslin cloths pinned in place from waist to feet, embroidered with jasmine vines, hibiscus flowers, and the heads of cobras. She went barefoot, her toes and ankles wrapped in rings and bracelets, and wore gold circlets on her black hair. She painted her nipples and draped herself with coral, pearls, copper, and silver—strung around her neck and waist and dangling from her ears. When Khema walked, she walked under a parasol of palm leaves, and when she didn't want to walk, she was carried, and when she didn't want to be carried, she lay on a chaise lounge stuffed with human hair. Each night she slept in a bed under a canopy, coddled on both sides by servant girls who massaged her to sleep.

Siddhārtha came to Magadha many times and preached often to the king and his court. Every time he talked about how nothing can be counted on, how everything changes and everything dies and the cause of suffering in the world is desire, desire of many kinds. Khema found his lectures irritating in the extreme. Sometimes it is exactly what we know and need that we resist being given. In her past lives she had been a queen, but she had also been a renunciant who had given away all her wealth to others, even her hair at one time. Khema was full of merit—she just didn't know it.

The king conspired with others in the court, all of whom loved Siddhārtha and Khema both, to get Khema's attention. He asked the court poets to write odes describing the loveliness of the Sacred Grove where the teacher often stayed. When Khema began to ask questions about the gardens there, he offered to take her for the day, for a diversion.

"Let me blindfold you, dear," he said, laughing, "to make it more fun. A surprise." Khema loved surprises, so she let him blindfold her with a length of silk and help her into a cart. She giggled now and then as the cart bounced along the road to the garden. Then he helped her out and took off the blindfold, and she saw Siddhārtha waiting for her. Khema was upset and demanded to return to the castle, but half pleading and half insisting, the king made her sit down.

"Enjoy the trees and the grass," he said. "Have some fruit and just listen."

Siddhārtha began speaking of nothing in particular, but as he spoke, bit by bit, there appeared a woman beside him—a stunningly beautiful woman, more lovely than Khema. At first Khema was even more upset. Then she found herself entranced by the woman—and what was even odder, she began to be envious of her. Khema had never envied anyone, but before she could get used to this feeling she noticed that the woman was beginning to change. Her skin was growing coarse and wrinkled. Her breasts softened and sank, her belly grew, and her hips got wider. The thick, black hair was fading, its color turning dull and then speckled with gray. She began to bend at the waist, and the skin on her arms loosened. Her ankles thickened, and one by one her teeth disappeared.

Khema watched this strange sight, all of it happening in a matter of moments, and felt the foundation of her life shift and fall. She was watching the world as she knew it disappear and die. Suddenly Khema realized what Siddhārtha had been talking about when he talked about desire—the desire that some things change and the desire that other things never will, and the impossibility of both. She saw that everything in the world was going to change with time, that she would change, the king would change, that all she knew was going to fade away.

"Look at this body, Khema," Siddhārtha said. "Don't delight in it. Yours will die too. Notice. Notice that everything rises and falls away." Khema had never admitted to herself that she was afraid—that the endless restlessness of her days was fear. All at once she admitted this and saw the secret demons that had driven her every choice and filled her dreams as the product of her self-obsession, and she was disgusted. Just as the illusive woman in front of her staggered and died, she felt the awakening of the Mind That Seeks the Way, the mind that lives in each of us, waiting to speak, and when it speaks, it is never silent again. She was filled with grief for herself, and for all beings bound to die. She was filled with humility when she realized we are all the same under our skin. In one moment, the deep and seeking voice spoke, and in the next moment the knowledge for which it sought was found. She relinquished her fear and accepted the truth simultaneously with seeing it, and her heart transformed completely. It took only this one time for her, a laywoman, to realize the entirety of Siddhārtha's meaning, to achieve complete understanding.

"I have been mistaken," she said out loud, looking around her. "I failed to see this. I didn't understand." When they returned to the palace, she had a surprise for the king—she asked him for permission to leave the court and join the nuns. This wasn't exactly what Bimbisāra had had in mind. He had hoped—well, he knew enough to know that hope is as lasting as beauty. So he said yes, a bit ruefully, with no one to blame for the loss of his beautiful Khema but himself.

The next day, without regret, she left behind everything she had held dear, everything she had considered herself to be, and knelt before the monks and nuns. She was given the robe and bowl, and she began to train. Being awakened is not the end of one's training, but as much the beginning of it as any other moment. When Māra came to tempt her one day, he said, "You are young and beautiful, and so am I; let's enjoy ourselves." But such an approach no longer appealed to her; once touched, impermanence is never completely forgotten. Khema replied, "Sensual pleasures are swords and snakes. I've let them go. No more of that pain for me."

Two weeks after her ordination, as she sat watching a lantern flame flicker in the evening breeze, she leaped out of herself completely, past flickering, past change. In the next moment she awakened to the world of change again, entirely renewed. From that point on she could always see both qualities of the world—the evanescent and the eternal, the solid form and the formless void. In time she became Pajāpatī's closest assistant in establishing the women's order. Khema, the lovely consort of a king, was given the right to ordain other women and to preach to the community, and she was always called the wisest among women.

Some years later her dear friend Bimbisāra, who had saved and then released her, was deposed by his son and put in prison. From the forest where she slept she could see the prison walls, and she thought of him with love. When Bimbisāra was executed, his son began a rampage that lasted a long time. Sometimes, like many of us, she cried for the terrible suffering of the world.

When she was much older and had begun to look like the bent crone of her vision, King Prasenajit of Kosala paid her a visit. He was earnest and seriously pursued the Way, but he had questions that couldn't be answered.

"Do sentient beings exist after death?" he asked. "Do sentient beings not exist after death? Do sentient beings both exist and not exist after death? Do sentient beings neither exist nor not exist after death?" he asked. With each question, she answered, "The Buddha doesn't say this."

The king became frustrated. "So what does the Buddha say if he won't say this?"

"These questions—and any answers—are irrelevant," Khema answered. "With great understanding, one no longer needs to ask. When you see that there is only this, which rises and falls, only this, one no longer speaks of either existence or nonexistence.

"It is quite profound," she said. She repeated herself, using many different images, until the king suddenly understood and was filled with delight.

Prasenajit would eventually be deposed too, and the king who replaced him would systematically destroy Siddhārtha's clan, the Śākya tribe. But first, while he was still king, Prasenajit went to the great teacher and asked the same questions, and he got the same answers. *Wonderful!* he thought. *Khema uses the same words exactly.* His exchange with Khema was recorded in the *Abyākatasamyutta* and made part of the permanent canon of Buddhism.

the slave
Punnika

In six different lives, Punnika felt anxious and sought an answer. In six different lives, she found the Dharma, she was ordained, and she lived in perfect virtue. In those six lives, she couldn't cut the root of her delusion. Punnika cultivated pride. There are few karmic knots tighter than pride, and none tighter than spiritual pride. Outside, she was calm and obedient. Inside, she refused to ask for help, to surrender, to let go of her self in any way.

Most tribes practiced the class system; a few did not. But every tribe at least distinguished between free people and śūdra—the slave class of domestic servants and laborers, and certain minor clerks, tradesmen, and craftsmen. The śūdra were generally the darkest-skinned people, the descendents of the tribes conquered by the Aryans. Because of this, they were impure and not allowed to read the Vedic scriptures. They processed food, spun fabric, and harvested crops, and they were owned, like tools—vital tools, but tools nevertheless. A śūdra's only hope was to achieve a better rebirth in the next life by assiduously performing the duties of this one.

Punnika was born at Savatthi as a slave, the hundredth child born in the household of Anāthapiṇḍika. Her duty was to carry water from the river, and she hated this chore just because it was her duty. She was treated well enough if she behaved, but she had no choice, and lack of choice is worse than being beaten sometimes. She belonged to Anāthapiṇḍika, and he could loan or sell her if he wished or punish her in almost any way he wanted. Not that he did—Anāthapiṇḍika was a devout follower of the Buddha—but he could, and she hated that. She stood up tall, refusing to bow an inch lower than required. Even when she was perfectly courteous and subservient, Punnika gave people the impression of thinking she was otherwise. The world said she had little worth, so with great effort she concentrated on her worth and nursed it so that others would see it.

Drawing water was tedious; it could be easy and it could be hard. There were wild animals along the river—fishing cats and tapir on the banks, water buffalo and alligators in the water. In the summer Punnika couldn't see the mountains through the haze, and there were mudslides in the hills when the monsoons came. The river's course could change overnight and farms disappear in half an hour. The air was hot before and during and after the rains, which came every afternoon, so that the streets and fields flooded and one's feet were always muddy. The light was dull and gleaming, the ground steaming as the rain hit the hot dirt. People were dazed with the heat.

But if the monsoon didn't come, drought and famine followed. Then drawing water meant a long, thirsty walk, and the water was silty and sometimes foul. All things considered, she preferred the rain.

One hazy, hot day, Punnika was lingering on the banks, in no hurry to walk home with a full bucket, when she saw a small crowd. In the center, Siddhārtha was speaking—a thin, ordinary man, but with a voice that carried through every sound. While she listened, he seemed to roar with a lion's roar; its noise smashed open her ears and left her ringing like a bell. Her mind was caught in the lion's jaws.

We think our suffering is always unfortunate. But sometimes (often perhaps) the nature of our birth, the peculiar details of our suffering, free us. Life as a slave had pressed in on Punnika like a shrinking cocoon until she had no room left in which to move. She had finally reached a life where there was nothing she could control, nothing she could demand, no one she could even *be.* Listening to this lion's roar, she saw all at once how falsely she had made the world in her own mind. Punnika had believed what she'd been told all her life—that people are high and low, superior and inferior, good and bad. She saw her pride all at once—how hard she worked all the time at separating herself from what she did. Listening to the Buddha's words, she realized how this had only enslaved her in a new way. Whatever she was, it wasn't a slave or a queen or any *thing* at all. She was just this, here, now, this body and mind, drawing water, walking, sleeping, as free and changing as air.

Not long after, she was on the banks again with her buckets. Once her mind had opened, carrying water became a simple task, nothing more or less than what she was doing. She felt at peace. When she saw a brāhman named Udakasuddhika bathing ritually, she was filled with her own lion's roar.

"I carry water because I must. Even in the cold, even in the rain," she said. "I am afraid of the animals, of the current. I am afraid of being punished if I make a mistake. What are *you* afraid of? Why do you come to the water?"

"You know the laws," he said. "I am washing away evil acts."

"Who told you that would work?" she asked, and she was talking to this man of the highest caste as though they were good friends, without pride or shame. "If this were true, frogs and turtles would go to heaven. Crocodiles, pork-butchers, fishermen, thieves, and executioners could all be cleansed with a bath." The whole of the world in which they lived was filled with tight cocoons, and in each one someone squirmed in pain. *Unspin them,* she thought. *Let it go.*

"Besides," she added, "doesn't the water wash away your merit too?"

That's all it took. It wasn't the words, but the force of her roar, of her knowing, the strangeness of a slave who seemed so calm and sure ofherself. His own mind opened, and he tried to give her his robe in gratitude.

"No, you keep it," she said, knowing it wasn't the robe for a slave—and she was a slave, after all. "I don't want it. But listen, if what you're really afraid of is pain, don't do things that can cause you pain. Don't do harmful things to others, or to yourself. Why do we find this so difficult?" she mused. "Well, I don't know. But that's the way it is. Why don't you go listen to the new teacher in town?"

"I will," he whispered. "Your words have washed me clean."

Punnika's owner, Anāthapiṇḍika, admired Siddhārtha's teaching so much that he had given him the woods that came to be known as the Jeta Grove. When he heard about his slave's conversation with the brāhman—and you can be sure he heard about it soon, because the brāhman was telling everyone—he was deeply impressed. From that day on he kept his eye on Punnika as she walked back and forth from the river, carrying water.

Punnika's heart had been greatly humbled. It is a strange fact that when we are really and truly humbled, when there is no longer anything we are trying to defend, there is nothing to be afraid of anymore. The next time she saw Siddhārtha she approached him, buckets slung across her small shoulders. Without preamble, she asked, "May I be ordained?" She knew it was impossible. No slave could make this choice, but she had to ask. She had to speak her own truth now, no matter what the consequences.

He smiled, and she left without a word—glad for the smile at least.

Siddhārtha then sent one of the monks to investigate her circumstances. When the monk explained her request to Anāthapiṇḍika, his heart was humbled too. Unspinning, one by one. Immediately he set Punnika free with a word, and with another he adopted her as his daughter. Then he gave her permission to devote herself to studies.

So deeply humble was Punnika's heart at this point that she could only put her palms together and weep with gratitude. Then she took up her practice, not to prove her worth or to be seen, not in dignity or fear, but as though she were giving her whole life away as a gift to the world with every step. With little effort she attained arhatship; she meditated on the formlessness of form—on the sameness of buddha and slave—every moment of her day and awakened freely.

cloak walker
Patachara

This one lived many lives: she lived through 20,000 years of righteousness. She made many vows—still not enough, not enough.

Patachara's father was a respectable banker. He arranged her marriage to an older man she didn't know, but Patachara was already in love with one of their servants. When her unwanted wedding date was set, they eloped and moved to a town some distance away, across the river.

It was traditional that when a woman married she left her parents' clan and became part of her husband's instead. Patachara's husband had no family, no security. To marry out of class, to marry for love—these were dishonorable things. To marry without security or support—this was just foolish. Patachara left everything behind when she ran away.

Their small farming village was surrounded by simple walls with gates that closed at night. The couple lived in a small hut made of clay and dung with earthen floors, a single door and window, and a roof of palm leaves, with a bed and a few big pottery vessels for storing food.

Patachara had chosen a hard and peaceful life. She walked every day to a lotus pond to draw water, a pond shared with water buffalo, crabs, cranes, heron, and mosquitoes. She cooked simple meals, swept the dirt floor, loved her husband. There was just enough food to get by; theirs was a world made up in equal parts of fecundity and hunger.

When she got pregnant, Patachara wanted to return to her parents, but her husband wouldn't take her. The next year she was pregnant again, and she longed for her mother's company. But her husband dawdled until it was almost too late. In spite of her weariness, she was glad when they finally left on the long walk back.

A great storm blew up just as they reached the riverbank. Her husband left her with the toddler while he went to find a tall palm, to cut its fan-shaped leaves and make a shelter. While he was gone, Patachara went into labor. Out of her sight, her husband reached around a tree and disturbed a snake. The snake bit him, and he died.

Patachara's husband didn't come back, but she couldn't go looking for him; she was in hard labor and couldn't even stand. She gave birth alone in the night, in the rain and wind, trying to shelter one child while delivering another. Finally, when the weather cleared in the morning, she wrapped the two children in her clothes and went searching for her husband. When she found his body, she collapsed in grief at his side and stayed that way for a day and a night. She nursed the baby, fed bits of fruit to her son, and tried to gather enough strength to go back to her parents and her new life as a widow.

But the rain from the storm had raised the river so high that she couldn't cross alone with two children at the same time.

Patachara thought a long time about what to do. Finally she left the boy sitting on one bank and carried the newborn across, swimming hard, holding his tiny body high. On the far bank she laid the newborn carefully on a palm leaf. Turning back to get her toddler, she found herself terribly anxious about the baby; as she swam she kept turning round and round to watch. Suddenly a hawk dropped down and stole the baby away. Patachara began screaming and shouting at the bird, beating its way calmly into the sky with the baby wailing in its claws. It flew away so fast, so far and high, and Patachara was screaming so frantically, slapping at the river, that the toddler stood to watch. He thought she was calling him to come. Hurrying forward, he slipped down the muddy bank and was carried away in the river. Just like that, he was lost from sight.

After a time Patachara wandered, numb with pain. She walked aimlessly until she met a traveler from her parents' village. He recognized her and called her name.

"Oh, sir," she cried, "I'm going home. How are my mother and father?" she asked him. "My brother?"

"Oh, miss," he said, with a terrible look, "don't ask."

"I don't care about anything else," she cried. "Tell me about them."

Seeing she meant this, he told her how the storm had brought the roof of their house down, killing them all, and that even now they burned together on a funeral pyre.

Patachara's mind began to give way like the hillsides in the rain, slipping, sliding, coming apart. "My two children are gone," she cried. "My dead husband lies in a bush somewhere, and my mother, father, and brother all burn. There is nothing left in all the world."

There was a class below the śūdra, a class so low it wasn't called a class. These were the untouchables, people who existed outside all notions of human decency. They were the executioners, butchers, ditch diggers, chariot and basket makers, leather workers, liquor sellers, street sweepers, hunters, fishermen, and gravediggers. They were the necessary ugliness of the world. Untouchables were allowed to wear only clothes taken from corpses, to use only iron tools and cracked utensils and pottery. To kill an untouchable was equal to killing a dog. They banged wooden clappers as they walked so that people of higher caste could move away. Even the shadow of an untouchable, even the air that passed over their bodies, was tainted. If a person of a higher caste saw an untouchable, even by accident, he would wash his eyes with perfumed water and fast overnight.

When Patachara lost her family, she became a crazed spirit, an outcast among outcasts, untouchable even among the untouchables. Her clothes tore, and she became known as Cloak Walker because of her nakedness. People called her names and threw mud and garbage at her and shouted at her to leave. She didn't understand; she was less aware of herself than the dogs they kicked. All she knew was pain—less pain, more pain.

She wandered in circles for a long time, growing thin and filthy and ill. She wandered through rice fields and groves of palm all the way to Varānasī, a city of narrow, slippery streets crowded with people and animals, stinking of dung. The buildings went straight to the edge of the river; columns and turrets and small windows framed in stone crowded together at the bank. Sailboats and small sculls passed, and birds perched on poles watching for fish. The river was wide and opaque in the hazy sun, and Patachara came all the way to its edge. Squinting, she watched the water, knowing only that this was bad, it had hurt her, and she wanted to hurt it back. She began to beat the water with her hands, screaming curses.

Siddhārtha saw her in the water, and he knew she must be close to being whole. You have to be broken in order to be fixed, and she was completely broken. There was no more of that work to do—she had nothing to let go of, having already let go of everything. So he followed her, with his disciples trailing behind, complaining.

"Leave that lunatic alone," they said. "Don't get close to her." Patachara's splashing was getting their robes wet, and several stepped away.

He said, "Don't avoid her." He stepped into the water, touched her shoulder, and said, "Sister, recover your presence of mind."

Just like that, she was brought back to clarity. She looked around in a daze, at the man beside her, the frowning men watching her, the city walls, the water. Seeing that she was dirty and undressed, she fell ashamed to the ground, trying to cover herself. A monk finally took pity on her and gave her his outer robe. Patachara wrapped it around herself and then knelt at Siddhārtha's feet, crying out the story of her loss. She had suddenly remembered everything, as a wounded man remembers when the anesthetic wears off.

"Help me," she begged. "Save me from this pain."

"I can't help you with this," he answered. "Nothing can save us from loss and grief. Family doesn't last. Kin doesn't last. Not in this world or the next. You're clutching at something that you can't keep, that you could never have kept." He smiled then, and it was so unexpected, so pure, that she stopped crying. He helped her to stand.

"This isn't the first time you've mourned children. An ocean of tears has been shed; an ocean waits to be shed. This is the cycle. No other being can shelter or protect us. But there is a path—a way out of pain. It's better to know the truth about the world for a single day than to live a hundred years without it, Patachara," he said. By the time he finished speaking, lightly, gently, almost in a whisper, she had become a Once-Returner, a person who needs only one more rebirth to realize enlightenment.

Patachara joined the women's sangha. She ripened slowly after that, never finding complete peace even after years as a nun. She was happy—happier—but something was missing.

One day she washed her feet and was deeply struck by how the water ran into the ground and disappeared. She saw the hawk again, hungry, with babies of its own to feed. She saw her boy slip into the river like the water sliding into the ground. Later that night, as she slowly turned down the wick of a lamp, she was awakened fully to the inconstancy of form—not as loss and tragedy but as the nature of all things. She watched the flickering of the tiny flame in the dark room and comprehended that change itself is an unchanging thing. As she extinguished the lamp and saw the flame die, she knew that form itself is this emptiness of form, and emptiness itself is this changing form. There can never be one without the other. Patachara had reached the stage of a Never-Returner, needing no more lives to understand the truth of all things.

I washed my feet, and saw the waters,
flowing from the high land to the low.
Like this I concentrated my mind.
Holding a lamp in my cell, putting out the fire,
My mind was released as quickly as the flame disappeared.

Patachara became a highly influential teacher who brought many women to the Dharma. Many of her disciples became teachers too. She was allowed to ordain others and converted more than five hundred women. Each one had lost a child. When a woman came, crying, she took her by the hand and said, "Ask yourself, where did your child come from, to spend a little time here in this breathing space? We come one way, we go another. We die and pass to other births." One by one the women's hearts were softened into peace, and they stood and hailed her as their teacher.

curlyhair
Bhadda

In a past life Bhadda had lived in a clansman's family and accumulated merit for several eons. In another life she was a princess who practiced diligently, built hermitages, and for 20,000 years never broke a precept.

It was a start.

Bhadda's father loved her. He was the treasurer of the city of Rājagaha, a wealthy man in a wealthy world. The kingdom of Magadha had fought and conquered its neighbors: Anga, Kasi, Kosala, and finally Vrjji, growing in power and reach into a great state. Rājagaha was one of its captured prizes, a great city that was home to 200,000 people who lived surrounded by walls that stretched for miles.

Bhadda was good-looking and intelligent, but finding her a proper husband wasn't easy because she was also headstrong and unhappy. She argued with life—she argued with everyone, even speaking back to her father, which had the curious effect of making him love and indulge her more. He wasn't sure what to make of Bhadda's difficult behavior, but secretly he knew she was often right. Her mind and wit were sharp and her logic precise.

Like her brothers and sisters, Bhadda was cared for by a retinue of personal attendants. Each day she and her siblings were bathed, dressed, and decorated. Bhadda ate rice cakes and sweets and peacock's meat, wore peacock feathers tucked behind her ears, and had her long black hair swept up by jeweled combs. Many of her hours were spent on flower arranging, embroidery, sleight of hand, and memorizing tongue-twisters. The rhythm of the day moved between the morning and evening devotions, the many offerings to the gods, to the other beings, to the dead, to the poor.

She recited the devotional songs of Veda, which meant *knowledge,* learning by rote and mnemonic devices. This is what they called studying for girls. Her brothers were allowed to read the analytical Brāhmaṇa texts, which described the minute details of the rituals and explicated the hidden meanings of the songs. She knew what they studied because she spied on them when she could, longing for the secrets they learned.

Bhadda had no peace. She stamped her foot in frustration at the meaningless replies her teachers gave to her searching questions. What, *what,* is this world for if it isn't for knowledge? She argued and analyzed until her schooling was done, her tutors exhausted and her parents distraught.

As she grew older her father considered husbands for her and silently rejected each one, knowing Bhadda would break their spirits and bring trouble to her in-laws with her dissatisfaction. By the time she was sixteen, Bhadda was shielded carefully from men outside her family, and she retreated more and more into her own stormy mind, spending days in silence by the window.

One day, steeped in a gray sorrow she didn't begin to understand, she heard a drum beating in the street and watched a procession of soldiers pass by the window. They were leading a criminal draped in red garlands to be executed at the Robbers' Cliff. The criminal was named Satthuka, and he was the son of one of the king's ministers. He was also a thief of a low and violent kind. Because he was of such a high caste, he had been spared the harsher punishments criminals of the lower castes could expect—impaling, drowning, beheading, being burned alive. Whatever he had stolen must have been important, though, because he wasn't given the lesser punishments of the upper classes, like paying a fine or having his topknot cut off. His was a moderate sentence: simple death, no extra pain, and a chance in the next life to improve his conduct.

Bhadda took one look at his face, his handsome, sly, deceitful face, and fell in love. She collapsed on her soft, embroidered couch, prone with desire, and declared to her father, the way only a sixteen-year-old girl can declare: "If I get him, I shall live. If not, I shall die! Oh, I shall simply die!"

Not even eons of rebirth in the realms of gods can save us from ordinary human desire like this.

Bhadda's father loved her much more than was wise. We mustn't suppose that he believed for an instant Satthuka was going to make Bhadda a good husband, but he found himself in a very delicate position. After all, she needed to get married, and svayamvara—a woman choosing her own groom—wasn't *that* rare in the higher classes. She could still have a religious marriage, and he didn't need to provide a dowry. So Bhadda's father foolishly agreed. Being a treasurer—treasurers are more likely than many people to know secrets that can come in handy in cases like this—he asked for a few favors and stopped the execution. Satthuka was pardoned, and he and Bhadda were married right away.

When at last they were allowed to be alone, Satthuka, who could hardly believe his luck, told the adoring Bhadda that he had to fulfill a spiritual duty before any of his connubial ones—he had promised the local deity an offering if his life was spared. Bhadda made up an offering, and together they went to the base of the cliff with her many attendants.

"Come with me alone," he pleaded. "Leave the servants behind." She was flattered at his attention, and the two of them climbed to the top. There he turned to face her.

"You silly cow," he whispered. "Give me your jewels." Satthuka was so greedy that he threw away a rich life in the future for gems right now. That was the end of her crush, which had been as frail as desperate love usually is. Bhadda was left with only a bereft clarity, her will, and her considerable mind.

"May I embrace you just once before I die?" she asked. Pleased even then, Satthuka agreed. Bhadda stepped forward, reached up her bespangled arms, and pushed him off the cliff.

As Bhadda stood staring at the valley below, at the splash of color where Satthuka had landed, the Cliff Deity appeared. He was really quite impressed and complimented her insight.

"Men aren't always the smartest ones," he said with a smile. "When women see clearly, they can be clever too." But the deity's words cut; this wasn't exactly the cleverness she'd imagined.

Cause and effect. Each moment, a new cause. Twenty thousand years of discipline will not protect you from the need to act, or from the consequences.

Eventually, after considering her few options, Bhadda simply walked away along the cliff's edge—away from her servants, her family, and her home. She walked, thinking of the ascetics she had seen standing in the street at the festivals, naked and dirty, the stories she'd heard of the men and women who left their lives and temple duties forever—disappearing into the forest, never to return. They were regarded with respect and a kind of dread; they had stepped out of destiny and, in doing so, made everyone's destiny less certain. Bhadda felt herself caught in a wave of change that extended from long before her birth and beyond anything she could see, a great wave rising up from the depths of the world she'd known and climbing, climbing, soon to break. She walked until she found a small order of Jain women. She asked them for renunciation.

Which grade? they asked her. How severe?

The hardest, said Bhadda.

So they took her clothes and jewels and gave her a white robe. When she stood barefoot and plain before them, they tore her hair out by the roots, one hair at a time.

She was to strive to care for nothing, to own nothing and desire nothing—not even death. She was to feel neither pleasure nor pain, neither hope nor fear, to neither turn from danger nor move toward comfort. She was never to harm any living thing. Her sisters in the practice were dour company—but Bhadda didn't long for company. She longed for an explanation, and none was forthcoming. She began to debate other Jains, and she won. She asked questions, and no one knew the answers. They told her not to care for answers.

Bhadda left and wandered alone through the world for fifty years.

She walked barefoot, wearing her one robe. Eventually her hair grew back, curly now, and then she was known as Bhadda Kundalakesa—Bhadda the Curlyhair. She passed through Magadha and traveled east to Anga near the sea, then north to Vrjji, and west to Kasi, where she entered its capital city of Varānaṣī.

She begged for a little food but didn't take much care with her body; her body didn't seem to mean much. Her mind strove ceaselessly, trying to find somewhere to rest. Whenever she came to a new village, she propped a rose-apple branch in a pile of sand near the town border. Then the curious children came to see her—themselves also half-naked and dirty, with sticky cheeks and dark eyes, also wanting answers. She told them to spread the word that anyone who wanted to debate her should trample the branch. She waited a week in each village, sleeping beneath a tree or in a ditch. If no one came forward, she traveled on. When she debated, she always won. In all those years Bhadda found nothing that could withstand her. She was alone in the world, without peace.

When she was seventy years old, with dirt deep in the wrinkles of her faded skin and her bones sticking out like winter branches, she reached the Jeta Wood near Savatthi. She set up her rose-apple and explained to the crowd of children, wiping a child's runny nose on her patched sleeve as she spoke, how they could announce her intention to debate. Then she went to beg a few bites of food for the day.

Śāriputra, Siddhārtha's chief disciple, was strolling along the edge of the village when he saw the branch. They had been in the wood at rest for some days, and he knew this was something new. When the eager, sniffling child nearby explained to him what it meant, his interest was piqued. What a grandly confident woman this disheveled philosopher must be!

"Knock down that branch for me, won't you?" he asked, and the child happily agreed. He was still kicking sand and twigs about when Bhadda returned.

Now and then in her travels Bhadda had met disciples of the Śākyan prince who'd left his kingdom to teach. They were strangely unwilling to argue. So when the child said that it had been Śāriputra, famous for his dialectical skill, she was glad.

Slowly Bhadda walked to where the monks were gathered. Their number surprised her—hundreds of men and women in a grassy verge under mango and palmyra trees. They wore simple robes and went barefoot like her, with their heads shaved bare. She was struck at their repose and at how quiet such a large group of people could be.

The monks watched as Bhadda approached Śāriputra and joined him under a tree, and when they were settled, the crowd gathered around. Immediately Bhadda leaped forward with her words, quizzing the renowned disciple. She asked him about the nature of self, how to know one's future, the way to transform evil, how to contact the hidden deities of the earth and sky, and what to make of the relentless permanence of Bhadda.

He answered every question, skillfully, surprisingly at times, never losing composure, never showing off. He quoted his teacher's simple stories about monkeys and trees, rivers and rafts, lute players and parents. He wove a picture of life as something moderate and true, parrying her blows without striking back. For the first time in more than fifty years Bhadda couldn't win. There was no target.

"All right, then," she said, frustrated at last, "you question me."

Śāriputra was a wise man in many ways. He saw Bhadda clearly, at least—how she clung to her loneliness, how she had tried to convert it into victory and knowledge. He saw the sharpness of her mind, her passion, her determination.

"What is the One Thing? The One?" said Śāriputra, gesturing vaguely.

Bhadda knew of the Vedantic One, of Atman, Brāhmana, Soul. But because she knew only ideas, she couldn't answer. She finally couldn't answer at all; her mind had come to a halt.

Does it matter to what Śāriputra gestured? In which direction he pointed? In her moment of not-knowing, Bhadda ripened as sweetly as a rose-apple blossom. What is it, this thing that she had sought for so long? In all those years she had gathered only the names of things. She knew endless names, a thousand labels, a million qualities and divisions and graphed matrices of the cosmos. They had never been enough. Śāriputra watched as old Bhadda fell to her knees, bowed for the first time since she had been a girl, and whispered, "I will take you as a teacher, Lord, and ask for refuge in the Order."

"Not me, Bhadda," he replied. "Go to the Blessed One tonight, just as you are right now."

These last words were whispered, Bhadda's head to the grass, Śāriputra bent low beside her gray curly hair. Intimacy, intimacy, in their exchange, and no victory, no loss.

The monks glanced at each other, at this mysterious end to a debate, and a rush of delight ran through the meadow, because it wasn't over yet.

She waited for dark. The Bhadda of debate was dead, but no new Bhadda had been born, and she waited in a strange state of calm. Looking down, she noticed for the first time in a long while her dirty feet and unkempt robe, the packed dirt beneath her nails, and went down to the river to bathe.

Night fell in the Jeta Grove, and the monks wrapped themselves in their outer robes. Finally Siddhārtha rose from his seat deep in the shadows of the trees and joined them. He began to speak without form or preamble. Bhadda, deep among the listening monks, drew forward without thought, as though he reeled her in on a rope tied around her waist.

And then she was before him. Their eyes met, and they recognized each other like old friends.

"Better than volumes of subtle knowledge is a single verse that brings peace," he said, very quietly.

Who knows which breeze opens the bud? This Bhadda flower has been blooming since the tree was a seed, and it will continue to bloom when the tree has turned to dust. But at that moment the last petal of her understanding opened to the earth and sky. Bud, flower, fruit, tree, seed. She was awake without barrier or lack.

"Bhadda, come," he said, holding out a hand.

Among all the women ordained, only Bhadda was ordained by the Buddha's own hand. She was famous forever for the swiftness of her insight. But we know, and she knew, that it was a long time coming. She left the Jeta Wood and wandered on for the rest of her life, which lasted a long while. She wandered freely, alone but never lonely, together with the world.

the widow
Dhammadinnā

Dhammadinnā was born to a respected family in Rājagaha, and her father arranged for her to be married to Visākha, a road engineer of good caste. On the wedding day he was rubbed with ointments, wrapped in fine brocade cloths, and led to Dhammadinnā's home. The servants washed his feet, and her father offered him a fine drink made of honey and rice and herbs. Finally he was led to his bride, who sat hidden behind a curtain in a great pavilion in the courtyard. As the priests intoned mantras and magical spells, Visākha promised Dhammadinnā that he would be faithful and pious toward her. Only then did someone pull the curtain so they could see each other face to face.

Then Visākha grasped her hand and helped her to stand; he knotted a corner of his robe to a corner of hers, and they walked carefully around the fire three times.

"I am he, you are she, you are she, I am he," he said. "We will marry and give our children to the world, and live happily together a hundred seasons."

They did live together for quite some time, in the mild happiness of two people who don't hope for more from each other than harmony. Having never met before, they became friends. As a married man, Visākha was expected to pursue only three things: religious merit through the study and rites of the Vedas, the accumulation of honest wealth, and pleasure of many kinds. This he did, while working to raise the roads, fix the canals lined with shade trees, post distance markers and signs, and care for the pilgrims' rest houses.

Dhammadinnā was in charge of their home. As a married woman, she walked with her servant to the trade district to go shopping among the covered stalls and small shops, buying from the milkman with his long ladle and big pail and the spice seller with his shelves of jars and pots. She visited the perfumer for lac dye and breath mint; the garland maker for flowers; the vegetable sellers for mangoes, peas, and lentils. Her life revolved around her husband; she rose first and retired last and made his needs her life.

Every day when he returned home, he saw her through the window and smiled. He was faithful; he was pious; they were at peace. One day, out of idle curiosity, Visākha went to hear Siddhārtha preach. As he listened, he was converted and immediately left home in his heart.

When he came home that day, he passed the window without smiling. Dhammadinnā went to greet him, but he didn't turn when she called his name. "What's the matter, Visākha?" she asked. "You won't even look at me. What have I done wrong?"

"It's not your fault," he sighed. "But I have to leave home. I've heard the truth, and I want to follow a teacher. I want to be a monk. From this day on I won't touch a woman. I plan to shave my head and leave this house forever."

"What am *I* supposed to do?" she asked.

"Do what you want—you can live here, enjoy our wealth, or return to your family."

This was a fine thing for him to say. When he left, he would leave her a widow, without children. Widows couldn't get married again, couldn't attend parties or ceremonies, couldn't wear makeup or jewelry. They were supposed to sleep on the ground and eat one meal a day, avoiding meat, honey, salt, and wine. Widows were avoided and, at the same time, watched closely to be sure they behaved. Many shaved their heads because there was no reason not to do it. At least the ordained were respected and had a kind of freedom. She saw no recourse but to follow him.

"Let me leave home too," she answered.

So while Visākha went about dissolving his household and finishing his business, he sent Dhammadinnā to the bhikkunis in a golden palanquin. After she was ordained, she asked permission to do solitary practice. "My heart longs for the retreat," she explained. In her mind, this was the funeral pyre; she believed her life was over. But in her hidden heart, where even she couldn't see, she was returning home.

So Dhammadinnā entered the forest and wandered. The days were humid, and every morning she rose from the ground where she had slept and walked to the river. The glaring sun seemed to crack against the flat blue water. Men slid out of canoes and disappeared beneath the surface, rising a moment later with an armful of dribbling jute plants. Ox-drawn carts rumbled along the banks, piled with bales of grass towering over the head of the driver. The sun rose and set in a dark blue sky that she saw through the black branches of the trees.

Sometimes she came to villages on begging rounds, and now and then she saw people from the east with eyes of a different shape, or northern people in rough clothing. She heard many languages and saw the practices of many religious sects, which seemed to arise and disappear as often as the sun. Almost every town had a guru on its outskirts, promising heavenly rebirth to anyone who listened. She watched the forest ascetics sometimes, with their long, tangled hair and uncut fingernails, standing for days on one foot or walking naked in the rain, with stones hung from their genitals. They seemed to think doing these things would bring them understanding. *Well,* she thought, *who knows?* Life was strange.

Dhammadinnā walked the forest, avoiding the dark, silent cobra, the tiger and leopard, watching the slow crawl of the sloth, listening to the noise of monkeys and unseen birds. She loved the banyan trees most of all, immortal giants whose roots spread in countless directions, providing shelter and wide, deep shade.

Dhammadinnā had been reborn many times. Her mind was prepared to die, and she took to the trees as though to her deathbed. Soon enough her ego, the small self she called *Dhammadinnā,* died. Her mind's complaints disappeared, her sorrow ceased, her body's needs faded away. On a quiet day like all the other quiet days, under a banyan tree like all the other banyan trees, the patience she had practiced in many Buddha realms was realized. When she returned to herself, newly awakened, it was as an arhat. She was filled with the absolute patience of all things, the end of fear and hope. When she awakened, she said,

She whose desire has finally come to rest,
desire that once filled all of her,

she whose heart is not driven by desire anymore,
she shall be called Bound Upstream.

After a time, she decided to return to the other bhikkunis. So in this way her solitary forest self died and a new Dhammadinnā was born, one who lived comfortably with other people. Her wisdom radiated in her speech, and she cut sharply to the heart of questions like a cook slicing to the heart of the lotus.

One day Dhammadinnā found her way back to Rājagaha, a huge city with hundreds of thousands of people, a city of gardens and temples. After joining a gathering of the devout in one of the big parks, she turned around to find herself face to face with Visākha. They sat down together under a sal tree near the broad main street, near rich houses with their gables and balconies and rooftop courts.

She was somehow not surprised to discover that he was still building roads, still keeping a household. After she had left, he found that home-leaving didn't suit him after all, and he became a lay teacher instead.

She felt no resentment, none at all; that Dhammadinnā was gone.

Her former husband was intensely curious about his wife, his widow, and he interviewed her, seeing with a single glance that she was a higher authority on the Dharma than himself now.

"What are the visible signs of meditation?" he asked. "Why must we do it, and how?"

"In meditation the heart is focused," she answered. "The practitioner gains four types of attention. We need four kinds of effort to do this, and we do it through practice." She went on for some time, in detail, and he asked many more questions, and she answered them all clearly, especially instructing him on the nature of emotions.

"There is nothing wrong with feelings," she said. "They shouldn't be suppressed. But we have to know how disruptive they can be, because over and over again we want to cling to them or push them away."

His last question concerned nirvana.

She looked at him for a long moment, with the quiet intimacy of an old friend. "You will always have questions," she said. "In nirvana, the question and the answer merge, the journey and the goal become one. Why not ask Siddhārtha if you'd like to know more?"

Finally, he submitted to her superior achievement, took her direction, and went to Siddhārtha. When he repeated Dhammadinnā's words, Siddhārtha was impressed.

"She is very wise," he said. "If you'd asked me, I would have given the same answers. You should listen to her."

Thus, Dhammadinnā's words were known as buddhavacana—Buddha words—and in time were preserved in their own section of the *Majihima Nikaya.* Siddhārtha called her foremost in insight and gave her permission to ordain. She became the master to many disciples and had many Dharma heirs. For the rest of her long life she stayed near Sarnath, the deer park, and strolled its paths, between spindly low trees under the pale sky.

the dutiful one
Sumanā

Sumanā's merit from many lives allowed her to be born the sister of King Prasenajit in Kosala. She had resolved to follow the Buddha in previous lives, so when Siddhārtha came to the court and lectured, she was immediately converted. So was her brother, the king.

The king had a kingdom to run and couldn't follow Siddhārtha. Sumanā was the chosen companion of her elderly grandmother, and in spite of her longing to go with the wanderers, she stayed with the old woman. Whenever the teacher came to town, they invited him to the court and spent joyful hours discussing the teaching with him. But he always left, and they always stayed.

Her skin felt wrong much of the time, too tight, too loose—someone else's skin. This wasn't her life, it didn't quite fit, and she wore it like the wrong clothes. But they were the only clothes she had—this was the only life she could lead, and she made do with it, hemming here where she could, shortening there. There was nothing else to do. She got very jealous sometimes, looking out the palace windows and noticing a shaved person in thin robes. How could she envy that hard, plain life? She wondered about it sometimes, and she cried sometimes. She thought something crucial was missing. It is very hard to be outside something for which we feel ourselves designed, to be forbidden to be the person we think ourselves to be.

But that was the secret for Sumanā. She had forbidden it for herself. Even in a life without choices, we make choices all the time. Late on a summer night, unable to sleep, she heard the frogs calling to each other in the garden—*brrribit, rribbit,* they called. Choose, choose! Choose your mind. She went to the window and stared at the heavy moon; an unseen bird gurgled like a baby. Choose—there is only now, this moment, and it is passing no matter what you do with it. It will pass if you spend it doing exactly what you want, and it will pass if you spend it longing for another moment, and it will pass if you spend it wishing for another life.

How could anything possibly be missing when this moment is everything?

After that, her distress and her excitement began to fade. Her life moved as softly as the fine, broken, pale clouds skidding like milk foam across the dimming sky.

Many years passed. By the time her grandmother died, Sumanā was herself old.

Sumanā and her brother walked to Siddhārtha's grove, carrying a treasure of carpets and fine weaving as a donation. Then they joined the community beneath the banyan trees as though they'd been away on a long trip and were finally coming home. The pipal trees heavy with sweet figs formed a soft wall around them, and the grassy field where the monks and nuns rested smelled fresh and clean.

When Siddhārtha began to speak, his words cut with the force of a tiny stream slicing rock, with the implacable power of a seedling breaking through the spring earth. Sumanā had already done all the important work —she had left home in her heart and mind, she had found the stream and plunged in, and she had begun to swim all by herself, by just going on, noticing and dropping the resentment, noticing and dropping the grief, noticing and dropping the anger, the yearning, the excitement. Noticing that she loved her grandmother and her brother and her own life just as it was. Having already done all that, she felt her mind open completely until it no longer existed as a separate mind, and then it became her mind again. She left the stream and stepped onto the Path of No Return.

In that moment, Siddhārtha faced her. "Lie down, now," he said. "Your passions are still now. You are cool, you know peace.

"There is nothing more to do."

Sumanā repeated this, quietly. *There is nothing more to do.* Then she repeated it with exultation, until it became her own poem. *There is nothing more to do.* There was nothing more to do but her own life. Prasenajit had to return to the kingdom; his entire life, until his death, was about being the king. In the end, she returned with him, the king's sister, to help. She was known forever afterward as the greatest of laywomen followers.

the seed
Kisagotami

Śuddhodhana was her uncle and Siddhārtha her cousin, but Kisagotami's own family was poor. She was pretty and well spoken, and from an early age she began to hope for a better life, for status, for recognition. When she married a man of higher class, it seemed she'd gotten her wish. Such marriages outside caste lines were frowned upon, though. Her in-laws belittled Kisagotami, talking about her behind her back and calling her "nobody's daughter."

A wife bears children; a good wife bears sons; an ideal wife bears ten sons. When Kisagotami had a baby boy, her in-laws stopped complaining. She was happy. Her son began to crawl, then to walk and play, and she was happier still. She had plans—more children, a big family of boys, higher status, a real place in the world. Then one day her son was feverish, and the next day he died. In just a day, everything changed.

To Kisagotami, it was worse than her own death, and she couldn't accept it. Her son was dead, so her dreams were dead, her aspirations, and who she'd thought she'd be. She wrapped the body in a rag and walked through the streets for days, showing the corpse to everyone she met and begging for medicine.

One person at last took pity on her and led her to Siddhārtha. "If anyone can help, it's him," she said. Siddhārtha looked at her kindly, and when she held the stinking body crawling with maggots out to him, he took it gently in his arms.

"Help me, sir," she begged.

"I will revive your child on one condition," he answered. "Find a household where there has never been a death, and bring me mustard seeds from there."

Kisagotami left the baby with Siddhārtha and joyfully began going from house to house.

"Has there ever been a death here?" she asked at each door. And at each door she was told, yes, yes, there had been a death. So many deaths. Oh yes, we can't recall how many. We no longer count them. I lost my mother, my father. We lost our children, our sister. My brother died, my husband died, my baby died. Died.

Slowly her hope faded and she felt dread, and then she felt simply hollow, and then at last quiet. How alone she had felt, and how far from alone she had really been. Finally Kisagotami stopped in the middle of the road, looking at the rows of houses still ahead, and thought, *This is how it will be in every house.* Her son was born, and then he died. She had been born, and she would die. Then and there, her life changed again. She awakened to the impermanence of form, bodies and selves, status and rank, love and hope, past and future, the fleeting life of each moment, not one of which can be captured. Then she returned to Siddhārtha.

"Well?" he asked. "Did you bring the seeds?"

"No," she answered, head bowed. "I don't care about the seeds. I only want peace." Then she took her baby back, walked to the charnel ground, and gently buried the decomposing corpse. Standing over the new grave, she said, "This is the universal law for all things: impermanence, impermanence."

After this, Kisagotami was ordained. First she vowed to keep the ten monastic precepts: not to harm living things, steal, indulge in wrong sexual behavior, lie, become intoxicated, eat when it was forbidden, indulge in entertainments, wear jewelry or perfume, sleep in a high or broad bed, or handle money. She also made a special vow to wear only the roughest clothes. In a previous life, she had been a devout Buddhist. In that life, she'd heard the teacher describe the practice of wearing rough garments and had vowed to do so someday. In time she was known as the first in humility among all the ordained.

One day in the grove Siddhārtha said to those gathered, "The person who lives a hundred years and doesn't see this path would be better to live only one day and behold it." With these words, Kisagotami was awakened further, beyond the impermanence of form to form falling completely away, body and mind disappearing altogether. Even one day of clarity is better than a life of delusion, and she was willing to make that trade, completely willing. Her body and mind fell away, and then returned, empty and clean. In a world of suffering, a world where no being can escape without pain, she found a way to end the pain. No self meant no death—just as not knowing what to do makes every act possible, not having a permanent self means no end to the selves one has, no loss, no extinction, no death. It was very curious and made her smile: after her search for a seed from the house where no one had died, she found the very seed inside her. She found the house where death had never been.

I practiced the Way until I reached the place of no death.
I have found great peace; I have seen into the mirror.
The arrow has been pulled out, and I carry no more burdens.
What was done, had to be done; I did it.
Kisagotami, with a free mind, says this.

beautiful eyes

Subhā

After lifetimes of accumulating merit, Subhā was born in this Buddha world as the daughter of an eminent brāhman in Rājagaha. She was raised in the midst of religious life, her days a long series of rituals, festivals, temple celebrations, and offerings.

"Fire became speech, and entered the mouth. Wind became breath, and entered the nostrils. The sun became sight, and entered the eyes." She knew these phrases of creation and source as she knew her mother's face. "The moon became mind, and entered the heart." She had to memorize the endless names and rituals, the pantheon of gods, the constantly increasing rites and rules, she had to know the taboos and requirements and do as the priests directed.

The Vedic texts called the universe a tension between the eternal and the transient. All forms, including Subhā, were only appearance. Her body was appearance, her chafing thoughts were appearance, her prickly feelings and secret longings were appearance. "That is Atman. That art thou. *Tat tvam asi.*" There was no place to look for the self. *Neti, neti,* she had always been told. Not this, not this. Not that.

Knowing this, she knew nothing, and she knew she knew nothing. Who is Subhā? she wondered. Why am I, me? Why am I bound to this temporary form? She questioned her parents and her tutors ceaselessly. What is this thing I feel myself to be, which does not feel like a dream at all? The religion was so complicated, the Vedic literature so long and dense, and the answers so opaque and confusing that she began to think people were evading the questions entirely.

"Just learn the rites, Subhā!" her father exclaimed in exasperation. "Let the priests sort out the rest."

One festival day Subhā and the other women carried lighted lamps through the streets to the temple, wearing the heavy jeweled headdresses she despised. "It is at the command of him who always covers this world," they chanted. "The knower, the time of time, it is at his command that this creation unfolds itself."

Then she shed her headdress and joined her sisters at a fair. She bought a length of cloth and ate too many jak-fruit candies. They watched elephants and acrobats, snake charmers and jugglers, and the rooftops of the city flew with commemorative flags and garlands. The air filled with the music of minstrels. *This is it,* she thought. This was everything for the rest of her life—hollow practices and brief entertainment. She was tired to death of it all.

When Siddhārtha came to speak to her father, Subhā overheard. Her father had demanded the audience, wary of this new teacher, this cult among cults that people were talking about. He was moved deeply by Siddhārtha's words, by the subtlety and radicalness of his teaching, but his priestly practice was his world. Subhā, already so anxious in ways she couldn't name, heard the teaching too and all at once saw sharply into the meaninglessness of her days. The idea of something immensely more simple and pure, like a small, still pool, filled her mind. Instead of ritual, freedom from ritual. Instead of volumes, a few words. Instead of complication and costumes, bare shoulders and plain cloth. Instead of a description of life, life.

There was nothing for her in the study of the Vedas, and nothing left for her in the world she knew. With her father's reluctant permission, while still young, she joined the women's community under Pajāpatī and quickly came to love the life they led.

One day, while walking in the mango grove near Jīvakamba, she was accosted by a young man from the town. Like many men, he saw all women the same way—they were either the property of a particular man or available to all men. Nuns and prostitutes were both endangered by the delusions of men like these.

He barred Subhā's way and made a rude request. He smelled of rice beer and swayed as he stood.

"Excuse me," she said. "This is against the rules, you know that."

He didn't move, so she tried again. "I don't want this," she said. "Please let me go." She was trying to be patient.

Instead, the man repeated his suggestion. He thought himself a grand lover, this one did, and described at some length what they could do in the beds of flowers, exactly how they could celebrate spring. Subhā was impassive, just waiting for him to get over himself, so he tried another tactic.

"Besides, you're alone," he said, in a louder voice. "You don't seem afraid. I think you really want this. And I love your eyes," he said with a gesture. "Your languid eyes like a forest sprite."

"This body is death," she answered. "What do you see worthwhile?"

"You have eyes like a gazelle's eyes, like a blue lotus bud. The lashes, their shape—your eyes make me more passionate than ever."

Subhā tried to teach him. It was impossible to get past him—she was sure she couldn't outrun him—and it seemed equally impossible to offend him, so she tried to teach him. At great length, she described the worthlessness of sensual pleasure and why she had chosen renunciation. She explained that she followed a teacher, she described the Eightfold Path, and she talked about the emptiness of human form and how all things will change and disappear. He only became more persistent. Whatever she said, he parried, and then finally he grabbed for her, catching the belt of her robe, laughing. "I love your beautiful eyes!"

She spun away, tearing the belt out of his hand. "These eyes!" she said fiercely. "These eyes are balls, bubbles, slime!" Saying this, she plucked her left eye out and tried to hand it to him.

"Come here, then! You can have my beautiful eye!"

The man was horrified. He stared in shock at her and then ran away. (For a long time afterward, his friends wondered what had come over him. Their noisy pal had become quiet and thoughtful and didn't seem interested in the local girls anymore.)

As for Subhā, she walked back through the woods, cradling her eyeball in one hand and holding her torn robe in the other. But she wasn't sad or scared. "The sun became sight, and entered the eyes," she remembered, smiling to think the old prayers finally meant something to her. This was real knowledge in her hand.

When she returned to Siddhārtha's company and saw him, her eye was instantly renewed. Her excitement disappeared, and she was filled with tranquillity. For a time she looked around the world with two good eyes and saw each thing clearly. Right there, as easily and quietly as she washed her face before breakfast, she attained freedom from all desire and delusion and thoroughly grasped the Truth. Then she saw with eyes completely new.

old bones
Dhammā

Dhammā was born into a respectable family. While she was still quite young, she married a man of good standing. After that, her life revolved around their household. She had servants but was responsible for every aspect of the home. She helped manage the endless rituals and propitiations of each season: raising the beds and having incantations said against snakes in the rainy season; monthly offerings to the ancestors; the ritual bathing in the autumn in honor of the king of the dead. She was expected to spend time every morning on her own ritual ablutions and to help her husband in his. She greeted him each morning by kneeling down to touch his feet and helped prepare his food, in spite of the servants, to ensure the purity of his meals, which she served him herself. He ate with his right hand. Only later, when he was done, did she sit down to her food.

The city streets were noisy places, filled with open stalls where housewives could buy anything from cucumbers and millet to flowers for the altar garlands. The spice suppliers gathered barks, leaves, seeds, and insects and prepared them for purchase. Huge ox-drawn carts filled the streets, the oxen with pierced nostrils and a cord drawn through the holes, their tails tied down so they couldn't swish the driver. The sound of rice pounding rang in every alley. Peddlers and craftsmen, musicians and entertainers harried the shoppers, who had to dart between porters, cattle and pigs, and women carrying great sheaves of wheat bigger than themselves on their heads, like vast hats.

Dhammā did not love this busy world. Shortly after her marriage, she was converted to Siddhārtha's teaching. Nothing had happened to her, no tragedy or loss, no deep longing. She simply turned toward it, like a morning blossom following the dawn, and was filled with contentment. She understood intuitively what an avowed life meant. All the things around her, the things everyone seemed to need, the things everyone told her she must need as well, she didn't need. She thought that needing was itself the problem. It was easy to be burdened by things when you had them.

One evening after dinner she knelt beside her husband and told him how she felt, how she wanted to leave the world behind and be relieved of her domestic role so she could be ordained. So she could have this one thing she needed, this lack of things.

Her husband refused. She accepted silently, eyes cast properly down, and went on with her life.

Her life was much the same day after day; only the weather and occasional quarrels or celebrations provided change. She and her husband offered rice balls and cakes to their dead ancestors on each full moon, and in the spring she cleaned the house carefully and fumigated. She shopped, managed the servants, and kept the fire going long after she ceased to believe it was necessary.

A year later she asked for her freedom again, and her husband refused again. She accepted in silence. She waited another year, then five years, then ten years, and every time she asked, he refused. She waited forty years, until he died.

Happiness needs things, so she wasn't happy. At first she had thought being happy was what she'd needed and could never have. But to her surprise, her slow and growing and then vast surprise, she found that she didn't need to be happy. Enlightenment, which is tranquillity itself, isn't happiness. Her housework and chores became the rules by which she governed her life. Step by step, she turned ownership into austerity. She examined her mind carefully and slowly, slowly, turned complexity into unity, too many choices and decisions into discipline. Her life was often tedious, so she worked at turning boredom into concentration. When she secretly resented her husband, she tried to turn the anger into energy and strength. When she was envious of others, she worked at turning it into generosity. When Dhammā stopped trying to be happy, stopped needing to have nothing to need, she found herself relaxing into peace. She found herself not happy, but completely at peace.

By then she was old and weak. Pain was with her whenever she was awake, an unwelcome but constant companion, as familiar as her own bed. After her husband's funeral, Dhammā walked slowly to a grove of trees near the village where several Buddhist nuns were staying and asked to be ordained as though she were a young woman, as though she had only then found the Truth. She was so old, so frail, that at first they wanted to say no; this bent old crone couldn't possibly have many days left. But Dhammā was past taking no for an answer.

After a while, finding without surprise that the life agreed with her completely, Dhammā took on the practice of following even the optional rules as carefully as possible. The monastic rules, for both men and women, were largely negatives—things not to do, actions to avoid. Dhammā lived her life within the structure of a set of guidelines that were prescriptive and positive, regulating almost every action, from eating and sleeping to interacting with other people. Her heart filled with joy in the narrow space of these rules, where she felt unbounded and free, and quite young. She had thought that this life of stricture, freely chosen, would be very different from the life she'd unwillingly led for so long. But one more surprise was in store for her—she was past this too. She'd learned the lesson the young nuns hadn't yet, the one everyone has to learn: no form is special. Every life meets itself, coming and going, and can't be escaped.

On begging rounds one day she tripped and fell. Her old bones were like the foam on fresh milk. She fell, spinning, hit the dusty ground, and heard her bones snap. Then her mind opened completely, with terrible pain and terrible clarity.

Before she died a short time later she gathered the other nuns around her and recited a poem.

I wandered every day, shaking and weary,
leaning on a staff, weak all over.
When I fell, I could see all at once—
The body is misery, but the heart is free.

teacher of trees

Sukhā

Sukhā means "bright and lustrous," and so she was. Young children of higher castes were not disciplined and knew a great deal of freedom. Sukhā's brothers often went naked, their heads shaved except for a top-knot, and played at cart-pulling or bow and arrows. They taught their pet mynahs and parrots to speak and had poetry contests to entertain the family. The girls wore miniature versions of adult clothing and played with dolls, and together the boys and girls played ball games, marbles, and spinning tops.

Childhood was lovely, but brief. Once upon a time neither girls nor boys married until they were ready. By the time of the Buddha, marriages were usually arranged in childhood. Girls married by sixteen, often by twelve—but always before adolescence, when their naturally libidinous natures were thought to be out of control. Like all the other girls, Sukhā began preparing for marriage while still very young. She studied literature, music, weaving and embroidery, gardening, the management of servants, cooking, painting, and many ways to please a husband.

Only one vocation was open to women besides marriage, and that was religion. One day Sukhā accompanied a group of women from her large family to a gathering of laypeople who had come to hear Siddhārtha speak. Without intending it, and never having imagined it, she was converted by his words and felt an irresistible vocation arise in her heart. It was as though she left home forever while still a child, while still with her mother and father.

When her parents saw the intensity and sincerity of her desire, their plans for her marriage were set aside. She was allowed to remain at home, even after her brothers and sisters had gone to families of their own, but she was not allowed to be ordained and not allowed to take a teacher.

How bitter a victory this was—no husband, thank heavens, but no teacher. No one at all. She was entirely alone and had nothing to do but study her mind in its aloneness. Sukhā talked to everyone she met, asking if they had news of the teacher, if they'd seen him or heard him, and she soaked up every word like rain. She had to be her own teacher, her own witness, her own critic, her own support. Loneliness overwhelmed her at times. But this was how she found her way to being a true student.

Once Sukhā lectured a group of followers on the road near her home. She had taken to doing this in the afternoons, when the damp haze of summer had faded, the air was sweet, and the clouds were spinning away into wisps. She stood near a huge, rose-colored narra tree, its buttressed roots almost fifteen feet high, and preached her understanding of the Master's words. Untutored in the Dharma, untrained in the practice, alone, young, but driven by a force in her heart she couldn't name, she spoke with such power that she converted the tree itself.

The small group who had gathered around her gasped at once, and Sukhā saw standing beside her the spirit of the tree, tall, fine, and strong. He gazed at her and then strode off, marching through her village, praising her name. For hours the tree wandered the countryside, singing in the humid sunlight, but wherever he went people scattered. Eventually the tree returned to its wooden home, where Sukhā waited.

"What has become of these people?" cried the tree. "They don't listen to you. They must be drunk not to pay attention; your words are as refreshing as rain."

"Sukhā," he whispered, bending down toward her a moment, already slipping back into the root, "live the life of this body fully, completely. I think it will be your last."

When she reached the age of twenty, her parents could see that she would never change her mind, and they allowed her to leave home. She joined the women's community, then led by Dhammadinnā, who became her true teacher.

Sukhā became a famous teacher too; her words were said to be as sweet as mead for her listeners to drink. She was eventually the master of hundreds of disciples. Never forgetting what it had been like to study alone, to be without a teacher, she was as kind as a parent to her students. It is said that she lived for centuries, solid and quiet as the tree.

shapeshifter
Uppalavaṇṇā

After being born under many Buddhas, Uppalavaṇṇā was born into the warrior caste in the town of Savatthi, capital of the kingdom of Kosala. Her skin was the color of the inner side of the pollen chamber of a blue lotus blossom, lovely to see. She was lovely in every way.

When she came of age, nobles from many kingdoms sent messages requesting her in marriage. Her father couldn't decide what to do. He knew that for the one man he satisfied, he would be making many powerful men unhappy. How could he possibly choose?

Uppalavaṇṇā didn't seem to care for any of them; she didn't seem to care for marriage, or for clothes, jewelry, garlands, or what she looked like in a mirror. Her father had an idea. Only a nun could avoid marriage, so he finally asked Uppalavaṇṇā to become a nun and spare him the trouble. To his surprise, she was overjoyed; her troubled feelings were instantly relieved, and as soon as possible she retreated from the world.

Once she joined the women's community, she was made pabbajja first, a novice. Shortly after she arrived, it was her turn to light and guard the lamp in the nuns' sleeping area. She lit the lamp, swept the room's bare earthen floor, and then contemplated the flame. With great concentration, using the flame as her ladder, she attained arhatship in the night, by herself. In all her past lives, she had made splendid offerings to others, and watching the flame giving its light and heat to the room, and to her, she suddenly grasped that the truth is a constant gift, that life itself is light and heat, life giving life to life.

As always happens when this occurs, the earth shook and flowers fell.

After two years of probation, Uppalavaṇṇā was ordained. She liked forest practice and often walked through the trees a long way from the other nuns. Accompanied only by her own mind, she gradually became master of the power of transformation, able to change her shape into many forms. As soon as she mastered this power, she saw it as empty and set it aside, telling no one.

Once, meditating under a sal tree, Uppalavaṇṇā was accosted by Māra, who saw that she was all alone and tried to scare her with threats, but nothing disturbed her.

"A thousand, a hundred thousand men, couldn't disturb me," she told the spirit. "You can't bother a woman who has mastery over her own mind."

Eventually, Siddhārtha announced to the community that Uppalavaṇṇā was foremost in mystical powers. She hadn't told him, but you didn't keep a lot of secrets around Siddhārtha. Once—only once, as a kind of lark—she and her master showed their powers to the other monks and nuns. When it was her turn, Uppalavaṇṇā transformed herself into a great ruler with a congregation thirty thousand leagues wide and rode a four-horse chariot through the sky.

Then she became Uppalavaṇṇā again, in a slim, dusty robe, and bowed at Siddhārtha's feet in humility. She was a little embarrassed for having shown off.

"You," she said, "are the refuge of the entire world."

Her cousin had desired Uppalavaṇṇā hand in marriage very much. He became obsessed with her after she retreated from the world and eventually discovered that she was living alone in a hut in Andhavana. One day he snuck into the hut while she was out walking and hid under her bed. When she returned, he raped her.

Now, Uppalavaṇṇā had no fear of Māra and none of her cousin either. She could have transformed herself into a man, a dragon, a tiger, a demon; she could have fought back this way, scared him, stopped him, even hurt him, if she'd thought it important. But she didn't. Homeless, free, knowing the realms of knowledge, knowing her past births and her future enlightenment, knowing how to perform miracles and to read the minds of other people, she didn't worry about a few moments' difficulty. His punishment was inevitable and not hers to give. When he finally left her, she bathed in a nearby stream and went to sit under a tree in the usual way.

Sure enough, he was condemned to hell, the fires of regret and loss. But we can still wonder what would have happened if Uppalavaṇṇā had resisted, because all the women were condemned too. Uppalavaṇṇā's experience meant more new rules. Even a buddha can change a world only so much; after that, the world has to change itself, which takes a long time. From this time on, women were forbidden to do solitary forest practice, go to the villages, bathe, walk at night, or ride a ferry alone. They had to be with a companion at all times.

Without complaint, Uppalavaṇṇā returned to the nuns' sangha. All the rest of her life, in complete control of light, air, color, and form, she stayed in her human skin and showed only joy.

CHINESE ANCESTORS

When Buddhism first came to China is an open question, but it was well established before Bodhidharma arrived and began to teach what would become the root philosophy and method of Zen. There is an excellent document from earlier centuries with biographies of Chinese Buddhist nuns, but I have chosen to begin with Bodhidharma's female heir, Zongchi.

The ancient system of Confucianism and the religion of Daoism competed with Buddhism for many centuries, giving way to each other time and time again. As Buddhism spread, it slowly took on many elements of Daoist thought. Zen, called Chan in Chinese, appeared over several generations, gradually dividing into several schools until the dominance of the two major sects of Linji (or Rinzai) and Caodong (Sōtō) was firmly established. It was after this time in China that Chan first came to Japan.

In the Chinese records, women appear largely as supporting players even when they are the main characters. (See the story of Ling Xingpo below for an excellent example of this.)

Zongchi, Shiji, Ling Xingpo and Lingzhao, women who clearly had achieved deep understanding and accomplishment in their Buddhist practice and whose wisdom was recognized, appear in the records of the male teachers with whom they studied—or, in a few cases, whom they bested. These are in the "Lamp Records," various collections of biographical religious writings about the lives and enlightenment experiences of Buddhist masters, and in koans. Other women are known from their own stories—brief and tantalizing koans, such as those few involving Liu Tiemo and Yu Daopo, and more extensive records for famous female teachers such as Miaoxin, Kongshi Daoren, Moshan Liaoran, and Miaodao. Their stories provide few biographical details and, as is traditional, are more concerned with their poems and sermons, the evidence of their accomplishment.

I wrote at length of Miaodao's experience because she is a rare case of a teacher whose awakening process was recorded in detail. For most of the ancestral women, we know who they became but little of *how* they became this. Miaodao is an exception to this rule; her teacher wrote and lectured extensively about her progress and how she came to her breakthrough.

Many stories are either not yet translated or have not been translated well. At this writing, Miriam Levering continues to work tirelessly to translate the stories of Chinese Buddhist women into English, especially the heirs of Dahui, including Miaodao. A group of women described here—Huiguang, Huiwen, Fadeng, and Wenzhao—are included in a largely untranslated thirteenth-century collection called the *Jia tai pudeng lu.*[1]

For the most part, the birth and death dates given for the women are approximate, based on the known dates of teachers, emperors, or male relatives. The Pinyin method of transliteration of Chinese is used here, except in certain circumstances where another version of a name is widely known—such as Bodhidharma, or the city of Changan, which is now known as Xi'an but was called by its former name for many centuries and is still referred to this way in historical contexts.

Chinese literature is filled with poetic imagery, metaphor, and simile, and Chinese Buddhist writing, taking from the culture as well as three major systems of thought, can be winding and difficult to the Western reader. I have offered my own humble interpretation of a few of these images in some cases, but I encourage the reader to let some of the poetry of these accomplished women flow in its own way. They are speaking the language of the unborn mind and saying what cannot really be explained in words as well as they can, and I have nothing to offer their efforts.

After the death of Siddhārtha, the monastics of India began to form small communities near villages. The sacred cities of India were buried under sand and rock; the wide Savasti River dried up and disappeared. Kosala and Magadha were conquered by usurpers, and the Śākya clan vanished. Buddhism bloomed in India for a long time and gradually spread north and south, east and west, carried by single people traveling great distances.

Some say that Buddhism came to China even before the great Nagarjuna was born, before the great Mahayana sutras were found, when a magician appeared in Prince Chao's court and created a three-foot-tall stupa on his fingertips. Others say that because of an emperor's dream, envoys were sent west. They met two Indian monks carrying sutras in saddlebags on the back of a white horse. The monks were escorted to Loyang, where they built a temple that came to be called the White Horse. There they carved the sutras, word by word, into the temple walls. The temple is still there.

flesh

Zongchi

(504–575)

The sixth century in China was a time of civil war, without a dynasty, and Zongchi's father had been emperor only a short time when she was born to his youngest consort.

Zongchi's mother taught her the Confucian roots: to respect her elders, especially her mother and father, and to treat her inferiors with kindness. Her mother was from the northern country, and a Daoist love of nature ran through her words, a stream within a stream. From the palace windows they watched fog and mist play through the spectral pines and across the snow-covered peaks on winter days. All the lowland trees, the pine, cypress, plums, and juniper, had already been cut for fuel and timber. In the sudden storms of spring the naked foothills fell apart into sluices.

The hills were hazy on the hot summer days, and Zongchi watched boys flying kites outside the gate. They were very different from her. Instead of rich clothes of woven silk, silk slippers, and intricate folded silk hats, they wore short padded jackets, short wide trousers, and shoes made out of straw. Different worlds, the boundary between them as strict and impassable as a wall.

Sometimes the eternal placid days in the women's quarters were broken by the sound of pounding horses and shouts from a company of armored soldiers carrying pennants, lances, and crossbows. They wore long leather helmets and buckled cuirasses and seemed to have no faces, no flesh. Even the horses wore armor, and people dropped their eyes and stood aside until they passed. More different worlds—defined, delineated, not to be crossed.

Her father was named Wu; he was an emperor of the Liang Dynasty in a time of change. Not far north, there was another dynasty, another emperor. More lines to cross, but not as much difference. Zongchi found the continual spasms of politics not so much confusing as irrelevant.

Fifty years earlier, a different Emperor Wu had tried to destroy the rapidly spreading foreign religion of Buddhism, first with restrictive laws, and then, in a final spasm, with executions and imprisonment. But that Wu died, and Buddhism seeped slowly out into the countryside. Sutras were translated and copied. More sutras came from India, and more teachers, until there were a thousand temples and then five thousand temples, and tens of thousands of monks and nuns slipping between the hooves of civil war.

When Zongchi's father took the throne, he converted from Daoism to Buddhism. He banned meat and wine from the imperial tables and ordered Daoist temples destroyed. Many times each year Emperor Wu invited monks, nuns, and interested laypeople to great convocations and assemblies, during which he pardoned criminals and invited lectures and debates on the sutras. The friendly court offered tax breaks and grants to new monks and temples. It was a good time and place to be a Buddhist. Zongchi saw the rise of Buddhism around her almost in passing, because what she attended to was the rise of its spirit inside herself.

Zongchi went to these lectures whenever she could. Accustomed to being silent and in the back of rooms, she slipped under tables and between the women's robes in order to hear. She was drawn to every part of it—the language of the sutras, the bare serene faces, the murmuring of ritual chants.

She heard about the Precepts, which seemed at least as sensible as all she had ever heard of filial piety; she met two nuns who had burned off the fingers of their right hands to show their dedication; she learned about the giant rock statues being carved into the riverbanks of the great Yangtze. She heard the *Mahaparanibbana Sutra* recited without a break from beginning to end by a trio of monks who stood the entire time without even shifting their feet.

One spring an assembly convened in a park near the imperial grounds. By then she was a young woman and should have been a wife or concubine, but she had managed to stay barely visible among the silk robes, working at this and that and slipping out whenever she could. There were hundreds of women at court, and a few were always happy to conspire at keeping Zongchi unseen.

For three days the park was a mass of ordained and laypeople, mingling together without distinction. She watched the silent nuns in small groups moving like cats among dogs. Flower-filled trees with orioles singing in the branches, snapping pennants, and silver lanterns—it was all marvelous, and in the distance she could see the gleam of the wide palace staircase made entirely of jade. The still reflecting ponds rippled with the breeze of snapping sleeves and the noise of lectures, debates, and ceremonies. In the evening palace guards lit the silver lanterns and pools of yellow light spilled into the black sky. For brief moments the solid world of class and difference in which she had spent her entire life seemed to disappear like mist on a summer morning. Then it was as though all beings were her body, and her body all beings.

Very quietly her determination grew, until it seemed as though she had never wanted anything else. When she was nineteen, a year younger than the usual age, Zongchi asked her mother for permission to be ordained. Her mother in turn begged permission of the emperor, who was delighted. He immediately sent her to a convent built for noblewomen.

As a novice nun, she vowed to uphold the Precepts and to follow a great many more rules defining the limits of her life. (The traditional Indian rules for nuns had finally been translated into Chinese.) But it wasn't a difficult life; many of the rules weren't enforced, and others were easy to keep because there was no opportunity to break them. The nuns studied and copied the long scrolls of scripture, and they dusted the massive statues. Little discipline, no teaching, and considerable comfort. After a few years she could see what her father had missed—that for the million peasants of China the new religion meant misery, poverty, and loss.

Most Buddhist monks refused to work; they claimed it was forbidden by the rules. Their job was to accumulate merit, and the peasants' job was to support them at it. Many monks were actually aristocrats, their ordinations nothing more than a tax break for their families.

The building campaign that Wu and others supported enthusiastically required so much labor that workers were drafted by force. Each great monastic complex used a forest's worth of wood. In the country the monasteries took farmland, and the fields that were left went unpicked for lack of hands because all the farmers were building temples. Sometimes monasteries took in criminals condemned to death and turned them into slaves, bequeathing them to each other in their wills. The monasteries grew so big they were like cities themselves, suborning entire villages to tend huge orchards and gardens, pastures and stock. The monks took some of the village children when they were toddlers and ordained them so that they could work as domestic servants inside the halls.

All this was paid for by appropriation of goods, by usury, by peonage, and by taxes. The Buddhist establishment had become just another imperial house—a huge, ungainly, top-heavy organization, dirty as mud.

Zongchi was disillusioned, which is to say she got rid of her illusions. She left the convent, with its pearl-encrusted statues and silver bells, and walked slowly through the streets of the city, watching, listening. Waiting.

Some years before Zongchi's birth, an Indian prince who became a monk had found his way to China. Eventually he traveled north of the Yangtze to the Shaolin monastery on Mount Song in the Wei kingdom, where he stayed a long time, although no one understood him. He just sat in the meditation hall alone all day, and so the other monks called him the "wall-staring brāhmin." They whispered in the halls that he'd refused to answer the emperor's question.

Such stories, told first to the watchers in court by the imperial priests, and by them to other priests, found their way into the Buddhist gossip, passing from city to city with the pilgrims. Everyone had heard of Bodhidharma—his coarse manner, his inelegantly large body, the way he seemed to ask for a sword across his throat whenever an aristocrat spoke to him. When she was very small, the Indian had come to the court at her father's request, and while not exactly refusing to answer the emperor's questions, he answered them in such a way as to make the emperor seem a child. Everyone had heard of him, but hardly anyone had actually met him. He didn't answer invitations, give lectures, or attend debates.

Zongchi traveled across the river, across the border between kingdoms, to see the Buddhist city of Loyang. She arrived in time for the Festival of the Buddha's Birthday, celebrated every year on the eighth day of the second moon. Half a million people lived in Loyang, and a huge crowd applauded when the priests bathed the statue of the Baby Buddha with sweet water. They admired the walls of flowers, parasols, pennants, and flags everywhere in the spring sunlight, the clouds of incense and drum rolls shaking the air. People laughed with their arms full of flowers, and the streets were so crowded that one could only roll with the wave of people.

Because she was an emperor's daughter, Zongchi stayed at the Jade Sparkle Nunnery on the north side of Imperial Way, not far from the palace. Many of the nuns were noble ladies or had been imperial consorts. It was a beautiful place, with a five-story stupa and five hundred rooms, luxuriously designed with lacquered vermilion doors and sumptuously carved windowpanes. The gardens were filled with rare trees and flowers. So many bricks had been required for the walks and walls that an entire quarry had been emptied into the casting ovens. Even the nails that held the walls together were made of gold, and the precious copper Buddha weighed thousands of pounds.

By accident, by design, by karma—who can know the difference?—Zongchi found Bodhidharma in Loyang, sitting in the central park with a few monks under the trees. Scowling, almost growling, he spoke quietly enough, and when the silent nun joined them, he glanced her way, nodded, and went on. One of the listening monks, she noticed, had only one arm.

When they stood and walked slowly to a nearby monastery and entered the zendo, she went too.

Bodhidharma had no fear in him, no interest in or patience with intrigue and status. He didn't care about convention at all. He perhaps did not know that Zongchi was the emperor's daughter, but if he had known, he wouldn't have cared. Zongchi never asked to stay, conscious of the rule that said monks were not allowed to consort with women—conscious too, almost against her will, of all she had absorbed about the Confucian order of high and low, which placed women forever below men. In the Buddhist world, people said men and women were equal in enlightenment, but that didn't mean equal in the world. Men and women didn't mix like this, didn't live together, and could be punished for it. If Bodhidharma had told her to leave, she would have gone—but he didn't, so she stayed. The three monks with whom he traveled merely made room for her in the small circle. If the monks at the temples where they stopped for a few nights' shelter complained to the muscular Indian about bringing a woman into their midst, she never heard about it. Perhaps no one dared complain to the monk who had turned his back on an emperor and lived.

She took on their poor and simple life, wearing rough clothes, eating plain vegetables and a little grain, rising early every day. They never stayed in one place for long but walked through the city streets and sometimes out into the suburbs, among the poorest of the poor, the rural peasants who had found their way, full of hope, to the city. Zongchi spent long, long days sitting with Bodhidharma in front of any nearby wall—the walls of city streets, the walls of cliffs and caves, silt walls and rock walls, walls of trees and walls of people. One year they walked north and went to gaze on the Great Wall being built block by heavy block for mile on endless mile. They watched the thousands of drafted men covered in sweat and sorrow, building the wall into the misty hills, and then they sat beside it a while.

The mind, he liked to say, should be like a wall. Then the Way is clear. They didn't talk much, but lived closely, depending on each other. Huike, with his one arm, had been Bodhidharma's student since they met in Shaolin; he was jovial where his teacher was stern. Daofu liked to chatter; Daoyu saved his breath for philosophy. They were companions and became friends.

Zongchi had grown up inside—inside the court, inside a palace, inside a world and a role. Now she was outside—outside her rank and status and even, sometimes, her gender. Instead of small rooms and screens and curtains, now her world was bordered by fields and storm clouds and steep mountain paths. She had grown up with precise instructions as to her place and purpose in life, and now she found herself with no purpose but her own.

"To find a buddha, all you have to do is see your own nature," said Bodhidharma, and around her she seemed to see her nature in rocks and trees: stationary, stolid, alive. "Your nature is the buddha," he continued. "And the buddha is the person who's free: free of plans, free of cares." And she was. She became a person without boundaries; she ceased to think in terms of in and out, high and low. She ceased to think of the edges of herself and the edges of the world as being different things.

One day, without formality or warning, Bodhidharma gathered them together and asked for a summary of what they had learned.

"What have I given you?" he said in his blunt way.

Daofu stepped forward immediately. "I have come to see that Buddhism is not about words, but we have to discuss it in words."

Bodhidharma said, "Yes, this is my skin."

Then Zongchi stood before her teacher, close enough to smell the sweat on his robe. "Joyfully," she said, smiling, "joyfully, I understand that knowing the Way is like seeing paradise. Once is enough."

"Yes," he said, "this is my flesh."

It was Daoyu's turn, and he let go of philosophy. "The elements truly have no essence, and the aggregates don't even exist. I cannot attain a thing."

"Yes. This is the bone."

Finally Huike, who was the oldest of them, stepped forward and simply bowed, slowly and deeply, and then stood aside in silence.

Bodhidharma said, "Yes. This, you know, is the marrow."

Skin, flesh, bone, and marrow—a body. His body—his teacher's body, and his teacher's teacher's body before him and back and back through time and space, a buddha body, needing all these things to live. The skin of form, the flesh of action, the bones and marrow of heart and mind—a whole body, nothing extra, nothing missing. Zongchi and the others wore the same robes and carried the same kind of bowl, and each was unique, each had received something else, something theirs alone, invisible to others and very precious.

The world was filled with chaos and wonder. First one rebellion, then another, and then border clashes on every side. Farmers and peasants were drafted by the tens of thousands to be soldiers, and the underclass grew larger and weaker at once. The shrinking aristocracy hoarded its wealth and built private armies and lived behind walls of servants and subordinates. The vast, great country divided into more and more layers—entire populations labeled high or low, clean or unclean, all of it marked by the wreckage of great poverty.

The governor of Loyang melted copper Buddhist statues into needed coin. Then the Erzhu tribe attacked, massacring the aristocrats. They pillaged Jade Sparkle and raped the nuns. They looted the mints—statues, coin, and contraband were all made of copper, were all the same to the usurpers—and a short while later the military staged a coup, taking advantage of the chaos. What little was left of the court fled, and the city emptied behind it.

One day Bodhidharma called them together and said that the world was changing; each moment was like a wall that had to be faced. Too many other teachers had grown jealous of him, he had done what he could, and the time had come for him to return to India.

"Endure what comes," he said. "Endure injustice. Whatever happens is somehow or other the result of your own past action—even if it is just a matter of what brought you to this place and time. Act according to the conditions you encounter, not the conditions you wish would be. Don't hang on to your hard feelings; let go of them, face the world like you face the wall, the way the wall faces you."

He looked around at them, unafraid, gazing carefully at each one, nodding. Everything was going to be fine. He sat up straight, and died. The four disciples buried him on Bear's Ear Peak and, knowing they were free to go anywhere they wanted to go, said good-bye. Huike smiled and left for the city of Ye; Daofu and Daoyu walked away, heads bowed together in debate. Zongchi went west.

She wandered easily amid difficulty. She saw coming storms, fading storms, clouds and clear skies giving way, the whole sky turning into storm again.

Once she saw Huike again. He had taken off his robes, left the mountains behind, and met students in the taverns, butcher shops, and public toilets. He was happy and loved by all he met; they parted friends. Occasionally she heard a rumor about Bodhidharma—that he had been seen walking in the mountains to the west, that his tomb was empty, that he was coming back. But she never saw him again.

Zongchi, her skin deeply riven by the years of walking in the sun and wind, resisted staying still. She liked the feel of the earth and the wind on her flesh, her strong and sensitive flesh, and felt no need to live inside again. One day she went to see the grottoes carved into the sandstone along the River Yi. Her father had sponsored many of them, and they were rumored to be beautiful. They were too—thousands of statues were carved into the rock, and crawling among them were sculptors who had already spent half their lives crouched in the cliffs chipping out the toe on a giant Buddha. She saw a cave filled with a thousand tiny figurines in a tiny world of awe and struggle, and panoramic Buddhas dozens of feet tall with hundreds of steps carved down to the riverbank. She liked the wide, quiet river, but not the statues. Her father was dead. Her teacher was dead. The people who had made many of the statues were dead. The granite faces of the cliffs were fine, just as they were, buddhas already. Why do anything to a wall? Why carve an image into a wall, which already is full of every image? Why waste a thousand men's lives?

After that, she found herself in the shadow of granite mountains, with green crevasses among peaks as soft as watercolors and hot springs wreathing the lacy, snow-covered trees in steam. To the east, peaks pierced the sky. She decided it was time to stay with this mountain, this particular buddha, this wall. First one, then another student came, and she made them sit for a long time, facing a wall of rocks, a wall of trees, a wall of mountains, the earth. She told them she had no patience with ceremony, that there is only knowing one's nature—only discovering the stillness of being a body, inside and outside.

She said the same thing after a new emperor, yet another Emperor Wu, issued a proclamation outlawing Buddhism. He demanded the destruction of all the temples, shrines, statues, and scriptures in the country and ordered monks and nuns to return to lay life. "Your skin, your flesh, your bones and marrow are part of the great body of the earth, running with its blood," she said, when she heard this.

the hat

Shiji

(500s to 600s)

Shiji was born in a village at the foot of mountains. The tall granite ranges stood side by side in a vast screen, a wall of mountains absurdly steep. Tiny pines clung to the shattered white cliffs, and cold, nameless streams filled the crevasses, spilling into deep blue lakes. Draped in a flowing skirt around the mountains were softer green valleys, melting into the patchwork of fields that filled a fertile plain.

Like many of the children, Shiji spent her spring and summer days on a little platform in the midst of the squash and millet fields. She wrapped her head in a white cloth and kept a pile of rocks beside her to throw at the scavenging birds. Other children guarded other fields, in sight but too far away for talking. Now and then the crows would come to feast, and Shiji would stand and shout or throw rocks and spin a noisemaker her grandmother had made until the birds flew away. Then the air was still again, with only the faint voices of the farmers calling to their oxen in the distance.

As long as her father could recall—as long as his own parents could recall—the only rule in life had been work and strife. "The people have four sorrows," her father would sometimes say, reciting an old poem. "The first is flood, the second drought, the third is locusts, the final warlords." Know your place, her father counseled the children in the evenings, rubbing his sore hands. Keep your place and you might be safe. People are for raising grain and paying taxes, he used to say, so you'd better do both these things well.

Hermitages hid in the folds of the weathered canyons, and in a small Buddhist temple that stood at the end of the village road a lone priest practiced odd magic and claimed to know the future. The roadside was marked with countless altars, a hodgepodge of statues and offerings. Her parents sent offerings to the Buddhist temple and the Daoist temple too. When Emperor Wu declared Daoism a heresy, the stone temple was pulled down and its beams burned for firewood. The small Buddhist temple nearby was suddenly wealthy, and her parents sent bigger offerings, and the children as well, to listen to stories told by passing monks.

One summer day when Shiji was fifteen years old, she was helping her father bring a cart of new melons in from the field. She heard angry shouts, a whip, and looked up in time to see the Marshal in Charge of Subjugating Barbarians appear, driving a line of prisoners along the road. The prisoners were barefoot and dirty, their faces tattooed with the marks of their crimes. A short way behind them came a pair of monks wearing wide hats that hid their faces. They stopped beside Shiji and her father, bowed their heads and clasped their hands, and asked humbly for some grain and a bed for the night.

Her father treated the monks with respect, but not with the same tense and fearful respect with which he treated the soldiers. With the monks he was relaxed, and she rarely saw him like that. She was struck by how they followed the criminals but didn't seem either worried about them or concerned with them. She wondered what it would be like to hide your face like that. When she left home some years later, she stepped outside of things just this way.

China was split by a great yellow river, the Huanghe, opaque with silt blown a thousand miles across the dry steppes. It was as wide as a town, and looked golden under the autumn sun and silver under a cloudy sky. Boats of all sizes crossed the Huanghe, but there were no bridges anywhere. The river was too wide, too unruly and turbulent, its banks too unreliable. So many people died in the Huanghe that many believed a great dragon lived in the river. Shiji, like everyone else, walked many miles to one of the few fords, where she joined the ever-changing crowd on the banks, people taking their turns and their chances. They crossed with courage and fear, some in groups and some alone, sailing on tiny rafts, buoyant with sheep bladder floats, or clutching the mane of a horse and keening a wild cry to scare the dragon away.

The peasants in the high steppes along the river built dykes and levees from dirt, rock, and silt. They posted flood-watchers along the banks during the rains, built carefully, and planned ahead, but still the land seemed to dissolve and disappear before their eyes. The floods always came, and now and then one effortlessly swept away crops, houses, and whole towns, until the valleys were a series of running low lakes and creeks all veined together, uncountable and unnamed.

Shiji walked for a long time in this land, in a nun's simple clothing, under a wide hat. She was looking for something worth seeing, worth taking off the hat to examine more closely. She was looking for something worth hearing in all the sounds of the world. What she saw, what she heard, wherever she went, was suffering. All things, all things, all things unsatisfied. All things changing, all things dying, all things being born, never still, never whole.

In this land shredded by the great river and its endless disciples, things were hard and soft at the same time. It was a land of ravines and canyons, broken cliffs, gullies scarred by flood, cracked and broken hills. She passed storm-carved pillars etched into strange shapes as though sculpted, inchoate forms that seemed either about to be born or already decomposing into earth. It was the same as far as she could see in all directions. The only way to live here was to live in this rolling river of change.

Many years later Shiji arrived at Jinhua Mountain, where Jinhua Juzhi lived as the head priest of a small temple along with several other monks. She didn't remove her wide bamboo hat when she entered the hall, as etiquette required. Instead, she walked around his seat three times, saying, "If you can say something, I'll remove my hat."

He sat mutely, transfixed by a sight he had never seen.

She repeated herself, circumambulating him as though he were a stupa, three times, and then once again. He had no answer.

"Anything?" she asked once more. "Anything at all worth saying?"

Silence.

Shiji marched through the hall past him, bowed before the dusty iron statue, and marched out without another word.

"Wait!" he shouted. "It's late, you should stay."

"Can you say something? If so, I'll stay." He had nothing to offer.

The other monks laughed at their leader. "Idiot!" they told each other. They'd always had a few doubts about Juzhi, and here he was, beaten by a woman. (None of them offered any suggestions for what he should have said. In fact, none of them said a word while she was there, hoping she wouldn't notice them.)

Juzhi thought, *I have the form, but I don't seem to have the spirit. A person of the Dharma should be able to speak, just like that. I'll leave tomorrow and see what I can find.*

Eventually Juzhi met another master and was enlightened by the sight of him holding up a finger. Juzhi was always known as the teacher of "One-finger Chan," because after that, he didn't say or do anything as a teacher but hold up a single finger. No matter the question, the comment, no matter what happened, all he did was hold up one finger. It saved him a lot of breath, and maybe it saved him having to figure out what to say that was worth hearing.

the footnote

Ling Xingpo

(600s to 800s)

When she was about fifteen, Ling Xing was sent with her uncle and cousin to the capital of Loyang to work in a lacquer factory. She was old enough to earn her keep, and there were smaller children at home who ate less and could help in the field just as well. Xing joined a great emigration of peasants to the new cities—peasants becoming servants for a growing aristocracy and laborers in factories and warehouses.

She pounded and stirred the darkening sap in shallow wooden tubs or ladled it through heavy hempen strainers. In winter she sweated over a fire, stirring the black liquid until it steamed, and in the summers she sweated in the sun, doing the same thing. One afternoon each week she was allowed a few hours of free time, and then she liked to walk to a nearby temple and sit quietly, doing nothing much.

After several years, when she was at the age of making decisions and most of the other factory girls were getting married, Ling Xing asked her uncle to release her so that she could enter a convent. Since the amount she earned and the amount she ate were almost the same, he saw no reason to refuse.

At this time a new school of Buddhism had begun to spread throughout China. It had begun with Bodhidharma, and after he died a teacher named Dayi Daoxin named it Chan, which means "meditation." This meditation, this silent sitting, this understanding outside of education and literature and class, was what the lacquer worker wanted.

When Ling Xing was a postulant, she was given a new character to her name—*po,* which means "old woman." *Mamma* means this too, so she was called Mamma Ling. One day she came to pay her respects to the teacher, Fubei Heshang. They sat together and drank tea, and she asked him, "If you have exhausted your effort and cannot articulate the bottom line, who are you going to instruct?"

Fubei simply said, "Fubei has nothing to say."

Mamma was unsatisfied. "One doesn't speak in this way," she said. So Fubei asked her to explain.

She placed her hands inside her opposite sleeves, drawing in, and at the same time cried out: "There is grievous suffering even amid a blue sky!" Again Fubei had nothing to say.

Mamma continued. "Discourse does not recognize distorted correctness. Principle does not perceive inverted depravity. To be a human being is to live in calamity."

Nanquan commented when he heard this story, "Poor Fubei, he was devastated by the woman."

When Mamma heard about this comment, she laughed. "Old master Wang seems to be deficient in a moving force." She meant that it was all about the point of view—moving or not moving, the trick was to do what was needed.

As Ling Xingpo won this debate, she won others; the attending monks stood in turn to test her after this fight. One by one, she defeated them. Chengyi of Youzhou met her by chance and decided to test her.

"So how," he asked, "does Nanquan 'seem to be deficient in a moving force'?"

"How sad!" she cried. "How painful!" This too is the trick. In the midst of heaven, suffering. In the midst of wisdom, ignorance.

He had no answer. "Do you get it?" she asked him pointedly. Chengyi bowed; clasping his hands together, he backed away in defeat.

"Brain-dead Chan associates are like hemp and husk," she added. Nothing worse than parroting the enlightenment of a distant teacher.

Some time later Chengyi described this encounter to Zhaozhou, who said, "If I meet this foul old woman, what I ask by way of instruction will leave her dumbstruck."

Chengyi wasn't so sure. He was still puzzled. "I still can't figure out what Fubei Heshang will ask her."

Zhaozhou hit him with his stick. "How long must this brain-dead man wait before he doesn't strike?" He beat Chengyi several more times over the head and shoulders.

This too came back to Mamma Ling; people were eager to share such conversations with her, as she seemed to be the source of them all. She said, "May Zhaozhou himself meet up with the stick in Mamma's hands."

Of course, a monk quickly relayed this comment to Zhaozhou, who responded by quoting her in his turn: "How sad, how painful!" he cried.

When Mamma heard of this remark, she put her hands together and sighed. His repetition was fresh and new; she was also deficient, as was he—as all of us are. She wished he really would come, and said, "The radiance released from Zhaozhou's eyes pierces throughout the entire realm in brilliant luminescence."

Zhaozhou told a monk to go ask Mamma Ling this question. "So, what are these eyes of Zhaozhou?" In response, she thrust a clenched fist into the air.

The monk hurried back to Zhaozhou and described this. He immediately composed a poem in tribute to her and sent it. The tribute read:

A straight face lifts up when regarding a moving force,
A moving force falls short when regarded by a straight face.
When responding to you, Ling Xingpo,
How can one lose by crying out?

In wisdom, ignorance—in ignorance, wisdom. There is always movement at rest, and resting in movement, if we only know how.

She then wrote a tribute of her own.

In crying out, the Master had already awakened,
But then who would have known that he had already awakened?
    In Magadha, at that time,
How many missed the moving force in front of their eyes?

The great Mamma Ling's wisdom is in the chapter of the *Jin de chuan deng lu,* the "Record of the Transmission of the Lamp," under the name of the first monk she defeated while still a postulant, Fubei Heshang. His own wisdom is not recorded. She has no chapter of her own.

bright sun

Lingzhao

(762–808)

Emperor Xuanzong, in his great capital of Changan, kept a troupe of four hundred talented horses. On his birthday each year they came into the court and danced and then, all at once, knelt with wine cups in their teeth to offer a toast for his long and healthy life. This emperor claimed to descend from Laozu himself, and Daoism was the country's official religion again. He filled his cabinet with young men who had passed a daunting civil service exam and welcomed Tantric teachers from Java and Ceylon, Muslim scholars, and Tibetan lamas along with many other foreigners and envoys. A grand military coup had taken both the capital cities for a time, and barbarians harassed every border. But a million babies were being born, and the country was swelling into greatness in an era that would come to be known as the golden age—the Tang Dynasty.

In spite of the Daoist court, Buddhism (much infected with folk magic) was practiced by people of all kinds. Most monks and nuns were ordained after passing an ordination exam, and most were content to stay in the lower ranks of the Buddhist hierarchy, since higher ranks required many more vows. Some were ordained at the favor of the emperor, and others simply bought their ordination certificates, the sale of which was sometimes a brisk business. The imperially ordained monks were likely to live in luxurious temples, and those who had bought their rank were frequently the private pets of aristocratic families, who enjoyed the tax break. According to the Bureau of National Sacrifice, there were hundreds of thousands of Buddhist monks and nuns in the country. But an untold number had refused to sign the bureau's census and either were pledged by small villages or wandered at will, calling themselves "monks of the people."

Pang Yun was very much a man of the dynasty. He was born in 740, the same year as the emperor's thirtieth son and twenty-ninth daughter. He was raised the son of a powerful and wealthy prefect in Hengyang city, far from hardship. Pang had an appreciation for the rarefied aesthetic of the times. With his father's help, he was able to obtain a great many books, and by the time he was a young man he had mastered Confucian scholarship, Daoist magic, and the Buddhist sutras.

Pang married a woman who shared his interests, and in 762 Lingzhao was born. Her name meant "Spirit Shining." Lingzhao took after her father; from her childhood, they read books together and debated them. She had a brother, Genghuo, and for many years they lived quietly in the southern part of the city. Confucianism briefly surged into popularity; the country was more cosmopolitan, more diverse, than ever before. Pang loved to debate, and debates were easy to come by.

Pang's wife was nimble too. One day she went to the temple with an offering. The priest asked her for whom she made the offering, so he could record it and the merit could be transferred to the proper being.

She took a comb from the side of her hair and stuck it instead in the back.

"Transfer of merit is done," she said, and left.

When Lingzhao was eighteen years old, Pang retreated to a hermitage in the mountains for several weeks. When he came home, he announced that he had given their house away to a temple and sunk his belongings and all their wealth into the deep waters of a mountain lake.

They all looked at him, Lingzhao, Genghuo, and their mother, for a long time, without comment. Then they began to pack, and soon they had moved in with Lingzhao's aunt.

Pang was content for a while after that. He wrote a poem about it:

My boy has no bride,
My girl has no groom.
Forming a happy family circle,
We speak about the Birthless.

But he left a few months later to travel to Heng Mountain and study with the famous teacher Shitou Xiqian. A year later Pang sent word that he had left Shitou, after taking all he had to give, and was on his way to study with the "Great Solitary One," Mazu Daoyi. He returned three years later, grinning. He'd brought a friend and fellow monk, Danxia Tianran, and they were both full of excitement.

"Just as I thought, just as I thought!" he shouted as he came through the gate and saw Lingzhao standing by the door with a whisk broom. He waved his bag, the one holding his transmission silks, over his head. "Moving heaven, moving earth!" Then he and Danxia doubled over in laughter, Pang hit Danxia on the head with his bag, and they went inside. "Bring me tea!" he shouted at his wife.

Danxia stayed a while; he and Pang were always making obscure pronouncements and shouting without reason. They didn't pay much attention to anyone else and held long discussions on the nature of selflessness—talking late into the night, keeping everyone awake with the noise, and calling for Lingzhao to make more tea. Pang liked the way she made it best, with a few precious cloves and a green onion for the spice.

Lingzhao was twenty-eight years old that season, and she had had enough. Her brother had finally gotten married, and he and his wife were willing to care for their mother—who, frankly, didn't want any help.

One day Danxia came to visit—his nickname meant "Spontaneous"—and he saw Lingzhao washing a basket of vegetables. He asked if "the Layman" was around. He liked to call Pang the Layman; it amused him. Lingzhao simply put down the basket, folded her arms respectfully, and waited. He asked again, and she picked up the basket and walked away. Danxia finally gave up and left, bested.

When Pang announced that he was leaving again, she recited to him the words of the *Vimalakirti Sutra:* "I have looked for the essential qualities of men and women and cannot find them," she quoted with perfect equanimity. "The Buddha said that no one is really a man or a woman. Such things neither exist nor do not exist. So I'm coming too."

This was unexpected. He decided to test her again. "What does this old saying mean: 'Bright, bright are the grasses in the meadow. Bright, bright is the ancient teaching'?"

"Such a wise man, and you talk like that," she answered.

He grunted. "So how would *you* say it?"

"Bright, bright are the grasses in the meadow. Bright, bright is the ancient teaching." Pang had no answer then. She threw his teaching of formlessness at him, and he caught it; she knew he would have to let her come along.

They traveled together for many years, beginning with a trip north across the Yangtze. They climbed slowly through towers and turrets of mountains—shadowed and difficult mountains, violet and gray in the twilight and blurred with mists and snow, until they reached a valley called the Land Within the Passes. It was soft, wet, green, and almost two hundred miles long, guarded by mountains and rivers on every side. At its heart was the capital, Changan, the center of China, the end of the Silk Road.

A great webwork of roads, rivers, and canals led to Changan, a city ideally placed, according to the geomancists. It was the greatest city in the world—a place to have one's fortune told, then to make that fortune, then to lose it again. Changan was square, the streets placed methodically in a pattern of broad and narrow avenues, each smaller section walled and gated separately. The people kept a curfew, and police directed traffic. It was a complicated, busy, and beautiful place; even the wells had tiled pavilion roofs. Splendid parks filled with willows and persimmon and apricot trees were spread throughout the city, and the willow catkins were so luxurious that the opening of their seedpods was known as the Snowstorm.

Lingzhao and her father wandered through the shopping districts, along avenues crowded night and day with people and merchants, carts, sedan chairs, and horses. Pang bought a calendar—365.25 days long—that claimed to hold all the auspicious and inauspicious dates of the coming year. "*This* will be useful!" he said.

As they were walking one day a few weeks after their arrival, Pang stumbled and fell into a ditch. Instantly Lingzhao threw herself down beside him.

"What are you doing, girl?" he mumbled, brushing himself off.

"I'm helping," she replied, and he chuckled at his surprising daughter and helped her stand.

When they left Changan, they turned west and then east, into the plateau where the great yellow river ruled. The land was hilly and broken between tall granite cliffs with bits of greenery clinging to them. Lingzhao picked bamboo and grass to weave baskets.

They stopped now and then to sell the baskets. During centuries of civil war and rebellion the Silk Road had stayed open, and it was still open; towns along its route had prospered. People planted hemp and mulberry trees beside the road, and rural markets were common there. Pang and Lingzhao never walked long before finding more people, another crossroad, another pilgrim or importer or gang of laborers. In the late days of summer farmers laid the raw millet and wheat on the roads and drove oxcarts back and forth over the piles to break the hulls. The women tossed the broken grain in trays to sift the seeds.

Pang wore the white robes of a layperson and the black gauze cap of a monk. He carried a priest's walking stick, and Lingzhao carried the baskets. Packed carefully in a wooden box was their portable shrine, a hinged triad a few inches tall of Buddha and his attendants. Every night before supper Lingzhao opened it and lit incense.

By then Lingzhao was well used to Pang's ways. He was immensely fond of debate, and since his time at the monasteries he had a particular appetite for Buddhist conundrums. In the lodging houses of monasteries where they stayed, he would soon set off looking for companions. After a while he would be engrossed in a bizarre conversation with other monks and self-styled wise men, all of them shouting and throwing water at each other and running away, yelling and grabbing and slapping each other like monkeys. Lingzhao sat in her room and wove the grass.

Pang was restless in the winter, wanting to move, to keep going, to find someone new, to see new things. He wrote poems huddled near their tiny fire. Lingzhao helped him with the crucial lines and kept a journal of her own, and in between her solitary dreams she made tea in a small traveler's stove made of clay.

Even when they were alone in the dry steppe, he would suddenly shout, "Difficult, difficult!" out of the blue. Once when he'd done this at home, his wife had answered, "Easy, easy. Just get out of bed, old man."

And once in the desert, on a cold late autumn day when the wind blew icy sand into her face as they walked, he shouted, "Difficult!"

"Neither easy nor hard," Lingzhao answered. "Just like the grasses growing." She walked slowly along. "Bright, bright grass."

They walked, rested, walked, and years went by. The court heard a fierce protest against Buddhism—that cult started by barbarians who didn't understand Confucius at all. Things were changing; things always changed. Lingzhao took care of Pang as he aged. She was his daughter, his helper, his sidekick in the moving adventure that he considered his life to be. The ancient Confucian texts teach that women are the cause of moral decay—the source of disorder in the world. Lingzhao was familiar with xiao, respect for one's elders. Because he was her father, because he was older, and because he was a man, she was supposed to defer to him all her life. Quite often, she appeared to be doing just that. But like nuns who tromped through monasteries without removing their hats, sometimes she didn't.

In 806, when Lingzhao was forty-three years old and her father an old man, they returned to the region where he had been born and settled in a cave several miles from Deer Gate Mountain. Every month Lingzhao walked nineteen miles to and from the city to sell utensils and buy food.

One summer day in 808, Pang announced—as he always announced things, all at once and brooking no dissent—that it was time for him to die.

"Make hot water," he commanded Lingzhao. "I must first have a bath." So she gathered kindling, made a fire, brought a bucket of water, heated it, and helped her father to bathe and put on a clean white robe.

He then sat up in the center of his sleeping pad, properly cross-legged, and said a few last words for her to remember. To her, they were no more or less interesting than all his other words.

They sat for quite a while, but nothing happened.

Finally he said, "Tell me when the sun is at its height. I'll die then."

Lingzhao went to sit at the doorway to watch the sun. After a while she said, "The sun is at its height, but its brightness is covered."

"What!" shouted Pang. "That's impossible!" He had to see such a thing and staggered over to the cave door.

While he was staring at the eclipse, Lingzhao quietly took his place on the sleeping pad, properly cross-legged, smiled, and died without a sound.

Pang finally turned from the doorway, excited by the strange light, and saw what she had done. "She has beaten me once more," he said. He was finally feeling a little modest.

the iron grinder

Liu Tiemo

(780–859)

As the aristocracy fattened, the peasants got steadily thinner. Sophisticated women read the classics, wrote poetry, and practiced calligraphy and music. Peasants wove fabric, made paper, or worked as tenant farmers raising rice, hemp, or cotton—backbreaking, endless work. Aristocratic women kept their hair tied up in buns and wore dyed silk robes with fantastic patterns. The peasants were taxed on land, food, salt, incense, clothing, tea, alcohol, grain, even spoons. Some babies weren't allowed to live long enough to steal the family's food, and others were sold as debt slaves as soon as they could walk.

Liu Tiemo was short, stout, and plain, with big feet. She had flat, hard hands; her fingers were no good for calligraphy and lutes. She didn't know anything about fashion. She grew up helping her father farm a small plot of someone else's land in a humid valley prone to floods and fogs. In the early morning mists, the village pouring men walked up the road, each balancing two heavy buckets of night soil on a pole slung across his back. They poured it on the crops and went back for more, collecting from travelers' buckets along the road. Tiemo worked hard, kept to herself, and made few friends. On the snowy long night of the New Year, she drank tea with the old women while the other girls pounded drums and blew horns.

They lived near Mount Hua, the sacred flower mountain in the Qinlings. It was the Number One Steepest Mountain Under Heaven, her father told her—a tantalizing, narrow cleft that seemed to go straight into the sky. Pilgrims had built a tiny pagoda near the top to show that they had been there. "There is one path, and only one path, to its summit," he said knowingly, and she knew he was talking about more than the mountain. "The hard way is often the only way," he added, shooing her out to the field at dawn.

When she was old enough, she left—simply walking away. If all life had to offer was hunger and work, at least she would choose where to be hungry. She walked through the Xiao Mountains and Xiao Pass. The loess plateaus there rose and fell like huge, eccentric steps gouged out by giant fingers. The round natural terraces wound everywhere, and every path was a long path. Giant rock Buddhas lined the cliffs by dunes of ochre silt smooth as wet clay, soft as flour. The river shot out of the canyons, spreading across the terraces, tumbling down the steps. So much silt was tossed out in the spray that the sun glowed golden through the mist.

All along the way Liu Tiemo stopped at convents for shelter. Many had become sanctuaries for poor and displaced women—childless widows, women beaten by their husbands. A lot of people thought convents were unsavory places because of the women they sheltered; certainly the nuns themselves weren't always well educated, and many couldn't even read or write. But the convents were safe and reliable places. The buildings were usually simple and rough, and sometimes lovely without reason, and so were the nuns.

Tiemo grew to love the carved statues, the serene faces surrounded by hair curls, eyes closed peacefully, sitting on lions, dragons, and raging waves with the same calm. Some of the statues had round faces, long noses, and spiraled hair and looked different from anyone she had ever seen. She imagined they could sit on anything with the same stillness—poverty, pain, injustice.

She aimed slowly for Changan because she had never been in a city before. Along the way she came to the Water and Land Convent, which had statues like nothing she could have imagined—thousands of them made of clay, covering every wall, telling the story of the Buddha's life. She stood for a long, long time, reading that story. The figures seemed to be alive, crawling up the wall into darkness near the peaked ceiling, disappearing behind beams, reading scrolls and speaking and sitting in pagodas and riding horses and swans, all of them surrounded by rows of arhats and wide-eyed, fiery-haired, multi-armed protecting demons. Can statues be teachers? Staring at the walls of that room, she saw her father's life, her grandfather's, her own. She saw how banal and ordinary evil could be, how distant and inattentive. She saw refuge and protection. She saw the power of not being afraid to die. There, like everywhere else, she sat on a mat in a cold hall and ate rice gruel by lantern light in a silence like that between breaths, between lives.

She went on to the city, just to see it. Changan was laid out so that most buildings faced the south. The imperial buildings were on the highest hills, the government buildings were in the middle, overlooking the lowlands, and the poor districts were built between the ditches and lakes in the low areas. The city had eighty-one monasteries and twenty-eight convents.

There was a lot of snow that year, and the people wore voluminous thick robes of fur and quilted silk, yards and yards of fabric bound and pleated together, knee-high boots, hooded coats and capes. Foreigners in turbans and headdresses sat on carpets on the ground, selling shoes. Tiemo saw big horse-drawn carts filled with bundles, ladies with hair piled high in combs and lips painted red. She saw dealmakers and profiteers and illicit wine shops and drunks. There were many strange-looking, oddly dressed people from Turkey and Arabia, from Korea and Japan, from Tibet and Mongolia and India and Persia. There were so many foreigners in Changan by then that the government had built special hostelries and provided interpreter services and protocol specialists. She entered the nearest convent and asked to be ordained. Tiemo had seen her city, and now she was through with it. After a while the nuns obliged.

According to the convention, female ordination candidates had to recite a hundred leaves from a sutra, give a lecture, demonstrate concentration, compose a text and memorize another, and analyze a scriptural passage. But those who couldn't do these things were allowed to offer an excuse and to be examined face to face instead, by government officials. A nun was granted about three acres of land by the government for her convent. Monasteries and convents ran hostelries, mills, oil presses, and even pawn shops; they kept donations in a storeroom called the Inexhaustible Treasury. But they were landlords most of all, and every acre counted. In due time, Liu Tiemo was examined, answered satisfactorily a few questions about her understanding of Buddhism, and was accepted. She gave the abbess her short string of money and her meager possessions, and in exchange for the land grant she was ordained. She put on a dead woman's old robes, shaved her head, and vowed to follow the Precepts.

Soon she saw that most of the nuns did little in the way of study or meditation. Many were members of wealthy families who had been ordained to create tax shelters, and they spent little time in the temple. She saw a few things she liked and many she didn't. Mostly she didn't worry about like and dislike so much. She dug in, worked like her meditation was a field, and stolidly plowed through. She had always known how to work. Not afraid of mistakes, she made a lot of them—and by making them, progressed fast along a path that scares most of us in its first few steps. She didn't talk much at first. After a few years she began to roar.

Once she started wandering, Tiemo met and beat many monks in debate. When she met the master Zihu, he told her he'd heard she was hard to handle. "Is that so?" he asked.

"Who says this?" she responded. She could name a few people who might have.

"It's conveyed from left and right," Zihu said, and they weren't just talking anymore. Zihu was testing her, testing her depth, her subtlety, and her courage. Were her words only words—was she confident or only clever?

She replied, "Don't fall down, master," and turned to leave. But Zihu's stance was very steady; he wasn't off balance at all. He jumped up and followed her, beating her with his stick across the back, with blows of compassion. Tiemo's understanding was deep and subtle, this was certain, but she was also attached to it. She won her debates like battles in these early years, beating her victims with her wisdom. Zihu stole that away and made her run from his own. It was all she needed; after that, she kept moving, examining herself for every hint of self-attachment, arrogance, and fear. She remained pugnacious and unadorned, and she became truly unafraid—she became a rock and then a boulder of the Truth. By the time she met Guishan Lingyou, she was as sharp and pure as a diamond drill.

To the south, Baizhang lived on Great Hero Mountain, inventing rules for monastics. Slowly his new discipline was spreading among the Chan temples. As it spread, the temples began to free themselves from the government's favors and sticky supervision. The monks and nuns learned to work instead of being served.

Guishan Lingyou was Baizhang's disciple. There was no shouting and whacking over the head for Guishan; he was a man of small smiles and patience. Like Liu Tiemo, he was an undecorated person. He taught with his body in the small moments of daily life, using garden hoes, the whisk, circles drawn in the air, the winter wind. When he caught a trace of enlightenment in his students, he wiped it clean with a brush of his hand.

Guishan took his name from the mountain where he settled down after leaving his teacher. It was a place of long, hard winters, but people said that no one was cold in his presence. In time, 1,500 students came to live there with the old man, who flared like a small sun in the deep snows. On his wall he wrote a poem: "Ten square feet of Guishan, too steep to climb. If anyone enters, he will become a great general."

Out of all those students, he transmitted only forty-three. One was Liu Tiemo.

A man already growing old and a tough workhorse woman pounding rudely on his door—human beings meeting face to face. Tiemo was fearsome by then; she struck like a knife or a bolt of lightning, and sparks flew where she walked. Yuan Keqin, in the commentary for "The Blue Cliff Record," said of her, "Hesitate and you lose your body and your life." She became known as the Iron Grinder, crushing delusion and pride wherever she went. Such a reputation that preceded her up the mountain! But she laughed when she met Guishan.

After a time at his side, she was transmitted as a teacher and went to live alone a few miles away.

The country was not peaceful. One emperor was murdered, while another was beset by small coups and connivance. A copper shortage led to a law against its use for statues, and many were melted down. In 840, when Liu Tiemo was old, Wuzong became emperor. He hated Buddhism and smashed it with a fist as big as China. Once again the government raided and destroyed the monasteries: copper bells and statues went to the Salt and Iron Commission, the prefectures took iron ones, and the Board of Finance took the gold, silver, and brass. Later, vast acreages and the Inexhaustible Treasuries were taken too. Most monasteries, convents, shrines, and temples were closed. Then the government ordered all monks and nuns over the age of forty—260,000 of them—to become laypeople again. Many did, fearful, giving up, and others put on lay clothes and grew hair in a disguise, hiding. Some slipped away, gliding into the clefts of the mountains to wait. Tiemo was one, but she wasn't entirely quiet.

The emperor tried to crush Buddhism, but finances crushed him first. When he died, the country fell into disorder. Bandits roamed the countryside, and the cities were dangerous and hard. Guishan liked to say, "A person of the Way is unconcerned." He was unconcerned, and so was Tiemo, who had nothing to prove and no one to impress and nothing to fear. The Truth is a plant that grows strong when pruned close to the ground.

When she was getting old and Guishan was frail, she went to see him again. What a noise these two made!

"Old cow, I see you've come," said Guishan, who liked to call himself a water buffalo.

She leaned on her staff in his doorway—still stout, implacable as a rock.

"Tomorrow there is a great feast on Mount Tai. Will you go?" she finally asked, gruff as always. Mount Tai was six hundred miles away—what was keeping him? To one who understands the nature of time and space, there are no real obstacles in time and space. Bodies are one thing—relationship is another. Can your mind go where it needs to go? she asked. Can you freely move, within all the restrictions of your old human body?

They were like two mirrors facing each other. Who sees, who is seen? Seeing each other like this, they experienced the recognition everyone craves—to be seen exactly as we are, nothing more, and nothing less. Seen like this, all the many forms in the world are the same as one's own hand, one's own face.

At her words, Guishan lay down, sprawling on the floor. The Iron Grinder turned and left, without another word. No need to talk about it anymore. When she was gone, Guishan smiled. He might as well die with a disciple like this.

the mountain
Moshan Liaoran
(800s to 900s)

Moshan Liaoran was famous in her own time, and she is still famous today. Her name means Summit Mountain; she was the first woman to hold an equal place in the Chan records, and the first recorded as an official Dharma heir. After her teacher, Gaoan Dayu, gave her the great mind seal, the emperor asked her to lecture.

Eventually Liaoran became an abbot. Once a monk came to her temple, tired and thin from his journey. When she commented on his leanness, he said, "I'm still a lion!"

"So why do you let Mañjuśrī ride you?" she asked him. He had no answer.

The most famous story about Moshan Liaoran concerns a monk named Guanqi Zhixian. Zhixian had studied with Linji, who was using new methods to knock his students' heads together. But Zhixian couldn't break free in spite of this, so he went wandering in search of a new teacher. When he came to Moshan Liaoran's temple, he said, "I'll stay here if the person is worth anything." Zhixian was desperate for awakening, but too proud to admit it. He covered up his need and his fear with bluster and clever words. He was always looking for someone to defeat, and when he did, it was both a relief and a disappointment.

Zhixian entered the hall where Liaoran was sitting. She summoned one of her assistants to go meet him.

"Are you sightseeing?" asked the young nun. "Or do you want real Dharma?" (She seemed able to see his mind better than he could.)

"Real Dharma!" he shouted, rather coarsely.

She led him to the teacher.

"Where did you start today?" Liaoran asked. "From the beginning of the road?"

"I left from the entrance," he said, leaving off all the small polite words strangers used with each other.

"Why are you so rude? Perhaps you should close your mouth," she said. He might have been a bit more polite, after all, since he didn't really have anything to say. And sure enough, unable to think of a reply, he bowed to his knees.

But this wasn't enough for him. He had to test a little more.

"What is Summit Mountain?" he asked.

"You can't see the peak; it's hidden by clouds," she answered.

"What is the hermit who lives there like?"

"Neither man nor woman—without appearance," she answered.

"Transform yourself!" he shouted. Liaoran looked at him.

"Why should I change?" she asked. "What would you have me become?"

Zhixian gave up and became the gardener at the temple, where he stayed for three years. Later he said he'd had half the teaching from Linji and half from Moshan Liaoran. Thus, she is also the first woman recorded as the primary teacher of a male student.

Surely this wasn't the first time such a thing had happened—but it took this long before the historians would record such things and make them official. Even then, the fact that she was a woman aroused endless comment. Centuries later, in the Song Dynasty, there was a famous poem about her based entirely on the surprising fact that such a formidable teacher was a woman. Even hundreds of years later Dōgen noted that Zhixian's willingness to be taught by a woman showed his true desire to know the Way, because so few men could do that.

wind
Miaoxin
(840–895)

Officially, Buddhism disappeared while Miaoxin was a little girl playing in the garden at her mother's side. The great monastic complexes were destroyed by the new Emperor Wu, their hundred-thousand-pound bells and copper statues bigger than houses melted into coin. But unofficially, Buddhism grew like vines in the hidden crevices of a wall, filling every gap. Linji Yixuan founded his Linji sect—Rinzai Zen. In the next century Dongshan Liangjie would take his vows and eventually found the Caodong School—Sōtō Zen. A while later came Xuefeng Yicun, whose line developed into the Yunmen and Fayan Schools. The great Zhaozhou Congshen was teaching, and Guifeng Zongmi wrote his commentaries at this time. How did Miaoxin find the Way? The Way found her, of course; it always will. And then she found another great teacher of the century. She found Yangshan.

Yangshan Huiji was Guishan Lingyou's main disciple and the co-founder of their Guiyang School. He was known as "Little Shakya," and he was a man of visions and dreams. He said to Miaoxin, "I speak only of the final matter. If you want to know the very base of things, right now, then go to the base of things."

She wanted to go to the base of things.

"Listen! Listen!" he urged. She listened; her name meant "wonderful belief."

The Guiyang School used many of the teachings and stories of Hui neng, the Sixth Patriarch of Zen in China who had lived more than a hundred years before. One story often told to the monks went like this:

> The flag above the temple gate was flapping in the wind. Two monks got into an argument about it. "The flag is moving," said

one. "No, the wind is moving," said the other. They almost came to blows. Then the Sixth Patriarch walked by, listened a moment, and said, "Neither the wind nor the flag is moving. It is your mind that moves."

The novices often took this story as advice to stop talking and sit quietly, waiting for their minds to settle. Perhaps the teachers intended it that way; novices can be a bit excitable at times. However, the monks at Yangshan's temple did a lot of talking about silence. Point at the wind! one said. Show me your mind, said another. What does it matter which moves? they asked each other. Pleased with their own insight, they raced through the chill halls of the monastery to beat the early meditation bell.

The older monks, having already felt the settling of the intellect into its base like a well-measured peg settling into its precisely cut hole, went deeper into the story. The mind is the base of all perception, they murmured to Yangshan, and to each other over tea. Past argument, past expression—the mind names *wind,* names *flag,* names *moves.*

The mind names *mind,* said one particularly adept fellow.

Only the very senior ones understood the great risk the Sixth Patriarch had taken. Only devils use words, but he couldn't help himself—he had to find a way to save the monks.

Yangshan sometimes smiled when he caught shreds of these conversations. *Still so many traces,* he thought. *Still a scent of something on the breeze. I wonder who will penetrate this one all the way?*

One season Yangshan asked his older monks for advice about who to put in charge of Secular Affairs. It was a moderately important job—attending to donors and other business, monitoring the provisions of grain and vegetables, taking care of the guests who came to the mountain to study—but not necessarily a lively one, and it meant living down below at the gate, outside the walls.

"What about Huaizi?" he asked. Huaizi—"child of the Huai River"—was his nickname for Miaoxin, who had been born on its banks. After listening to their advice, Yangshan announced that he would appoint Miaoxin because she was the most suitable person for the job. A few of the novice monks weren't happy with this, but they kept their grumbling to themselves around the abbot. The seniors agreed with the abbot. Miaoxin just bowed when she was told of her new job and moved down to the gate.

One day seventeen monks from Szechuan came to visit the famous teacher. They were put up at the guesthouse. Miaoxin prepared their rooms, took their dirty cloaks and shoes to wash, cooked the special partridge and duck dishes reserved for honored guests, and silently served them tea after the meal. As the sun went down and a mountain chill came in through the shutters, she lit the lamps and built them a fire without a word.

The monks gathered by the hearth, eating small cakes off lacquered trays. They would meet the great Yangshan in the morning, and they shared a self-conscious pleasure at the long distance they'd come. Yangshan was famous for answering questions with silence, yet they expected to debate him. A few thought they might win.

"Shall we start with 'the flag and the wind'?" asked the eldest. "A good one!" his friend answered, and they started arguing over the meaning of the story.

"The Great Ancestor said too much," complained one monk, a chubby fellow with mud on the hem of his robe.

"How can you defame him like that?" replied another. "He gave them only what they could understand." *We,* he seemed to imply, would have been given more. The debate went on like this for a long time.

After a time, out of the dim shadows scented with charcoal smoke, came Miaoxin's voice.

"You are all a bunch of donkeys," she said firmly, silencing the room at once. These were almost her first words since the monks had arrived. "What a waste of good sandals! You wouldn't know the Dharma in a dream." And she rose and left the room to tidy the dishes in the kitchen. "What a shame," she murmured as she left.

Finally, the monks, chastened and uncertain, followed her into the kitchen. They shuffled their feet and cleared their throats, but she wouldn't turn around.

"Please, can't you explain?" one finally asked.

Her hands in the water, brow damp with steam, she looked over her shoulder at him. "The flag is not moving. The wind is not moving. The mind is not moving. Hand me that towel, please."

In a daze, a monk handed her the towel, and one by one they left the kitchen and went to their beds and fell wordlessly into the great sea of understanding.

Miaoxin washed the dishes, shut the gate, doused the lamps, and retired. She knew that the flag moves, the wind moves, and our minds move too. But that doesn't mean we have to be blown around by the things we meet. Miaoxin was truly free, like wind is free—moving and not moving, speaking and silent, standing still and bending down, slipping gracefully between obstacles, through every gap.

The next morning the seventeen monks put on clean robes, offered incense, and renewed their vows with deeply felt intention. Then they took their leave without meeting the abbot and returned directly to Szechuan, their task fulfilled. They had found an enlightened teacher; they had been given turning words. When Yangshan heard about this, he was pleased that his student had done his work for him; that way, he could take his tea in peace.

Like her teacher, Miaoxin practiced silence when it was best and saved her words for certain uses. In 881 bandits overwhelmed Changan and slaughtered thousands, targeting especially the writers and artists. The city was looted, the crops withered, and the beautiful buildings were burned down. What was moving then?

purple robes

Huiguang, Huiwen, Fadeng, and Wenzhao

(1100s)

In 972 the emperor issued an edict that nuns were to be ordained only by women, and only in convents. This may have been intended to keep the convents pure and the nuns and monks separated, but the result was that women could do things their own way for a change. Many traveled to study with famous male teachers, and some became independent and powerful teachers in their own right, teaching men and women both.

HUIGUANG

Huiguang was from Chengdu. Her uncle was Fan Zuyu, a Confucian scholar-official who wrote *The Mirror of the Tang.* She studied with Kumu Fazheng, a Caodong priest who had taught Hongzhi. He emphasized sitting zazen day and night; Huiguang did this very thing, broke through, and Fazheng made her his Dharma heir.

Huiguang was noted for her skill in debate, her intelligence, and her deep study of the texts. She was known as Great Master Jingzhi. In the springtime, in the third year of the Xuanhe reign, what is now called the year 1121, she was appointed by the Song emperor Huizong to be abbot of the Miraculous Wisdom Convent in Kaifeng. She received the imperial purple robe that designated a Buddhist master.

When the Great Master arrived, she wrapped herself in the purple robe and climbed to the highest seat. There she told the story of Zhaozhou and the old woman who had confounded a monk. The monk had asked her which way to go to get to Mount Wutai, and she answered, "Just keep going, straight ahead." Zhaozhou went to see about this woman and asked her the same question. He got the same answer, and as she had before, she added, "Another good monk goes on the way." Zhaozhou simply told the monk he'd checked her out and didn't explain further.

Huiguang repeated this story, and then said:

Tongue of Zhaozhou,
Day after day, an old woman.
Radiance of the urna canopies the earth,
Investigating and shattering with distinctive brilliance.
Going back to that which knows no bounds
Is to enter calmly a state devoid of insight.

Huiguang quietly stroked the center of her forehead, between her eyebrows, as she spoke. Here a buddha has a curl of hair, the urna, a sign of enlightenment, and it radiates wisdom for everyone. The old woman didn't have this, but then, she didn't need it. She knew the way, and she was without excitement, without drama. To know this old woman was to know the same boundless understanding.

The emperor asked that Huiguang teach and give sermons to mixed groups of monks, nuns and laypeople together. When she died in 1165, she was buried on West Mountain in Jianxi province. A collection of her writings was found some time later by a famous Song Dynasty poet named Lu You. He greatly admired her poems and wrote an homage to her.

HUIWEN

Huiwen was the Dharma heir of Foyan Qingyuan, who was known as Longmen; Foyan was a famous teacher in his generation, known as one of the "Three Buddhas" of his time. His Dharma brother was Yuanwu Keqin, who finished "The Blue Cliff Record." Huiwen was appointed to teach at the Jingju Convent in Wenshou. When she arrived and ascended to the highest seat, she first cited the words of Fayan Wen'i for the edification of her audience:

With three strikes on the drum,
up they come in clusters.
Dharma of Buddha and matters of humankind
Fully completed at one time.

Huiwen then said, "This hillbilly monastic says as well, 'With three strikes on the drum, up they come in clusters.' Fayan had no walking stick at hand, so he just gave thirty [blows] with the handle of a broom."

FADENG

The nun Fadeng was Huiwen's heir and also taught at Jingju Convent in Wenshou. She was known as Great Master Wuxiang. Remembering her teacher's words about Fayan's lack of a stick, when she ascended the seat in the hall, she held her walking stick firmly in her hand. Then she said:

There goes Avalokiteśvara,
Here comes Samantabhadra.
There's Mañjuśrī standing on water, wearing boots.
Look up, there goes a sparrow hawk tearing across the kingdom of Silla.
Sparks from flint and rays of lightning can't catch up, oh dear.

The chance of enlightenment passes through our lives as freely, as often, as elusively as the hawk. All of it is right before us—wisdom, action, compassion, available in a single breath, gone in a flash of light. The only one who catches it is the one who is also flying, like Fadeng.

WENZHAO

Wenzhao was born in Wenling in the province of Fujian, in the family of Dong. After becoming a nun at the young age of seventeen, she wandered for a long time, meeting and seeking teachers. Eventually she was given authority by Ganlu Zhongxuan. The governor heard of her abilities and ordered her to be the abbot of Miaoshen Temple in Pingjiangfu.

When she arrived, she put on her transmission robes, climbed to the high seat, and said:

Should wellsprings of numina fail to stir,
On what may the embodiment of wonder rely?
Solitary brilliance of utter distinction
Is the radiant splendor of whom?
Were we to speak of bhūtatathatā, or genuine suchness,
Realm of reality is what it most resembles.
To dig out an ulcer from unblemished flesh
Is to render the concept of "patriarch."
To deliberate that which is just so
Is foolishly giving preeminence to recognizing shadows.
Forty-nine years, the old barbarian
Spoke on dreams and thereupon ceased.
Within the Sangha Hall, Senior Kāṇdinya
For each of you, one and all,
Took up "restoration of bodhi," do you recall?

After a long silence, she added, "Let's be sparing in grasping eyebrows."

Wenzhao had at least one male heir. She became abbot of five different Vinaya convents in her life. The Vinaya nuns kept the letter of the rules carefully, but their spirit was lacking. Each time, Wenzhao gradually reformed the method of the convent from Vinaya to Chan. She taught the nuns to look for the nature of their own minds, to practice for all beings, because they were all beings at the source. Thus, it is due to Wenzhao's efforts that Chan spread among so many women of the time.

the bathhouse attendant

Kongshi Daoren

(1050–1124)

Kongshi Daoren's father, Fan Xun, was shidafu, part of the educated class—a scholar, official, and gentleman of the Song Dynasty. He was an archivist. The civil exam system had given birth to good schools and widespread literacy for boys and girls alike. Print shops using carved blocks produced bound books at the rate of a thousand pages a day, and Kongshi had grown up with much to read. Her father had manuals of advice on medicine and fortune-telling, her mother liked books of aphorisms and popular stories, her brother studied for his exams, and she was drawn to the Buddhist sutras and stories of the masters. Several decades before her birth, the *Tripitaka,* the entire original Buddhist canon, 130,000 pages long, had been printed, each page requiring a separate carved block.

Kongshi's name meant "empty room." She was quick and clever; she loved to study, and her teachers thought she was quite sharp and intelligent. She even mastered algebra, which her brother couldn't do. When she was the right age, her father made her an advantageous match with Suti, the prime minister's grandson. She was more serious than her husband, more serious about everything but politics. Marriage and courtly life was a never-ending series of petty amusements—jugglers and storytellers and poems—and malicious gossip. These small concerns seemed so large to everyone around her, and she tired of it all quickly.

After a few years, she left her husband. She was willing to be divorced, if her husband preferred; divorce was shameful for a woman, and she couldn't initiate one. Her husband preferred not to divorce, since it wouldn't affect his behavior very much. He let her go with little regret; they'd never been close.

She returned to her parents' home. When she found within herself the desire to be ordained as a nun, she asked her father for permission. He refused, and then she had no choice but to stay home.

Fan Xun had his reasons. The government was top-heavy with tens of thousands of bureaucrats in endlessly replicating administrative layers. The country was divided into almost three hundred prefectures—the bureaucracy was impossibly big, and inequities of tax and marketplace impossible to correct. Government control eroded with the country's borders. There was too much change coming too quickly, and many people blamed Buddhism, which seemed to defy authority in slippery ways. The northern tribesmen who harried the borders, attacking villages and leaving a trail of bodies wherever they traveled, all called themselves Buddhists. Even the peaceful national temples had begun to give off a faint scent of decay. The Chinese were great metalworkers. In their furnaces they cast stoves, pans, coins, lamps, knives, axles, temple bells, and Buddhas. It was not a good sign, Fan Xun thought, that the bells and statues produced for the Buddhist temples were the largest cast items in the world.

Ordination certificates were sold everywhere; criminals bought them so that they could get sanctuary. Even the "Master of the Purple Robe" certificate was for sale to those who had enough strings of coins.

A new emperor had taken the throne in 1101. Huizong was a Daoist, and one of his first acts was to declare that Buddhist monasteries would now be Daoist temples. After centuries in China, Buddhism was once again declared a foreign religion. Only a few Buddhist temples were officially recognized and protected by the government in return for government control. The Dharma was studied most sincerely in the small private monasteries scattered throughout the provinces, but these now had little protection from capricious laws and wandering discontents.

For these reasons, and because he loved her and enjoyed having her near him, Fan Xun refused to let her go.

Many women couldn't be ordained because they didn't have permission or they were raising children. A few men couldn't either, because of household responsibilities. There were enough that they became known as daoren, people of the Way. This was Kongshi's only choice. She ate a vegetarian diet, fasted regularly, and practiced a simple meditation she'd learned as a child—sitting and allowing her breath to rise and fall.

Her brother passed his exams and became shidafu, like their father. Her parents' hair grew gray. Kongshi attended to chores, took regular exercise, rose early, kept her room neat, and studied. She refused to wear elaborate clothing or fancy hairstyles or ornaments. She served tea to her father, sat with her mother in the evening, and gradually grew, if not old, no longer young. She wasn't content, but she did learn to do what needed to be done.

Kongshi studied most carefully a strange, brief instruction on meditation called "Contemplation of the Dharmadhātu." "One includes all and enters all," it said. "All includes one and enters one; one includes one and enters one; all includes all and enters all. They interpenetrate one another without any obstruction." In this way, one could see the Indescribable Indescribable Turning of the World.

By herself, in her room, Kongshi gradually came to see that every "thing" is part of a whole—that each thing in fact *makes* the whole. No one thing is important or unimportant, since all depends on all. She remembered a mosaic she had seen as a child, an elaborate mural in which endless little bits of colored tile were fitted together into a beautiful, complicated picture. It had seemed magic to her then, and it seemed magic to her again. The universe was a mosaic, perfectly laid so that each tile fit exactly. If one tile shifted even the tiniest bit, all the others had to shift too. This had to be true—the world fit together this precisely, this neatly. How could there be any extra pieces or extra room? Those things nearest us seem to move the most, she reasoned. But if it were possible to measure such change, one would see that every single tile in all dimensions also shifted some tiny bit with every change. It was unimaginable, but it was the only explanation.

She wrote two poems about her understanding. The first said:

Bhūtatathatā, embodied within the vast realm of dust,
Together with Vairocana is densely interwoven.

If a wave in its totality is one and the same with a stream of water,
The wave negates the stream of water.
If a stream of water in its totality forms a wave,
The stream itself obliterates.

The second poem went like this:

Matter and self are wholly lacking in discrepancy,
Identical to the likeness of countless mirrors.
To deliver host and companion in shining brilliance,
Penetrate the true lineage with clear awareness.
A comprehensive corpus embraces manifold dharma,
Interlocked within the net of Indra.
One after another, inexhaustible abodes,
To stir or be still is entirely one and the same.

One winter, both of Kongshi's parents died. They were old, there was a sickness; many died that year. One day not long after her parents' memorial service, she asked her brother for permission to be ordained.

"Your place is with me," he answered. He had never been patient with her studies. She was a little embarrassing, plain where all the other women he knew were fancy. "We're family. You stay here." When she asked again, he simply said, "No."

The Laws of Avoidance mandated that government officials couldn't serve in certain offices in their own provinces, to prevent favoritism. When Kongshi's brother was promoted to Concurrent District Defender and sent to a new posting, she went with him. When one sees into interdependence, one sees that every thing depends on every thing—each life depends on every other life. To see this is to see how fragile one's own life truly is, how little a life depends on wishing or desires or hope. We are the product of all that we encounter. We are the product of all that is encountered by all that we encounter. There is no such thing as a single life.

My life is the child of beings beyond counting, she thought as she packed her belongings for the trip. But her chest felt as though it had been cracked open with an ax. She tried to tell herself not to fret, that everything fit together, that this was just another unopened gift. And in the cracks of her sorrow there was a glimmer of peace: as she contemplated the indescribable web of being, she saw that it was just a single step to gratitude, and from there, one more step to giving everything away.

They traveled to Nanjing, arriving in the chill, late days of winter in time for the end of Spring Festival. The city's doors were decorated with gods to ward off evil, and the streets, bright with lanterns, were crowded with people in animal masks, men in women's clothing, and drunken revelers waving incense and drinking pepper wine. This was an altogether different place than where they'd been before.

Nanjing was modern. It had regular garbage service and street maintenance. The marketplaces had bookstores, flower shops, groceries that sold red lotus-seed rice and rare herbs, jewelers that sold ivory and rhinoceros horn. The cries of porters and laborers filled the air, and traveling salesmen went door to door with tea, candy, and toys. Customers paid with paper money instead of coins. Singers, acrobats, and puppeteers crowded the streets.

Kongshi saw the growing abyss between the rich and the poor. She saw that beneath its pretty skin the city, the entire country, was filled with beggars and criminals. Emperor Huizong's main concern had been pleasure. At enormous cost, he'd built a huge park in Kaifeng, with rare plants and exotic animals, artificial waterfalls running down an artificial mountain, a pond, herds of deer, a family of screaming gibbons, and a mysterious beast spoken of with dread and seen by few. He sent emissaries throughout the empire to find more strange animals and rare gems, and when someone found a giant boulder said to have divine power, he had a giant ship built especially to transport it back to Kaifeng, tearing down bridges and carving riverbanks to make way for it. The park alone cost so much that new taxes had to be levied.

Wealthy men visited beautiful courtesans, small women with petite figures and pale skin, their black hair in huge buns held up by combs of ivory and gold, their cheeks red with rouge. Afterwards the men returned to their luxurious homes decorated with terra-cotta dragons and phoenixes under green tiled roofs, which rose uncaringly above the streets where more and more people went hungry.

Meanwhile, an anonymous inventor had discovered how to make things explode.

In 1111, Kongshi's brother died. She held his memorial service, packed up his belongings, and then considered what to do. He had left her with enough money, and she was free.

From one perspective, it had seemed more important than anything in the world to be ordained and to leave the ordinary world behind. But now she could see that robes were no different from anything else. What mattered wasn't what you wore, but how and why you wore it. What mattered was a mind of clear awareness, a mind that could see how shifting *this* here moved *that* there. This meant knowing that what seemed crucial from one point of view seemed unimportant from another. There was no single "correct" position within interdependence from which to see the "real" truth. Vital or meaningless? Everything depended on where you stood, what place in space-time you occupied—which depended entirely on your position in the mosaic, which was changing all the time.

She found herself near the monastery of the Linji master Sixin Wuxin. His name meant "dead mind," a compliment to his serene nature. Sixin Wuxin had a birthmark on his right side and both shoulders; he looked as though he were always wearing an imperial robe.

She came to hear his lecture and then respectfully asked permission to come back whenever she could.

"You are already awake," he told his students. "You just don't know it yet. First you have to understand what a 'person' is. Then you have to understand the 'half-person.' Finally, 'no person.' That's the way." He saw Kongshi's sincerity and invited her to come every day.

One day he asked her, "Whom did bodhisattva Sadāpralāpa, flaunting his intellect, instruct to take up a study of prajñā?" Sadāpralāpa, also called Bodhisattva Always Weeping, is a character in the *Prajnaparamita Sutra,* where he weeps continually at the difficulty of finding a true teacher. It is said that he "sold his heart and liver" by showing off this way; such an act kills our inner truth, and we have to look elsewhere for a path.

She answered, "If you're not of a mind to do so, then I can stop now too." She was ready for more—she dared him to come closer.

Then he asked, "As for that which a single rainfall nurtures, roots and shoots are different. What comes from the earth where there isn't sun or shade?" That single fall of rain, that Dharma pouring down on every thing the same, leading to endless roots, each different—what a miracle that flowers come from dirt!

She answered, "Five petals of a single blossom come," referring to the Five Schools of Chan.

Another afternoon he asked Kongshi, "What wall will you face day and night when you settle down and get on with your pursuit?"

"Oh, reverend," she answered, her voice shaking with intensity, "you are good at borrowing eyebrows."

"This woman messes up the order," he said at last, and hit her. She bowed deeply.

Kongshi was filled with gratitude for Sixin's efforts on her behalf. She composed a poem of appreciation for him:

His dead mind is still thriving—
The source of the luminous is deep!
He sees colors with his ears,
He hears sounds with his eyes,
  And the peasant understands while the sages remain ignorant.
Behind, one is rich; ahead, one is poor.
He benefits all beings, frees all things, by
Turning a bit of mud into gold.
No colors can make his image,
Which lives neither in the past or the present time.

She gave the poem to Sixin, and in reply, he composed a poem of challenge for her. She studied it deeply.

One day, as she walked up the long path to the monastery, the last obstacles fell away. There it was: everything. The mosaic. The whole view, right now: an interpenetrating tapestry of atoms and seeds, her feet, desire and pain, her parents' ashes, her brother's opinions, the building she approached—her mind, her teacher's mind—the stone path and the moss along its edge, her sore feet—her broken heart, the dead men frozen in Nanking's doorways, the crowd of crows complaining from a cypress tree—everything and at once, *pffft!* nothing, a tiny wave lost on the sea, a little cloud gone in the spring sun, a leaf blown by, a spark a dream a light a shadow. Her many broken views, seeing only part of things, seeing only *this* and not being able to see *that*—this was also part of it. Just as everything was broken and gone, at exactly the same time and in exactly the same way and for exactly the same reason, every atom and seed and mind was essential, eternal, joyous, and pure.

When she arrived, she went straight to Sixin's room. "I make the universe," she said to him. "I unmake the universe." Then she spontaneously recited a poem:

Self and other are never different.
The many things in the world are just reflections.
Bright, full, holding both principle and practice,
Completely experienced, filled with the absolute.
Every single thing holds all things,
All things are connected to all things,
This continues layer upon layer without end—
Moving, still, it never stops, this interpenetration.

For some time, they exchanged poems. He made puns with her name, pointed her first in this direction, then in that; she stood her ground, asking more intently with each verse.

After he approved her awakening, Sixin sent her away. Real awakening is just like everything else—a whisper, a slight tilt of a hand, a wink of the eye; it is almost silent and doesn't need attention. They understood each other very well, these two—so calmly did they say good-bye that anyone who didn't know better would have thought they had barely met. This intimacy was as invisible and strong as air, it could not be grasped. The spark exploded silent fire; the cloud vanished in the sun.

Kongshi went to the Baoning Monastery and built a bathhouse outside its walls. She hung a pot over the door, the sign for bathing, and put a painting of Lingzhao and Layman Pang on the wall. On the door she wrote this poem:

If nothing truly exists, what are you bathing?
Where could even the slightest bit of dust come from?
If you say one sentence worth hearing, you may enter the bath.
The ancient teachers can only scrub your back;
How can I clarify your mind?
If you want to be free from dust,
Sweat with every part of you.
Perhaps water washes away dirt,
But do you understand that water is also dirty?
Even if you see no difference between the water and the dirt,
It all must be washed completely away when you enter here.

Then she posted signs around the bathhouse with other poems she'd written, challenging the bathers to consider the real meaning of washing, cleansing, and dirt. Right there she expressed the Indescribable Indescribable Turning of the World.

Many people came to Kongshi's bathhouse, some of them every day. Most wanted a simple wash in cold water, leaning over the wooden and iron tubs. A few wanted hot water, so Kongshi heated big stones and blocks of iron in the fire to set in the tubs. She hired assistants who could give massages, set up screens to hide the women when they washed, and help her empty and scrub the tubs at the end of the day.

Every day she laid out clean towels for the bathers, and every night she gathered up the dirty ones and washed them out and hung them up to dry. In the morning she gathered the dry towels together and folded them as carefully as if they were the ordination robes she'd never worn.

She tried to explain her understanding to the customers who took up her challenge, but few of them understood. The traveling monks were especially dense. She would lean over the tub in her faded skirt and jacket, a strong, lean woman growing old, and slap the water to make waves. "Watch the waves," she would try to explain. "Where do they come from? Where do they go?"

The world is nothing but dust and suchness.
Up and down, forward and backward, everything is marked by Buddha.
What is a wave but water? But water isn't just the waves;
Even when the whole sea is wild, it is still just the sea.

Kongshi spent her evenings writing a commentary called "The Record on Clarifying the Mind." She carefully copied it and sent it to Sixin as a gift. He had more copies made and sent them to other masters. Eventually someone else paid for Kongshi's commentary to be printed, and others bought copies and passed them from temple to temple and hand to hand until it circulated throughout the entire country of China. Several teachers appended their own comments and compliments to the pamphlet. Kongshi was held in high regard, but few thought they'd met her. It didn't occur to anyone that the old woman in the bathhouse, with her crazy poetry, was a great Zen master.

In her old age, Kongshi finally closed the bathhouse and moved to the Xizhu Convent in Jiangsu. When people realized who she was, they came with questions, laypeople and ordained people alike. Many people came, and many went away awakened.

When she was very old, as an afterthought, Kongshi was finally ordained. Every day she put on her robes, and every night she took them off, folding them as carefully as if they were bath towels.

no robes

Yu Daopo

(early to middle 1100s)

When she was a young woman, Yu Daopo heard Langye Yongqi speak of the teaching of *true person of no rank.* When Yu Daopo heard of this, her eyes half opened. A short while later she was taking pastries she'd made to the local temple. She and her husband were walking down the road when she heard a voice chanting, "Happiness in the Lotus Land!" They turned around and saw a beggar in rags, skipping about, singing. Without thinking twice, Yu Daopo threw the tray of food on the ground.

"Are you nuts?" her husband cried.

Yu Daopo slapped him, crying, "This isn't your realm!" He had his areas of competence; this, his dear wife knew, wasn't one of them. To see that there is no true rank, no true mark, no true difference in the midst of difference—what a gift. She made a deep bow of gratitude to the beggar and her husband both.

After that, she studied with Langye in earnest. At a lecture he shouted to the audience: "Who is the true person of no rank here?"

Yu Daopo stood up in the midst of the crowd, with no rank at all, no robes, no stick, and shouted back: "A person exists who has no rank, but does have six arms and three heads. With her full strength at work, Mount Hua falls in two. As strong as flowing water, unstoppable, not caring about the coming spring!" Her claim was outside the status that any official world could give her. The *po* in her name means "old woman," and this she was, at every age.

Langye was very pleased with this answer. Eventually he made Yu Daopo his only Dharma heir, but she refused to be ordained. What was the point of being a monk? A monk took rebirth without resistance, becoming whatever circumstances required, she explained to Langye. Therefore, it was pointless to take on such a form artificially. He had to agree.

So if that's what a monk is, she went on, rebirth as required, then what does it matter what a person wears? Hair, bare scalp, loincloths, robes!

"It doesn't matter!" she said. "It doesn't matter, Mr. No Rank."

Instead, she and her husband, a man she'd known since she was quite young, opened a doughnut and pastry shop in Jingling. Whenever she served a monk or met one on the road to the temple, she addressed him as "son." If the monk complained, she shut the door of the shop or turned her back.

Fodeng Shouxun came to the shop to test her understanding of the Dharma—her reputation was getting around.

"What do you want, son?" she said as soon as she saw him, refusing to kowtow to his robes.

"Do you see my father?" he answered.

Yu Daopo turned around and bowed to a post near the road.

Shouxun kicked over the post and said, "I thought you'd have better answers than that." He turned to leave. He couldn't accept her rudeness as wisdom; he wanted the bow.

"Son, don't go!" called Yu Daopo, just doing it again. "Come back here and let me cuddle with you." But he left anyway, disgusted with her disrespect.

Another monk came for pastries and combat. She immediately asked him, "Where are you from?" (This is a dangerous question when asked by a Zen master; it always means more than one's daily travels.)

The monk answered, "From Deshan's place."

Yu Daopo threw up her hands in delight. "But he's my son!" she cried. She felt herself higher than the monk's own teacher, higher than Deshan himself—junior to no one, she said.

The monk found this offensive. What made her the senior? "Whose son are *you?*" he asked with a sneer. She was no one's son, after all—she was a woman, a layperson, his child in the Dharma.

Yu Daopo dropped her hands in disgust at his answer. "Oh, that just makes me want to pee on you!" she said. She really had expected more than that from a good monk. "You're not allowed to leave." He just stood there, without making another move. Never had he heard such callous, rough talk.

One day she climbed Mount Jia in Hunan province to hear Yuanwu Keqin, known as Fuguo, give his first lecture as the new abbot of the monastery. As he climbed the high seat, she ran out of the crowd, gave him a great shove, and then ran back into the audience.

The next day he came to see her. Pretty little flags hung from the eaves of her shop, flitting in the breeze. The smell was enticing. He called her name, but she refused to come out of her doughnut shop.

"Such a yellow boy!" she shouted from the back room. "And you say you are a master!"

Yuan Wu shouted back. "Stop bragging, you! I've already noted your accomplishment."

Then they laughed together, and she served him fresh cake made with candied fruit.

She wrote a poem about the great teacher Mazu:

Sun face, moon face,
An empty sky filled with lightning.
Mazu shuts up all the skin bags in the world.
He tells half the truth.

What a great eulogy; even Mazu barely deserves it. The laughing Yu Daopo is serious for once. Mazu's teaching lives forever, and only a moment, and in the flash of his insight he brings wordless insight to everyone. Half deluded, half enlightened, she goes back to her baking, content. For the rest of her life many monks come to eat her doughnuts and her words.

the silence
Miaodao
(1090–1163)

Miaodao was born near the coast in Yanping, where the winters were severe. Snow sometimes fell for many days without cease. The spring was drizzly; the summers were thick with heat and rain; the autumn was so dry the crops would sometimes fail. No one liked being there. But her father, Huang Shang, was head of the Ministry of Rites. He had the highest score in the national metropolitan exams of 1082 and was deeply immersed in questions of public education. He was a great lover of art. When the brash passions of the Tang Dynasty ended, they were replaced with great delicacies—subtle porcelain, tender calligraphy, ink paintings like faint dreams. Huang Shang could never get enough of these gossamer arts.

For a long time people had been migrating south to a milder climate, away from the dust storms and floods of the Huanghe Valley, away from the endless border clashes with the northern tribes. Farming was easier in the south, and the soil more productive. Miaodao's family, like many in government, had moved north against this slow tide. Eventually her father was transferred into a financial department, and they left the coast. They moved all the way to the capital at Kaifeng, at the end of the Grand Canal and the great river so rusty with silt it was like a river of flowing soil. The city was the hub of a web of waterways—all of China was connected by river, canal, and delta through Kaifeng. Large boats pushed by poles and shaped like smiles plied endlessly up and down the river roads; the city's life took place on riverbanks and endless small bridges.

Huang Shang put lifts in his shoes, covered his topknot with a black cap, wore clothes of a single color, and went to work in a world of trade organizations and guilds. He argued over monopolies and price-setting while Miaodao and her two brothers studied at home. Her father still valued education, for women as well as men. There was a lot to learn—the written language had more than ten thousand separate characters, and after it was mastered came Confucianism, history, poetry, and classical literature. For Miaodao, there was also music, household management, and minor healing remedies: ephedra leaves for bleeding and asthma, mercury for wounds, arsenic for rashes and sores. To please her father, she learned to recite from memory long passages of Confucius's "Classic of Filial Piety."

For her own pleasure, she sat in meditation every night, wrapped in silence.

Miaodao learned to dress in bright colors, layers of silk vests, skirts, and jackets with ribbons for decoration. Her ears were pierced, her brows tweezed, and she wore makeup to pale her skin, the mark of an indoor life. Kaifeng was bustling, filled with markets and crowded streets of shoppers and sellers—but almost all of them were men. Women's lives were expected to be private; many wore veils on the street. As Miaodao grew into a young woman, she retreated more and more behind the screen, into the women's quarters and a woman's occupations.

Her mother and aunt steadfastly opposed the new custom of footbinding, although it was increasingly popular among the upper classes. In Hangzhou, women with unbound feet were said to be "planted on the ground"; this was an insult. A woman who had been bound as a child was never active or strong. She sat instead of standing and preferred to stay home. Her weakness meant she was delicate and soft, and her very dependence was a sign of wealth. Many people, men and women both, found tiny feet attractive. But Miaodao's father was indulgent toward his daughter, and his good sense led him to agree with his wife. Miaodao was quiet, which was to be expected, and she was small and neat, but he couldn't bring himself to think of her as weak. In fact, her confidence and iron discipline made him uncomfortable sometimes.

These qualities also made finding a husband problematic. It was harder than ever to get worthy men as sons-in-law—there didn't seem to be as many worthy men anymore. When she first brought up the possibility of becoming a nun, Huang Shang didn't refuse. "Let me think about it" was all he said. Many of the better families had a few women devoted to Buddhist studies, after all. But she was so young. She was too young still.

His sister, Miaodao's aunt, worked in the palace. Like many of the three thousand palace women, she had been recruited for her position and worked under the Supreme Commander of the Palace. Huang Shang decided to place Miaodao in a similar career for a time. When she was fifteen years old, her aunt came to get her. She was placed as an apprentice in the Department of Lighting.

Miaodao watched palace life from her position in the hallways; it was her job to light the lanterns at dusk, change the wicks, report problems, and dim the lights in the morning. In the labyrinthine hallways and courtyards, she made her way from lamp to lamp. The concubines, their children, the other female servants, and the myriad eunuchs who guarded them were always about, but she was invisible in the way young girls and servants are often invisible. Thus, not speaking, she saw and heard a lot. The courtly ladies played on swings under the peach and willow trees. The men played polo and two-man football in the inner courtyard. The palace was a noisy place, with hundreds of people about all the time, the halls filled with commands and songs and speeches, endless intrigues and whispered assignations, gossip and scandals, people jockeying for position and power. The more Miaodao heard, the less she said—not that anyone asked her opinion or would have listened if she'd given it. She began to feel an oceanic silence inside, a silence that was not the opposite of speaking—a silence in which speaking couldn't be imagined. She lit lamps and watched the soft darkness instantly disappear into shadows; she extinguished lamps and watched the details around her vanish into black.

In 1110, when she reached twenty, the traditional age for ordination, Miaodao quietly came to her father and told him she had done her duty. She had tried. She could not imagine herself married, or staying in the palace. Could she be ordained, please? This time he agreed, with blessing and sadness, and she left forever. She bought a silk map, rolled it up in a traveling case, and left.

For more than twenty years she wandered, training with different teachers but mostly being alone, cultivating the sound of not speaking and the meaning of light and dark. At one time she found herself in a northern province, a flat hard place north of the yellow river. In the open, windy reaches, people dug their homes into the ground, hollowing out dark, cool rooms in the hard soil, away from the wind and sun and storms. There were only spindly plants and long flat farms and distant hills, the river and the sky, until she came to a town filled with forges and blast furnaces.

Iron was vital for machinery, tools, Buddha statues, nails, chains, and weapons—so many weapons, many thousands of swords, shields, spears, and suits of armor, made by a thousand artisans and ten thousand laborers. Most of the trees in the province had been cut down a century before, whole mountains denuded, burned to make charcoal for the iron factories. Now, progress: instead of charcoal, there were giant holes in the earth and another thousand people digging coal by the bucketful.

The town was bare and gray, the people broken and filthy. All day and night she could hear the roar of the furnaces and now and then an explosion in the mine, opening a new vein. The air stank of smoke, and she wiped black soot off her face. Yet she stayed a while; she felt she was on a visit to hell, seeing the suffering of people who had committed terrible acts in a previous life. They didn't seem to know why they were living in a place like war, like the end of the world, like a prophecy bearing down. Light and dark, sound and silence.

The whole world was like hell, in a way. Even when it was beautiful, anything could happen; terrible change could come. In 1127 the Jurchens, a tribe from the north, attacked. After a long and terrible siege, they captured Kaifeng. The northern Song court collapsed, and everyone who could get away fled to the new capital at Hongzhou. She never heard news of her parents again.

For Miaodao everything had turned gray. She could remember the heaven she'd glimpsed in the silence of meditation; she saw hell all around her. Her own life—her very mind—seemed stuck at the crossroads between. She saw details without clarity, heard words without meaning, silence without peace, and she had begun to doubt if there was such a thing as a great awakening at all. She went to study with Zhenxie Qingliao, who ignored convention and took a few women as students. He was abbot on Mount Xuefeng in Fuzhou at the time, and Miaodao was one of hundreds of students there.

During the summer of 1134, in a strict practice period, Dahui Zonggao came to give a lecture. Dahui was a bit of a prodigy—he had still been a young man when he was given a purple robe—and when he came to Fuzhou, he was the leading master of the Linji sect. Whatever he said in his lecture, it was enough to make Miaodao break her vow to study under Zhenxie. She was forty-four years old when she followed Dahui to Guangyin Monastery.

Dahui had attained enlightenment studying the koans collected by Yuanwu Keqin known as "The Blue Cliff Record." Afterward, distressed at his students' confusion, Dahui burned every copy of the collection that he could find. He taught men and women, monks and laypeople alike, not caring what a person looked like or where he or she had been.

Miaodao requested entry into Dahui's chamber three times. She asked formally, bowing to the ground between each request. She felt very solemn. He invited her to sit, and suddenly she started talking, an ocean of unspoken words pouring out. Her own voice seemed to surprise her.

"I am here—it seems the only reason to be anywhere—to investigate the Great Matter," she said, finally. "It seems to me that we get old and die with such astonishing speed, with such pain in birth and death. Cities appear and disappear just like that. Families vanish. This endless cycle seems urgent to me, but I still don't even know my own mind. Please help me, please teach me."

There were about seventy people at his temple, and a number were women. One was Lady Ch'in-kuo, an aristocratic laywoman, but all the students were treated the same way. Twice a day, each of Dahui's students came to see him for a brief interview.

When it was her turn, Miaodao would come to the door, light a stick of incense, make a full bow, and then speak. She couldn't seem to stop talking; in fact, they would converse for long hours, late into the night when most of the other people were asleep. Sometimes he lectured her, sometimes she implored him, and sometimes they simply talked—about demons and gods, the nature of meditation, the labyrinthine paths of the mind, the vow to help all beings to attain great enlightenment, her fear that her own karmic past was an obstacle to her enlightenment, her desire to pay endless gratitude to the Great Buddha with no idea how to do this—because she didn't know what the Great Buddha *was,* not really, not at all. They spoke for hours, days, and weeks, and yet she didn't know the base of her own mind.

On a muggy afternoon when the cicadas buzzed continually in the shrubs outside Dahui's rice-paper window, she said, almost in tears, "Please, just point out the doorway. I know it's there! I know there must be a key to all this. Please just give me the key!" That day he laughed at her and sent her away.

It was a terrible summer; the haze hung in the valley all day long, and the sun was sharp and hard. When the ninety-day practice period began, all the students were expected to work twice as much. Dahui told Miaodao that he wanted her to study the koans he had learned from his own teacher. "I don't know what else to tell you," he said. "You must reach a point where you can't use your mind. Concentrate on what Mazu said: 'It is not mind, it is not Buddha, it is not a thing.'

"While you concentrate, follow these principles," he added. This was an experiment; he had never tried this with a student before, never tried to clarify the method he used before. "Don't assume it's the truth. Don't assume it's not important to do something about it. Don't take it as a 'lightning flash.' Don't try to figure it out. Don't pay attention to the context. Just concentrate on the crucial lines."

It is not mind, it is not Buddha, it is not a thing. What is it?

Twice, a third time, she came to him in hot excitement, unable to hold back what she'd understood. Twice, a third time, he shouted at her before she finished speaking, flicking his horsehair whisk like a whip, and sent her running away.

Then, on a sultry August afternoon, when their robes stuck to their skin, she bowed at his seat and said, "I found the doorway in."

He smiled kindly, suddenly like a mother to her, and said, "It is not mind, it is not Buddha, it is not a thing. How do you understand this?"

"I only understand this way—"

"That's extra!" he broke in.

And the words cracked open—she fell with a crash into a silence so deep it seemed to echo upon itself. This was not the silence when no one is talking, she realized. This wasn't the silence between the words when someone is talking. This was the silence inside the words—the silence *of* words. She was home.

Great Chan masters said of her, "You only see a woman when you look at her, but she is ta-cheng-fu." This word, *ta-cheng-fu,* means a lot of things. Usually it means manly or heroic. It's a compliment: it means having courage, firmness, and determination, and it also means being undeterred, being able to concentrate fearlessly, and, in Zen, aiming for enlightenment without hesitating for a moment. Women generally were never paid this compliment, but Miaodao heard it and ignored the half-intended slap inside. She was the first person to follow the way of the koan that Dahui Zonggao created—the way of deep investigation of koans—all the way to its end, to the great awakening. She was his first Dharma heir, and eventually she was known as the Great Teacher Light of Concentration.

Dahui eventually made several of his female students Dharma heirs, including the aristocratic lady. He spoke of Miaodao often, saying once, "Can you say that she is a woman, and women have no share? You must believe that this matter has nothing to do with male or female, old or young, monk or nun or lay. Breaking through, you stand beside the Buddha."

Miaodao returned to her hometown and became abbess of the Convent Fuxingsi there. Later she was head of Zisheng in Changzhou and of Jingju in Wenzhou. She had a great many students for the rest of her life. Dahui was caught up in political unrest not long after she left him and had to flee again and again. One season half his monks died of plague and famine, but his method of working with koans still thrives. It was with Dahui that Miaodao became a true student of the Way, and it was with Miaodao that Dahui became a true teacher of that Way.

The Dharma is inexpressible, but sometimes we can say it with words. That this works, that it's possible, is as mysterious as the flame rising from the wick at a single touch. Her sermons often left audiences speechless, which was just as well.

After her first sermon, a monk asked, "When words don't do it and nothing is heard, what then?"

She answered, "You fall into the hole before you've even defecated. Don't ask a lot of questions. Before the Blessed Teacher appeared, there was nothing to be done. Then Bodhidharma came to this country, and many monasteries followed, facing each other across the mountains like pieces on a chessboard. Finally it leads to me standing here in front of you, making little bits and pieces of a rumor of truth.

"It's like light—can you hold it? Shout, and life and death disappear. Shout, and the buddhas and patriarchs can't be found. Shout, and enemies attack. Shout, and you can't be saved. But you tell me, in which shout is life and death extinguished, the buddhas lost, the enemies born, your life taken?

"When we discuss the meeting between two people, we don't need higher and lower ranks. But forms arise out of conditions, and today the authority is mine. So I respond to these conditions. Sometimes I block the student's way, and sometimes I'm a gate.

"Every person is complete, nothing missing, and every thing is as it should be. Spring flows among the myriad grasses, and the moon reflects off a thousand waves. There is nothing lacking, and nothing extra, in things as they are.

"Do you want my power? Take my power away! Get it for yourself. Grab the weapons away from the buddhas and ancestors and wield them yourself."

She picked up her horsehair whisk. "Can you see it? If so, sight is in your way." She hit the whisk handle against the sitting platform. "Do you hear it? Sound is in your way. But if you can step out of sight and sound, you can ride sight and sound. Let it all go, gather all of it, and you can move freely between form and emptiness. It is said that one can know Buddha Nature by knowing the causes and conditions of this moment. So tell me, all of you—what is this moment?"

Then she threw down the whisk and left. What daring! Her Dharma had already filled the world, but Miaodao had more to say.

JAPANESE ANCESTORS

Buddhism first came to Japan in the sixth century, before the country was called Japan. The central region at the time was known as Yamato. Technologically and politically, it was far behind China, and most of the country was still a violent place of clan warfare. At this time, Bodhidharma had already come and gone in China, where Buddhism was widespread.

Over the centuries, just as Buddhism had absorbed elements of Daoism in China, Japanese Buddhism was able to absorb many Shinto elements and folk beliefs of the rural people. Japanese Buddhism was dominated by the Tendai and Shingon sects; Zen was a comparatively late arrival. The first Zen, or Chan, monk came to Japan from China in the mid–800s, and the Zen school was not strongly established in Japan until medieval times.

Sources for the lives of Buddhist women in Japan are, as in China, both scarce and fertile. Some women are barely known, such as Zenshin, the first ordained Japanese; she is mentioned briefly several times in the ancient Japanese history *Nihon Shoki* but is virtually unknown today in Japan. Likewise, the accomplished female disciples of the masters Dōgen, Keizan, and Hakuin are little known today, and few facts are known about their lives. I have been unable to learn much at all about how these women practiced from day to day with their teachers and the monks who were their Dharma brothers; many records (and entire temples) have been destroyed, and the answer to many questions about the lives of medieval Buddhists is simply, "No one knows for sure." The details I've included are inferred from the facts we know—for instance, since we know that Keizan gave transmission to a couple of his female students, we have to assume that an intimate teacher-student relationship was in place. What that looked like at the time will probably never be known.

Certain women, such as Mugai Nyodai and the early abbots of Tōkeiji, were famous in their time and are still honored today; their artwork, graves, and relics are marked and their memories cultivated. Ryōnen Gensō was famous outside Buddhist circles; her story became both fiction and fable and was included in tourist brochures of the time.

The line of Japanese women included here brings us to the nineteenth century and through repeated arcs of experience for Buddhist women: times of independence and accomplishment, times of suppression and frustration. The Tokugawa era (1600s–1867), when Japan closed its borders and rigidly controlled the population in specific classes, was a time of unusual stricture for women and nuns. There are far fewer records and details of the lives of Buddhist women in this later period than in the medieval and earlier eras. The eighteenth and nineteenth centuries are especially lacking in details. In some cases, such as that of Teijitsu, I am basing a story on little more than a known name, dates, place, and context. When I imagine the lives of these women, the few among many anonymous and forgotten people whose names, at least, are known, I imagine loneliness, great effort, and—I must imagine this last—a reward of understanding in the end.

The land of Yamato was a place of continual civil war. After a warrior woman named Pimiku rose and united much of the country, ruling as a queen, the people lived in interlocking spheres of clan and community and worshiped the spirits that inhabited the places and objects all around them. Above all was the Sun Goddess, Amaterasu Smikami, who gave birth to their leaders.

the first
Zenshin
(approx. 572–640)

Asuka was the center of the kingdom of Yamato, on the central island of what would become Japan. It was a green, wet land, split by rivers. The sky was often heavy with rain, and the hills grew thick with bamboo. Even on hot summer days a fine drizzle fell. The rulers of Yamato held a tenuous authority among powerful clans. When they died, they were entombed in vast burial mounds the size of hills. Then the capital would be moved, usually only a mile or two, until more than forty abandoned government compounds dotted the land for a long way around.

Sometimes in the winter it snowed, and drafts filled the chill dim rooms of the wooden houses, making the lanterns flicker and smoke. But in the late spring the sky cleared, flowers leaped across the hillsides in a shower of color, and the rice stood up in its precise embroidered rows like needle holes through the still water in the fields.

Across a small sea, the Korean peninsula was divided into warring kingdoms. One, Paekche, had known Buddhism for almost two hundred years, thanks to Chinese monks fleeing persecution. King Syūng-Myōng was pinned down between neighbors who couldn't be trusted, so he sought the favor of the Yamato court. Around the year 538, he sent a small Buddha statue and a few scriptures.[1] Buddhism, he wrote, was admittedly very difficult to understand. It was even more difficult to master. But Buddhism was also the highest doctrine the king of Paekche had ever found, and he deeply hoped the people of Yamato would adopt it.

There was nothing strange to the people of Yamato in this intersection of religion and state. In the Japanese language, the earliest word for government is matsurigoto—"religious observances." Nor was the new religion's language strange. The Yamato court knew that China was a great country, and they admired it deeply. They had adopted Chinese as the written language of government more than a hundred years earlier, and they used it for the keeping of all records and laws. They also admired the various clans of the Korean peninsula who had defeated them in battle more than once.

Yamato was controlled by three large, extended families—the Soga, Nakatomi, and Mononobe. They fought both openly and secretly with each other, sometimes brutally and often with more subtlety. The powerful Soga family immediately adopted Buddhism, while the other ruling families rejected it. This was a touchy choice. Perhaps this foreign religion, so important to the Chinese and Koreans, was a powerful tool, conveying spiritual power—but it hadn't brought peace to either country. And who knew how the local deities would react. More importantly, what about the peasants who worshiped the deities? The leader of the court, one of the first to be called an emperor, couldn't decide what to do, so he waited for a sign. When an epidemic broke out, he took it as an omen and had the Buddha statue thrown into a canal and the Soga temple in which it had been housed razed to the ground. That day the wind blew wildly and rain fell from a blue sky.

Teachers kept coming from across the sea, however, and could not be resisted for long.

She was called Shime, after her family, which had emigrated from Paekche long before. Shime Tattō, her father, was a citizen now, and closely aligned with the Soga. By 572, when she was born, Buddhism was established in Asuka but not widely accepted.[2] Since she was connected to the Soga, Shime knew about Buddhism from the beginning of her life. Everyone around her was concerned with the kami, big and little spirits inhabiting trees, rocks, birds, and watery places. Strange occurrences might be kami, strange and wonderful people could be kami. This was normal, the way of things. But Shime also knew the Buddhist priests—odd, entrancing men from other countries, chattering in Chinese and Korean. She liked their statues and bells and books and ideas, in which the kami were not in charge.

In 584 another Soga patron built a new temple to house some of the Buddhist statues. Shime went to the temple every day and sat in a silent contemplation that came naturally to her. Sometimes her best friends, Toyo and Ishi, came with her. They did whatever Shime wanted, they loved her that much; the three girls could often be found in quiet relaxation there.

Shime was made to marry Kimatsu when she was still a girl. He was the son of a powerful man, and it was an arrangement of land and position. Then Soga no Umako, the leader of her clan, decided to strengthen the position of Buddhism (and with it, the Soga) in the government. He sent Shime Tattō with two other men to look for practicing Buddhists across the countryside. They found only a few, and Soga wanted to change this. He told Tattō to have his daughter ordained as a nun. She was then twelve years old. For some girls, such an order would have been a terrible thing, but to Shime it was welcome. She knew what she wanted, and it wasn't marriage to Kimatsu and more of the same. Toyo and Ishi, who had also been married by this time, wanted what Shime wanted, and agreed to be ordained too.

The few Korean monks were pleased. This was a great development, this first-stage ordination of a Japanese person. But it couldn't be completed, since the proper number of ordained priests weren't there. The girls received only the six novice nun precepts—not to kill, not to steal, not to tell lies, not to engage in sexual activity, not to become intoxicated, and not to eat after the hour of noon. Their heads were shaved, they put on simple robes, and their names were changed. Shime became Zenshin, and her friends became Zenzō and Ezen.

The Soga leader gave the girls into the protection of Tattō and his friend Hida no Atahe and ordered them to provide clothing and food so that the girls could devote themselves to services. Tattō built a hall for them on the east side of his house on the Soga estate and installed a statue of Miroku Buddha, the Buddha who will come in the future. Zenshin and her friends were servants of the Buddha now, no longer important members of an important family. They cared for the grounds and altars and began to study the Paekche and Chinese languages so they could study the sutras.

One day a priest brought a miraculous relic to court, a bit of yellowed bone that he said couldn't be destroyed. The emperor gave it to the nuns and their protectors. It was important to test such things; the last thing the emperor wanted was to look like a fool.

"See what you can do with it," he told Tattō, so he and Atahe and their friend Mūmako no Sukune tried pounding it with iron blocks and sledgehammers. They threw it in the river, but it floated back to shore. The little bone was an eerie thing and made the men nervous, so finally they gave the bone to Zenshin and asked her to protect it. Then Sukune told the emperor what had happened.

"I'm convinced," he said, "that there is something quite profound at work. It seems a good sign. A strange sign."

The next year brought an epidemic, and the Mononobe clan took it as an opportunity to complain again about Buddhism, the foreign religion that seemed to displease the local gods. The clashes continued, and when Zenshin was fifteen, a rebellion broke out. One day they heard shouting in the roads, and by nightfall the Soga had been disarmed and the Mononobe were in charge.

The emperor, as emperors do, followed the will of the winners—who, after all, had the weapons now. He issued a proclamation against Buddhism and sent his soldiers to seize the nuns. When the men came to the hall, Sukune was there, but he didn't dare to disobey. Already men were pulling down the altars and tearing the scrolls of copied sutras. Weeping and afraid, torn between his vow to the girls and love of his own life, Sukune made the girls go with the soldiers. The nuns were marched down muddy roads in the rain to the public square.

The leader of the Mononobe, Moriya, was waiting. He dismounted, a smirking smile on his face, and strode over to them. Soldiers held the arms of the three young women with shaved heads and no shoes while he tore off their robes, growling in his disgust. He hated Buddhists. Ezen began to cry when he grabbed her, but Zenshin silenced her with a hush. When they were half bare and in rags, the men surrounded them, and Moriya flogged them with whips. They held each other, and Zenshin started chanting, under her breath so just the other girls could hear, and together they prayed to the Buddha what prayers they could remember as they gasped for breath, helpless tears of pain running down their faces. The blood streaked their arms and legs, mixing with the mud. Rain pattered on the green water of the rice fields in concentric circles, circles circling each other endlessly, soft and green.

When the beating was finally done, they were given their torn robes and taken to the prison.

It wasn't long before the emperor got sick, with weeping sores that spread across his body. Then his ministers became sick too, and the pustulence spread throughout the town. Finally the emperor called Sukune to him. Sukune wasn't sick, and this confirmed the problem for the emperor.

"All right, all right," he said, scratching at his legs. "Take the nuns back. You can fix their rooms and do rites. But just you—no one else. Now go."

Zenshin and her friends sewed new robes and changed their bandages and cleaned up the temple. The pus sickness finally ended, and for a while things were quiet. Mūmako no Sukune became the Oho-omi, a powerful regent who advised the emperor himself. A spell of calm, a spurt of fighting, an unexplained death, then calm again—over and over. When Mononobe no Moriya himself died, two princes attempted a coup. Once again it seemed there could never be peace. The day after the princes' execution, on the ninth day in the fifth month of that year, Zenshin came to speak to the Oho-omi, whom she had known for a long time.

"I beg your permission to travel," she said, eyes properly downcast, but her voice carrying throughout the hall. "We study every day, but we need training. We need to complete our vows in order to help the people of this land. We rely on discipline. Discipline is the way we renounce the world and find peace." He had known her since she was a child, he had seen her devotion, he had seen her whipped, watching from his hiding place under a stack of hay. He knew she was disciplined.

"I beg your permission to travel across the water to Paekche and be fully trained and ordained, so I can make Buddhism truly ours."

The Oho-omi was an astute man. He'd seen the relic that couldn't be broken, and he'd seen how quickly the winds of power could change. Buddhism seemed to be one possible future for his country, part of a faint vision he had of a greater world, an alliance of many clans, even countries, sharing this one way. If it worked, he would be in the center of it all. He agreed to her request. Several Korean envoys had recently arrived, and he instructed them to take the nuns to Paekche, see that they received instruction, and return them safely. Zenshin's mother cried when she said good-bye, and a short while later the three teenagers left with the Koreans and their servants.

It was a fearful journey. They had never been more than a few miles from home before, and now they walked for weeks to the southern end of the islands. There they got on a boat with a rough sail and a primitive rudder and traveled more than a hundred miles on open sea, trusting to the prevailing winds and their own good karma. Some of the monks with whom they traveled were kind, but others disapproved of their presence and tried to humiliate and confuse them. They arrived in a strange place and were taken to a temple in a cold hard valley with many new rules—many, many rules they'd never heard before. There was no comfort, only work and training going on under watchful eyes.

To be fully ordained, they had to stay in the monastery for at least two years to prove they weren't pregnant—this was one of the first new rules they learned. Two years with nothing to do but go forward. Bit by bit, they perfected the forms, the language, the methods of Buddhism, studying the ceremonies and sutras, learning to open them to the world all at once by unrolling the scrolls. They called it "turning the sutras," and to Zenshin it was a kneeling dance of chant and rhythm.

Finally, in March of 590, when Zenshin was just eighteen, they became the first Japanese to be fully ordained.

Then they returned to Asuka—another long and difficult journey—arriving in the height of summer. The rice was green and tall, and every morning hazy with the heat. Zenshin's mother cried again. The Soga niece, Daidaiō, gave Zenshin her imperial quarters, and there the young nuns established Sakurai-dera, the first Buddhist temple made by the Japanese. Remembering how their first rooms had been destroyed, they had a secret repository built, collected the original sutras brought from Paekche many years before, and hid them there.

The rains fell—the endless rains, hard and then soft, waxing and waning. The rice grew, and the weeds began to cover the water until it no longer reflected the sky and clouds. Frogs croaked all day at the edges of the fields. From the small courtyard of the temple, Zenshin watched egrets and herons stepping carefully like dancers through the green shoots. The carpenters scraped and pounded, adding rooms and storage cupboards to the princess's quarters, and the nuns tried to keep the altars clean in the midst of the dust and mud.

The rice flowered at the end of summer, and a yellow harvest moon hung over the valley. Then the fields were crowded with people, cutting down rice, swinging their sickles back and forth and back again. The dikes between the fields were piled with sheaves, and then the sheaves were carried off to hang from the eaves, including those of Sakurai-dera, where they turned yellow and scented the rooms.

The weather hardened, and frost bit into the ground. Zenshin kept the shutters closed all day, so that even at noon they had to read by tallow lamps. The women of the town began to heckle the rice, dragging each plant through a sieve to pull the seeds off so it could be winnowed. Flecks of icy white frosted the hills and roads, and three more young women came to the temple and asked to be nuns. Zenshin welcomed them quietly, taught them to make simple robes, and put them to work. They had rice to heckle and winnow too, and much more to do, before the snows came.

Zenshin's brother, Be, had already converted and been ordained. Over the winter seven more men were ordained as monks by the Koreans, and then it was spring, and summer again, and it seemed as though life was going to continue in this tranquil, fragile way for a long time. Zenshin was content, but not forgetful.

In 592 her friend Sukune, the Oho-omi, sent an assassin to kill the emperor. Change wasn't happening fast enough for him, so he sped things up. The princess Daidaiō was installed as the new Empress Suiko, and her nephew became the crown prince and was called Shōtoku Taishi. Shōtoku and Zenshin had been children together; he was a few years younger than she was and had always liked her. By the time he became prince, she was famous throughout the country—the little nun who had been beaten and then traveled across an ocean and back. He could see what she had done, as well as the force and power of the sutras and the rites she'd learned. He began to take his own Buddhist training more seriously.

The next year, through the empress, Shōtoku ordered the building of a major temple, a central temple called Asuka-dera. When the foundation stone was laid, he placed relics of the Buddha underneath. Foreign priests supervised its construction, which took years, and when it was finally done, foreign priests were in charge. Asuka-dera was the official temple, the imperial temple, the country's temple. Zenshin's nephew, Kuratsu Kuri no Tori, made a statue of the Buddha for it—a big, dark, hulking statue, with big flat hands open in a mudra. Privately, she thought it wasn't half as nice as the small Miroku Buddha she had. But it was big, she granted that.

Many more foreign priests came from China and Korea, and laypeople too, escaping the endless civil wars in those countries. Though refugees, they were well educated, and many were scholars—calendar makers, astronomers, magicians skilled in the art of invisibility and telling the future, geomancers, physicians, musicians, and architects. Monks began mastering these new arts. Prince Shōtoku read and lectured on sutras, especially that of Queen Śhrīmālā, wrote moral doctrines, and built more temples. Sakurai-dera was one of many temples now.[3]

The new temples had new statues, done in a style of realistic carving that seemed empowered with the teaching itself—baby Buddhas and many-armed Kannons, masculine generals and feminine bodhisattvas, small and elaborately dressed guardian kings with living faces in blue and red and green made of lacquer, clay, and bronze, eerily alive. The images became commonplace, and Japanese people, ordinary people, began to be converted to Buddhism.

Zenshin was there at every temple dedication. She always stood behind the men, giving way, bowing to each one, even the young Japanese monks who were her junior. It was one of the rules she'd learned. But they watched her surreptitiously, trying to copy the way she moved, the graceful precise forms she'd embedded in her body from youth.

After many years, the nuns were able to build a separate temple on a hillside of Asuka, looking down on the rice fields. They called it Toyuradera.

After the ceremonies but before the feasts, the nuns went back to little Toyuradera, remembering their vows. They tried to keep all the rules, which was quite difficult at times. But there is joy in following a form for the sake of following it, discovering in one's obedience to things the emptiness at the heart of those things, of all things. They did their chores and meditation, ordered supplies, and filled out receipts, placing the temple seal carefully on the documents. When the rain stopped, a pearly color filled the sky and colored the tendrils of fog in the hills.

Shōtoku controlled an entire country's fortunes. With his power, he built temples and monasteries and pagodas and shrines; he filled them with beautiful art, and in so doing he ensured that his family's fortunes would be entwined with those of Buddhism forever. The world was changing very quickly—men were changing it—trading and conspiring and fighting, warring and diplomatic by turns. Zenshin established several other convents and, after a great deal of effort, an ordination platform where eight women were fully ordained, right there.

When Shōtoku died in 621, on a spring day, Zenshin was an old woman of fifty-two. The chronicles say that every person in the country cried as though they had lost a child. Women couldn't taste salt and the farmers quit plowing because the great Buddhist prince was gone.

Over the next several years the country darkened again and again. Terrible things happened, terrible omens—heavy snow in the winter was followed by famine in the spring; hail as large as peaches smashed the summer crops; an infestation of flies was followed by a drought; and a total eclipse seemed, for a few days, to mean the end of everything. In 623 a monk killed his grandfather with an ax. Empress Suiko was infuriated and afraid. This was just one more very wrong thing. She called every monk and nun in the country to an audience, forced them to confess their mistakes, and was about to punish many of them severely. One of the elderly Korean priests talked her out of it at the last minute, reminding her that only a few of them had had real training. Only

Zenshin and her close friends had even been to a real training temple. The empress agreed to punish only the murderer, but from that time on the temples were inspected and records of the ordained kept.

When Zenshin died a few years later, it was very quiet. She was a brave and persistent woman, and she was the first one of all, but by then her name was already fading. No one wailed except the nuns at Toyuradera. No farmers stopped plowing. But the morning and evening bells she rang every day for fifty-six years are ringing still, and the sutras she learned to turn are turning still. They are turning themselves, for the sake of turning.

the empress

Kōmyō

(701–760)

She was born into the center of the world, the whole world. Yamato had become Nihon—Japan—which means the "source of the sun." Her name, Kōmyōshi, meant "luminous brightness." She was the brightness at the center of the sun.

Her grandfather had been a Nakatomi, the family that traditionally held Shinto rites, while the Fujiwaras were responsible for administration of the government. Kōmyōshi's grandfather was granted the name Fujiwara as a gift from the emperor. After that, the family business became government instead of religion. So they became Buddhists, because Buddhism was part of the life of the court, and worked as government officials. Kōmyōshi's father, Fujiwara no Fuhito, was a minister of state affairs. Her mother, Agata Inukai Tachibana no Michiyo, served as a lady-in-waiting. Kōmyōshi's half-brother, Michiyo's son by her first husband, was a prince.

The imperial administrators were trying to wrestle control from the traditional clan leaders and centralize power. The state began keeping a census, making maps, building a central arsenal, registering land, and appointing judges. When Kōmyōshi was a baby, her father helped to write the Taihō Codes, which created an enormous bureaucracy of ministries and commissions. Nihon was officially divided into 66 provinces, each with a governor, and each province was further subdivided into 592 districts; a network of seven major highways was built to connect them.

This newly powerful government created a class system based on Confucian principles of social order. The three main divisions were the aristocrats, the gentry, and the slaves. Each of these levels was then subdivided into grades—thirty grades just for the aristocracy. Carefully defined roles and duties were assigned to every citizen. Men stood above women, the old above the young, the educated above the ignorant, and scholars and ministers above farmers. There was a place for everyone, and everyone was expected to know his or her place. The future of Japan lay in careful organization, forward thinking, and discipline.

Nara, called Heijōkyō, the Citadel of Peace, became the first permanent capital of Japan in 710. Builders had modeled the new city on the great city of Changan in China, using Chinese ideals: eight wide streets and nine avenues; the palace in the north end, surrounded by nine walls; rectangular buildings in groupings of three, five, eight, and nine. The symmetrical and grand architecture was a new blend of Indian and Chinese ideals. Asuka was done, and entire temples in Asuka were dismantled, moved, and rebuilt, board by board, in Nara. Fujiwara no Fuhito moved the family temple there, reassembled it painstakingly, and renamed it Kōfuku-ji. In spite of an edict in 713 that monasteries across the country stop taking all the good land for themselves, the land around Nara was quickly buried under splendid temples, tall pagodas, walls, and enclosed grounds.

Little by little, but quite deliberately, the Buddhist priests worked at controlling the Shinto shrines. They began by claiming that kami were manifestations of the bodhisattvas and Buddhist gods and so Shintoism was actually a primitive form of Buddhism. Buddhist priests began performing minor rites usually done by the Shintoists, pushing them further to the edge of city and court life.

Nara was a cosmopolitan place: hundreds of government clerks and scribes in indigo blue robes with little black Chinese caps milled about, running importantly from errand to errand. It was a kind of university where the favorite sons mastered the intricate Chinese language so they could read the sutras, the classical poetry, the *I Ching,* and the works of Confucius.

In 720, when Kōmyōshi was a young woman, her father died and her half-sister's son, Shōmu, became emperor. A year later, mourning her husband's death and the illness of her beloved Empress Genmei, Kōmyōshi's mother became a Buddhist nun. Michiyo tried to give up her fortune and lands then, but Shōmu refused. Instead, against her wishes, he promoted her to imperial rank. She resigned herself to things as they were, as they always had been, and retreated into contemplative practice, leaving well enough alone.

Omens and signs were everyday occurrences—strange clouds, flocks of birds, odd animals, dreams, and unusual noises all seemed to be portents of one kind or another. Now and then the entire earth trembled and shook. A white tortoise was found and brought to court—an amazing omen, a sight no one had seen before. Shōmu decided that it meant he should get married. He didn't look far—only as far as his aunt, Kōmyōshi. They were the same age, after all. Born into the highest circles of court, she was educated, courteous, skilled, and devout in her daily Buddhist practice.

Kōmyōshi's world had always been full of servants, but after she married the emperor, the doors of privilege closed tightly. She began to understand her mother's frustration with court life and its lifelong requirements of devotion. Shōmu was trapped too, his time divided between Buddhist and Shinto rites and the business of state. He attended endless ceremonies and committee meetings and had several consorts to attend to, delegations to meet, and proclamations to sign. He was never alone either, and on their rare quiet evenings he would complain to Kōmyōshi about the nitpicking regulations his court officials seemed to invent without ceasing.

A few years after their marriage, the new crown prince was born. They named him Motoi. This was a great omen, and they were happy. Then Motoi died. Shortly after that, Shōmu made Kōmyōshi the empress and not just his wife. After that, she was known as Kōmyō.

Endless fighting over power and succession roared on around her. Death seemed to be everywhere, and it didn't favor the rich or poor; it didn't care about Confucian ideals and rank. Shōmu was rather given to proclamations and speeches; he spoke often and at length of the duty of the state to its people and the importance of harmony and humility. Then he imposed new taxes. Most Japanese lived in a way that had hardly changed in a thousand years, with bronze tools and bare shelter.

The one change that made a difference was paddy-field rice farming, which created close-knit villages but required exhausting labor without end. The peasants were subject to conscription at any time, and many were drafted to build roads and move the temples. They often came a long way from home to reach Nara. Some died working, and others starved or froze to death on the long walks home.

All over the land people died, children died, babies died. As empress, Kōmyō had real power and began to use it. She had a temple called Kinshoji built in her baby's honor, far from the court on a wooded hill, and then established the Hiden-in and Seyaku-in, charities that gave medicine and food to the poor. She insisted that Shōmu build way stations so that laborers could eat and rest on their way home.

Now and then the empress visited her mother at the hermitage. Nara was Buddhist not only in name but in shape and color and design. All its rooms and courtyards and gardens were filling with beauty and art in a great accumulation, a surfeit of images like endless mirrors reflecting each other: tiny and intricate, grand and imposing, Kannons, Bosatsus, and Nyorais, on panels and canopies and tapestries and rugs. Even bowls became more beautiful, more perfectly shaped, more correctly weighted, more wonderful to hold. The hermitage was no different. One day Michiyo showed Kōmyō a box made of betel palm wood, plum bark, and red sandalwood, decorated with jasper and pearls, and painted in gold and silver with a design of waves. In it was a copy of the *Lotus Sutra,* a scroll of yellow hemp paper with seventeen perfect characters in each precise line.

"I copied this myself, dear," she told her daughter. "Wonderful practice."

Kōmyō began copying. She commissioned a sutra desk of her own in dyed persimmon wood, with black bamboo fittings and gilt bronze edging, engraved with clouds. She invited her chief maid to join her, and then her other maids, and they began to spend long afternoons over reams of paper, practicing each elaborate Chinese character time and time again before committing it to the scroll. The *Lotus Sutra* was a life's work, wonderful practice, and yet not enough for Kōmyō's exploding devotion. She would copy it all, she told a priest who had spent many years in China. She would copy the entire canon, every word, and he began to help her, providing books.

As Kōmyō sank deeper and deeper into the work, hours and weeks slid by. She dipped the tiny spoon shaped like a lotus petal into the little bowl of water, sprinkled the ink cake and mixed it until the thickness was just right, dipped the brush, drew a character once, then twice, and started over. Everything disappeared while she copied, even her sadness. Shōmu came to watch at times, bemused, all the maids dropping to the floor and hiding their faces when he entered the room.

Before the end of the year they had a new baby, a girl named Abe. Kōmyō set aside a building on the family estate she had inherited, called it Sumidera, and dedicated it to copying.

Shōmu felt himself changing too. His daily life was full of noise and ritual. The empress's world was a quieter one, and he envied it. Her effort moved him, as did his daughter, as did Kōmyō's oceanic tranquillity, which grew by the day. He began to copy too, but of course then he created a Bureau of Copying, an entirely new department devoted to copying, binding, and distributing the sutras, filled with clerks and managers, ink makers, paper makers, pen makers, binders, and especially copyists. Skilled calligraphers were hired by the day, given clean clothes, and paid with a day's food and drink.

Michiyo died without a word one winter. Abe grew taller. A plague of smallpox struck the city, and Kōmyō's four nephews—her stepbrother's sons and the most powerful ministers of the government—died, one after the other. Shōmu felt a terrible guilt; he really did believe he was the Son of Heaven and the Father of the People, and he assumed he had done something wrong to cause the epidemic. One evening he and Kōmyō sat side by side in their quarters, their elaborate silk and brocade kimonos spilling in folds across the floor.

"We can't copy fast enough," she said. "There isn't enough time in our lives, in a hundred lives. Everyone must do this so that everyone can read the sutras." Shortly after that, he issued an edict commanding the provinces to erect statues of the Buddha and to copy a chapter of the *Lotus Sutra.*

"It's not enough," she told him firmly a few months later. "There need to be temples where people can train seriously. You see the lax discipline, the inconsistent practices. There aren't enough teachers to go around. We need a better system—a real system of training temples."

He called an audience of provincial representatives. "It is Our error," he said. "Awake and asleep, We are ashamed of Our failures. We will establish training temples. For men, We create the Konkōmyō Shitennō Gokoku shi Ji, the Golden Light Temple for the Protection of the Country by the Four Heavenly Deities. Men must pray for the country's well-being. For women, We create the Hokke Metsuzai shi Ji, the Lotus Temple for the Atonement of Sins. Women must pray for the country's purity. The residents must read the *Lotus Sutra* and the *Sutra of the Sovereign Kings of the Golden Light Ray.*"[4]

So it was done. Abe was growing up, and Kōmyō had perfected a lovely script. She copied with ease and speed. But she was painfully aware of her power, his power, their privilege, their responsibility, and how much there was to be done. So many words—so many books—so much to do.

"There should be a head temple, don't you think?" she asked Shōmu one day. "The training temples need central administration, and perhaps—well, I had this idea. For a great statue. A great Buddha, a Lochana Buddha so big it could bless the whole country."

So, on the fifteenth day of the tenth month of 743, Shōmu issued another edict. He did enjoy edicts. He declared that a Great Buddha would be built for the temple Todaiji, which would be the head temple of the provincial system.

Their first attempt was a failure—a big building with a large Buddha was planned, but when only the first supporting pillar was up, an earthquake destroyed it. The priests thought this was a bad omen, and they decided the temple had to be moved to another location. They chose the huge hill on the far side of the city, where Kinshoji, the temple dedicated to their dead son, stood. The first job was excavating. This time they would do it right, constructing not a big building but the biggest one possible, for a Buddha beyond imagination.

So began the great work, with shovels.

Kōmyō watched from the confines of her palanquin, pushing aside the silk curtains. Now and then she was allowed to walk carefully along paving stones with her maids to see the work more closely. Men worked day and night, wearing jackets in the cold and loincloths in the shriveling heat, felling trees and moving soil. The winter rain turned to snow, geese clattered in the fields, bonfires flickered all night, and the men dug.

Finally, the hill was terraced, and they began building furnaces, scaffolding, and foundations. The noise increased—pounding, scraping, shouting, the roar of the fires. In the summer the mosquitoes bred madly in the sewage canals, and the smoke from the furnaces hung over the city under the gray bruised sky of summer rain.

From the palace balcony Kōmyō watched the herons swoop across the pond like brushes, trailing ink.

First, a huge clay statue had to be made as a model for the metalworkers. New noises—angry shouts, the clang of tools, and now and then a crash. Every day the priests went to the construction site and chanted for harmony and safety. When the copper was melted, the air stank with fumes. First one casting failed, then another and another, seven times. Finally a Korean sculptor arrived. He commanded changes, and the work began again. Copper was mixed with lead and tin to make an alloy for the body, and gold was dissolved in mercury for the gilding.[5]

Many men had died by then, from accidents, sickness, exhaustion, and the metal fumes. Kōmyō prayed for them in her nightly devotions, wishing them a happy rebirth.

When gold was discovered in Japan in 749, Shōmu made a proclamation. He brought the entire court to the site of the temple. It was summer, and the air was as sticky as cobwebs; Kōmyō's skin swam with sweat underneath her embroidered kimono and sashes. The emperor faced north toward the still headless statue, with the empress and crown princess behind him. Noblemen, representatives of the hundred government bureaus, and commoners were divided into ranks and drawn up at the rear of the hall. The Junior Third Rank Minister of Central Affairs spoke for the emperor first, declaring the Son of Heaven to be a servant of Buddha.

Then Shōmu spoke for himself. "We have been so anxious about the gold," he said. "I'm so relieved. This is a great omen. Buddhism is the best way of protecting Our nation." It was a sly and effective speech, and he ended magnanimously by giving lands to provincial officers and local temples and other gifts to the elderly, the poor, his ministers' sons and daughters, his scribes and scholars. Finally, with a wave of his hand, he pardoned many criminals.

As they turned to leave, Kōmyō saw the laboring men resting while they could, out of the sun, their bare backs shiny with the heat. Nothing much had changed for them.

Later that year the emperor abdicated to his daughter, Abe-naishinno, who was also called Kōken. This was one of Shōmu's greatest moments. Again he had a minister speak for him, using the language of an inferior to his master, and declared himself the servant of the Three Treasures of Buddha, Dharma, and Sangha. By stepping aside without really stepping aside, by throwing himself at the foot of the Buddha who blessed and protected the entire nation, he became more than a leader. Without realizing it, he had begun the tradition of the cloistered emperor, the power hidden behind an empty throne.

Nothing much changed. Shōmu issued judgments, signed official papers, heard quarrels between his advisers, and made policy, while Kōken managed the ceremonial role. Kōmyō copied and supervised copying. She visited the orphanages. Using the ash from her altar, she made dog charms, for safe childbirth, to give to the poor. Now and then she rode miles to the temple, leading a line of carts filled with barrels of cool water for the laborers to drink.

The entire head and neck of the Great Buddha was cast as a single piece taller than two men, and one day it was lifted slowly with ropes and set in place. Nine years had passed in the work.

Priests came from India and China for the dedication. Before the ceremony, draped in so many layers of brocade that she could barely walk, Kōmyō stood at the edge of the compound, looking at the enormous mountain gate before her. The sun was falling behind the hills, the sky rosy and gold. Then she followed Shōmu and the priests down a long stone path, between trees, through the great gate. The scale of what they had done was overwhelming. Every step, door, post, and hinge was larger than life. Each pillar was a whole tree.

And in the center sat a Buddha more than fifty feet tall, on a bed of bronze lotus petals. His right palm faced outwards, and his left hand lay open in his lap, large enough for eight men to stand there at once.

More than ten thousand monks and nuns watched while six men climbed a scaffold of bamboo into the Buddha's palm, where they picked up an enormous brush. The lantern light flickered, and the Buddha's vast, tranquil face seemed to move slightly in a tiny smile. The priests began to chant as Shōmu and Kōmyō climbed up the platform beneath the great statue. A famous Indian priest named Bodhisena climbed the scaffold to the Buddha's hand, Shōmu and Kōmyō held cords attached to the brush, and Bodhisena painstakingly painted the pupils of the eyes until they were opened.

Kōmyō watched the play of the lantern flames, heard the pennants snapping, and thought, *His body is the universe. What could stand against such a guardian? All sounds are his words. All beings are his breath. How can we be the servant of that which has no single nature?* She didn't know, but she was glad to try. She felt safe. She knew she would come here often.

Another ten years passed before the construction at Todaiji ended. Meanwhile, Kōmyō commissioned other temples. Though it was not the custom for women to spend time in the Buddha halls of the temples, she did go to the hall at Todaiji often. She had seen it in her mind before the first shovel of dirt; she had held the cord at the end of the brush and helped to open his eyes.

When she came to pray at the Buddha's feet one day, she was stopped at the gate. A priest walked out, shutting the gate carefully behind him so that she couldn't see in, and told her that it was a consecrated place now and not for women.

This was just like her baby dying before her eyes, it was like she herself was dying. Shōmu kept his distance; he didn't know how to comfort her, didn't know if he should, if she wasn't better off just listening to the priests, who had to know best what to do.[6]

Finally, she lifted her head. Everything died. She converted the family estate lands into a convent called Hokkeji. It was far from Todaiji on the other side of the city, on a slight hill looking over the land, with a lovely garden filled with azaleas and lotus and lilac. She asked a sculptor to make a large Kannon for the central hall, and he carved a single block of precious sandalwood into the very image of Kōmyō herself.

When Shōmu died a few years later, she commissioned a remarkable building known as the Shoso-in, tucked into the hills behind Todaiji. Triangular logs of Japanese cypress were laid tightly atop each other to form a long, narrow room, and all of it was lifted off the ground on high stilts. Inside the temperature and humidity remained perfectly even at all times. On June 21, 756, the seventy-seventh day after Shōmu's death, Kōmyō filled the Shoso-in with many of Shōmu's possessions—tools used to make the Buddha (including the giant paintbrush), pottery, records and receipts, notes and calligraphy, weapons, medicines, rugs and tapestries, jars and vases, musical instruments, manuscripts, paintings, jewelry, toys, and costumes. Then the doors were closed.

The Shoso-in still stands, undisturbed. The Kannon with Kōmyō's face is still in the hall at Hokkeji, and the nuns there still make dog charms in the same way she did. The Great Buddha of Todaiji is visited by many thousands of tourists and pilgrims every year—men and women, foreigners and Japanese, Buddhists and the curious, who come to stand below its benign and far-seeing eyes.

the independent one

Seishi

(809–879)

The emperor of Japan wished he were Chinese. Emperor Saga Tennō especially loved Chinese poetry—he was inflamed by it and never traveled without a poet in tow. Many aristocrats loved to make waka poems, with a total of a mere thirty-one syllables arranged in a pattern of five lines of five, seven, five, seven, and seven syllables each. But Saga preferred the elaborate Chinese arrangement of six and four characters—so much so that the form was used in legal documents and court pronouncements. Japanese had long been a spoken language only, a language of family, peasants, domestic life, the ordinary. When a set of symbols to represent its syllables was finally invented, it was left to women to write in Japanese. The emperor sponsored elaborate collections of formal verse in the foreign tongue of Chinese, still considered the only truly civilized language. At summer parties he gave Winding Water Banquets—with guests stationed along the banks of the small stream that ran through the palace gardens, he would place a cup of wine in the stream. As it floated daintily past, each guest was required to pick it up, take a sip, and recite a poem.

Seishi, Saga's eldest daughter, practiced a fine hand of calligraphy and learned to be a lady of the court, not at all a bad thing to be. The length of a woman's hair was a sign of her class—the longer her hair, the higher her class and position. Seishi's hair was several feet long, a river of hair, and when it was loose, she draped it over her clothes like a scarf of black silk. For formal occasions her hair was wrapped and pinned into elaborate buns with decorative combs as forbidding and confining as her formal clothes.

Seishi's mother, Empress Tachibana no Kachiko, had once met a nun who did severe ascetic practices. This nun had predicted that Kachiko would be the mother of both an emperor and an empress, but it was the terrifying mortifications she practiced that Kachiko remembered most vividly. All her life from that day she was plagued and blessed with prophetic dreams.

She became a devout Buddhist, a less common practice among the upper classes and courts than it had once been. When the capital left Nara in 784, largely to separate the government from the increasingly powerful and demanding Buddhist church, the court settled in nearby Heian, the City of Peace, which would become Kyoto. The Tendai sect built its center on Mount Hiei, destined to become the largest Buddhist center in Japan, and then the Shingon sect built its central temple on Mount Koya. Women were forbidden to set foot on either temple grounds.

In the ranks of the lower and middle classes, Buddhism was popular and practiced actively by both men and women. This was nothing new. Once upon a time—in Zenshin's time, in Kōmyō's time, as long as there had been Buddhism in Japan—there had been ordination platforms for men and women both, official places set aside for the ceremony. There had always been head temples, subtemples, and training temples for both men and women. But by the time Seishi was ready for it, the women's ordination platform was gone. It disappeared bit by bit, through obfuscation and complication, through bureaucratic regulations and neglect and passive resistance, until finally it was eliminated. If a man of court made monastic vows, he received a new name and entered an official hierarchy. If a woman made monastic vows, she retained her name and entered nothing.

Princess Seishi was married at a young age to Junna, who was the same age as her father. When she was fourteen, her father abdicated and retired to his country palace, where he disappeared into the stanzas and sounds of poems. Her husband became Emperor Junna, and thereafter she was often referred to as Empress Junna.

When she was sixteen, she gave birth to a son, Tsunesada. With his birth, the politics of court overwhelmed her other priorities, her other desires. The hidden deals and hopes of various courtiers and relatives in turn overwhelmed not only the empress but also her son, and brought her husband to his own abdication just a few years later. At the age of eight, Tsunesada was made crown prince in place of his father. Junna retired to the Junnain, his personal palace west of Kyoto, and Seishi remained to protect the interests of her young son. A few years after the retired emperor died, when Tsunesada was seventeen, both mother and son were thrown from palace life after another uproar in court politics.

Seishi's life had been one of court and only court, until that day. Shortly after her ungentle retirement from politics, she cut her great river of hair off at the ears. This was called a half tonsure, taken by women who longed for ordination—a public proclamation, an announcement of her unfulfilled desire for renunciation. The head of the Tendai sect, Ennin, gave Seishi the Precepts, and she and Tsunesada went to Junnain together. They devoted themselves to religious rites, and Seishi began to call herself a nun.

There were still ordained nuns, under monastic supervision. They were given a little government support, though unlike monks, they were required to pay taxes. Men pursued a series of ranks once they were ordained; most nuns were considered to be novices for life. Only a woman ordained on an ordination platform could be a full nun equal to a monk, and there were no ordination platforms for women. Only a nun who had properly taken on the rules of the Vinaya and followed the standards given at ordination was considered fully ordained—and there was no ordination platform, no Vinaya given, no standards declared.

Seishi tried. She petitioned the priests who made these decisions. She offered to sponsor the ordination platform, to build what needed to be built, to do whatever needed to be done. But the priests weren't interested; few even answered her letters or agreed to discuss the matter. It was of little interest to them. She begged Ennin to intervene. He had been to China, he had seen women's ordination platforms, and he understood Seishi's need. But the institution that he headed wasn't his to run; when he carried Seishi's request to the governing councils, they simply ignored it, as they had ignored it from her.

Without official recognition, the nuns could not achieve any institutional rank; they had no power, and they would have no power; they had no privileges and would be having no privileges. When a priest pointed out to Seishi that it was inappropriate for anyone but a fully recognized nun to approach the priesthood on such doctrinal questions, Seishi quit asking. Ennin simply invited Seishi to receive the bodhisattva precepts, publicly this time, when he gave them to a group of a few hundred people. A few years later she did the same thing, with 170 other people, but in her mind she was all alone, bowing before Ennin on the platform.

Seishi studied; she had access to many sutras and histories, and she read about the Buddha's stepmother. She read about Pajāpatī's desperate act, the act of the five hundred women begging to be ordained when there was no ordination platform and finally ordaining themselves. After all, the Buddha did accept her in time; her self-ordination was finally recognized. Seishi felt there was a clear lesson for her there, and so, alone in her room one night, she declared the bodhisattva vows and shaved her head completely. From then on, she wore only a nun's robes and did daily rites.

After Tsunesada had been forced from court, Seishi's brother, Ninmyo, had become emperor. He ruled for seventeen years, while Seishi lived in the Junnain, practicing and praying, alone now. Tsunesada became a novice in 848 and lived a life of study and careful cultivation of his superiors. He devoted himself to earning the monastic privileges and rights his mother was denied.

Because of one of her dreams, Seishi's mother, Kachiko, made a set of Buddhist robes and sent a monk named Egaku to China with them. She wanted him to present them to an image of a bodhisattva there, the one she'd seen in her dream. But China was a big and complicated place; through one unexpected turn and another, Egaku ended up giving the robes to an abbot in the lineage of Mazu. He returned in 847 with the abbot's disciple, a Chan monk named I-k'ung. For the first time, the teaching that would be called Zen came to Japan.

Kachiko ordered a temple built for I-k'ung, a great complex with twelve chapels called Danrinji, near Saga's country palace west of Kyoto. She made it a convent at a time when there were no official nuns in Japan, a Japanese nuns' world run by a Chinese man at a time when nunneries weren't officially recognized. This was the temple the Empress wanted. Not happy about this, the Tendai and Shingon establishments did nothing to help I-k'ung in his efforts to teach. He remained at Danrinji, with little to do. Shortly after his arrival, Japan had begun to sever ties with China, and much of the fashion of Chinese imitation disappeared from public life. As a Chinese, especially as a Chinese bringing something altogether new, I-k'ung was almost an embarrassment.

When Ninmyo died suddenly in 850, Kachiko also cut off her hair and declared herself to be a nun. She moved to Danrinji, and I-k'ung began to instruct her intensely in Buddhist practice, before her death a few months later.

I-k'ung had no more patience. He decided that the Japanese people would never accept or understand Zen. The vast sects of Tendai and Shingon held their hearts in a vice, and they would never let them go. After Kachiko's death, he left Japan and was never heard from again.

Meanwhile, Seishi devoted herself to service. She gave much of her wealth to children, building orphanages and hiring wet nurses for abandoned babies. She built a hospital for sick monks and nuns and sponsored religious conventions, lectures, and meals serving tens of thousands of people.

In 860, Tsunesada was fully ordained and given all the rights and privileges and support of an official priest. He devoted himself to cultivating his image as a priest in the establishment and developing all the connections and power denied his mother.

When Seishi was sixty-five years old, the Junnain where she had lived for decades burned down and she barely escaped. She petitioned the court—her great-nephew was emperor by then—that her father's long-neglected country palace be given to her to be remodeled into a temple. Sagain was dilapidated and required a great deal of work, but with her single-minded effort she remodeled it into a temple called Daikakuji. Here, Seishi declared, she would live for the rest of her life in a woman's temple, doing a nun's traditional practice—whether anyone saw, whether anyone cared, or not.

But Tsunesada had other plans. His many years of cultivating influence in the Buddhist world as though it were another court had marked and changed him. He needed a temple to call his own. With his now-powerful ties, he had Daikakuji declared a monastery. He installed six images of Amida Buddha and brought fourteen monks there to live. As residents of an official monastery, the monks—and Tsunesada—would be granted special favors and privileges.

Seishi was moved to a small building on the grounds, behind the main hall.

The decades of discouragement, the sharp wounds of disappointment inflicted time after time after time, had slowly scarred over in Seishi's mind. Sometimes she forgot them while she was at her prayers, or rocking a baby in the orphanage, or repairing a tear in her robe and listening to the cheerful chatter of a bird nearby. She could forget all of it—her court life, her mother, her husband, her denials. Her son's betrayal was like a rusty sword drawn across the scars, and she burned with a kind of strange rage for weeks. Winter was coming, and she was busy making the little outbuilding a place to live. But she was never distracted. Each step was like a step in glass, and she died alone a few years later.

Seishi lived out much of her life in a terrible solitude, but she had many followers. More women shaved their heads and lived as nuns, regardless of official rules, often retaining their worldly names and doing their practice in private, never leaving home. Many were aristocrats, and some were imperial princesses. These women of wealth and education gradually developed a parallel system of women's temples and convents largely outside the hierarchy.

In 927 the government declared that nuns couldn't participate in state rites anymore. This had long been one of their main sources of income, and from then on nuns were thrown back on the benevolence of their families. Many had to leave their temples and return to live with their parents. Others became servants to monks, doing laundry, sewing, and cooking for the monasteries simply to survive.

After Seishi died, Tsunesada had Danrinji and Junnain put under the administration of the Daikakuji. Now both had official status, and it was the official status of subjugation.

In his will, Ennin wrote a request that his religious heirs follow Seishi's wish and create an ordination platform for women, but it was a long time before that happened.

Junnain continued to be a place for women; eventually it was called Saiin. In the last years of the tenth century, the women there remembered Pajāpatī and how she had inspired Seishi, who had inspired them. They created a special ceremony called Anan Koshiki in honor of the Buddha's disciple Ananda, to thank him for his help in letting women be ordained. The ceremony was performed in secret without the knowledge of any man for a long time.

the marrow

Ryōnen, Shōgaku, and Egi

(approx. 1165–1240)

For centuries court life in Japan didn't change much—a perennial round of banquets and ceremonies, moon-viewing trips and poetry contests, affairs and scandals. Now and then emperors died mysteriously or disappeared, but that was nothing new. For the clans, though, things changed. For a long time emperors had given land to favored people, and finally the gifts began to backfire. The court gave away land and then more land, until the clans became the true rulers of the country, the Fujiwara clan being the most powerful of all.

Extended families became huge organizations. To protect their growing territory, the leaders of the clans, who called themselves daimyo, or great lords, developed local militias. They had dozens, then hundreds, and finally thousands of men in armies ready to fight at the slightest provocation. These soldiers were the samurai. Loyalty was their first virtue, and the cherry blossom, which falls to the ground in the slightest breeze, was the symbol of how easily they would give up their lives to their lord.

Kyoto, the capital still, had been carefully designed at first, but it grew without following the plan, turning into a city pockmarked with large open fields, rice paddies, and farms, a place where old and new sat side by side. In 1180 the Gempei War began, and it would last for decades, a chaotic clan war engulfing the entire country. In Kyoto the fighting caused a great fire, followed almost immediately by a hurricane and then a drought. Beautiful Kyoto was half in ruins, filled with rubble and hungry people. Then came a plague; the rivers filled up with bodies, and men who had once been aristocrats begged for food in the street.

The lord Minamoto no Yoritomo, the ultimate victor both in imperial recognition and in military reality, did not settle for defeating his enemy lords. He consolidated his power province by province until, almost by accident, he had made a new government altogether—a military government. In 1192 he was given the title Shogun, and his government was officially the bakufu, which means "tent city," a government of the military, the shogunate. He chose the little seaside town of Kamakura to be the new capital, a place he could manipulate, a place where the warrior class would be at home. One by one, Yoritomo appointed his own men as military governors and stewards across the land; each new step was approved by a weakening court, and in the end he became Seii Taishōgun—"barbarian-quelling generalissimo." With brutality and efficiency, the shogunate unified the country once again.

Buddhism was embraced by people of every class. A man named Eisai had returned from China nearly a century before with the teachings of Linji Chan—Rinzai Zen. He met resistance from the establishment in Kyoto, but it wasn't long before the samurai in Kamakura welcomed him. Zen gave them courage in death; it was disciplined, simple, and precise, with its own aesthetic—its own architecture, vocabulary, and scriptures. Zen was ritualistic and offered vast intellectual challenge. Very quickly, the monasteries with their plain rooms and quiet gardens became refuges of a kind for the samurai. Eisai was followed to Kamakura by many other Rinzai masters.

Meanwhile, Kyoto remained the center of Tendai and Shingon Buddhism, esoteric sects that were elaborate where Zen was plain. Both were hugely popular; their mystical practices appealed to people who were used to multiplying spirits and unpredictable tragedy. But neither sect welcomed women, and they despised each other. Like the provincial lords, the monasteries had built armies of soldiers who looked like monks but fought in the streets, rioting and brawling. People were caught between the crushing power of the shoguns, the lawlessness of the streets, and their own constricted lives. Some Buddhist priests said it must be mappo time, the long-predicted era when the teaching of the Dharma would degrade and the True Way be lost.

In 1200 Dōgen was born. He was the son of a Fujiwara woman and should have gone to the court, but he ran away to be ordained, entering Mount Hiei, the center of the Tendai School. He was driven to understand why people failed so completely to express their Buddha Nature. There weren't any answers to this on Mount Hiei or anywhere else in Japan, so he went to China. There he met his true teacher, Rujing, who was born the year the great Miaodao died. When he returned a few years later, he was determined to transmit true Buddhism to Japan—a Buddhism he thought no one in Japan really understood, a true Zen he considered the original heart of Buddhism. Dōgen stood out instantly in Kyoto—he was impolitic, cranky and sarcastic, and he insulted priests of other sects without hesitation.

The large, complicated Buddhist world of Japan was a man's world. There were few ordination platforms for women, who had begun following Seishi's lead and ordaining each other. Mount Hiei, the center of Tendai Buddhism, was forbidden to women. Mount Koya, the center of Shingon Buddhism, was also closed to women. Todaiji's inner doors had long been closed, and the main training halls at virtually every monastery were kekkai, a "bounded area," the Enclosed Realm where women were never allowed to set foot. At women's funerals, priests announced that now the dead person could shed the defiling body of a woman and be free. Sometimes the *Ketsubonkyō*, the *Menses Scripture,* was laid in a woman's coffin at her funeral so that she wouldn't go to the blood hell caused by the poison of her menstruation.

A woman named Ryōnen, thirty-five years older than Dōgen, had left the troubles in Kyoto to enter the Daruma-shu, a new Chinese Buddhist sect led by Chinese priests. They began with and expanded Bodhidharma's teaching that the self is transcendent Buddha Nature. Ryōnen thought perhaps this approach would help her see something transcendent in herself, and in others. After years of practice, at the age of sixty, she was considered highly mature in her understanding. At some point in her years of steadfast effort, she had come to terms with the suffering that surrounded her—it *was* pointless, in that it could be avoided, and it was also inevitable, because people didn't know how to avoid it. She worked at avoiding it. She was well advanced, and advanced enough to know that something was missing. If the self itself is transcendent Buddha Nature, why was it so hard for people to realize that transcendence? When she went looking for more answers, all she found were closed doors. The main

Daruma-shu temple was on Mount Hiei, where she was not allowed, and temple after temple, priest after priest, refused her entrance.

Dōgen claimed not to be bound by doctrines or rules, and his radical comments made it clear that he didn't distinguish much between types of people. "All Being is Buddha Nature," he said, and sometimes shouted: "*All* Being *is* Buddha Nature!" to get it through the thick heads of his uncouth students. Ryōnen went to An'yōin, the decrepit temple in Fukakasa where he was staying. She came to question him, half expecting to be turned away—she'd been turned away from many places. Instead, he offered her tea, which he had become quite fond of in China. She saw immediately that Dōgen didn't mind having women around. Myōchi, a laywoman from Kyoto, had been a devoted student and patron of Dōgen's since shortly after he returned from China. Dōgen had also ordained the aristocratic lady Shōgaku, a wealthy widow and one of his distant relatives, shortly after he returned from China.

Dōgen and Ryōnen were at ease with each other from the beginning—the young, obsessed man and the old, strong-minded woman. Teacher and student, but also student and student, teacher and teacher, friend and friend—they met face to face, and Ryōnen decided to stay. She became Dōgen's disciple on August 15, 1231.

Two years later Dōgen founded Kōshohōrinji, a temple south of Kyoto on a hill beside the Uji River, the first truly independent Zen temple in Japan. He was mostly trying to get away from the prying and the complaints of the Tendai establishment. Shōgaku gave him the funds to build. A sloping lane led from the river up to the temple between rows of trees. The small buildings were close together, intimately close, facing inward on the terraced hillside. The women had their own quarters, down the lane at the bottom of the hill.

After Ryōnen came and the community moved to Kōshōji, Egi arrived. She'd been a Daruma nun as well, and remembered Ryōnen. Then a Daruma monk whom Egi and Ryōnen both knew, Koun Ejō, came. He'd met Dōgen once before and had never been able to forget his strange new teaching.

Dōgen had a huge impact on Ryōnen's life and practice, and she had a huge impact on his. Their questions about perfect nature and human delusion were reflections of each other; they spurred each other on to express the understanding of how these two things fit together, how simply doing the practice that expressed the understanding somehow *was* the understanding. In a Dharma talk to the community, Dōgen commented on Ryōnen's wisdom, her compassion toward suffering, her loving heart.

Just a month after her arrival he composed the *Bendōwa,* an essay that included questions from his closest students. "Is this practice only for monks, or can women and laypeople do it too?" was one such question. "There is no difference between men and women in the ancient teaching," wrote Dōgen, "and no difference between the noble person and the common." He would say this again and again over the course of his life—it needed saying more than once.

Ryōnen was so very much older, not only in years but in the settledness of her practice and her comfort with herself. She was like a lake of still water by then, all the silt settled, the water cool and clear, heavy, powerful. Dōgen had spent his first years as a monk on Mount Hiei, where women were never seen. He liked having women around, but sometimes he forgot them too, lecturing spontaneously when they weren't around. Ryōnen reminded Dōgen more than once of the story of the Naga princess, the goddess who challenged Śāriputra, and of his own comments about the universality of Buddha Mind.

Several times a month, men and women, laypeople and ordained people, came to hear Dōgen lecture in the Dharma hall in the afternoon. He sat on a higher seat at the front of the hall, and the monks and nuns and lay followers sat on the platform below him. After his lectures, there was always a little bit of debate and discussion between the teacher and students and between the students themselves. Now and then, late at night, he would speak spontaneously or read one of his poems; in the shadowed corners of the meditation hall, facing the plain wall, Ryōnen could see only the small space in front of her eyes. When he finished, she could hear only the brief shifting or indrawn breath of the monk or nun who sat nearest her and the occasional cry of a night bird; all else was gone, was not real, was not worth concern.

Kōshohōrinji was outside the establishment, free of the central authority; it was also without support when difficulties arose. A few powerful men and women became patrons, offering protection and funds. In 1237 Shōgaku paid for more building. Others in the upper class and the court found Dōgen and his little community weird, a little amusing, a little strange. A few traveled all the way to the temple and all the way up the hill, laughing at their own effort, to watch the eclectic mix of people sitting in silence, as still as rocks, staring at a wall in a plain room. The Tendai establishment was openly critical of a community where men and women practiced together.

When he wasn't lecturing, Dōgen wrote study guides on abstruse topics like the nature of time and insisted that his students study them carefully. This was what he wanted—to teach, to find a way to explain in words the extraordinary space he experienced inside, the space where nothing got in the way of anything else, where ideas about sects and class and jealousy couldn't exist. He was tired of the rounds of ignorant remarks by recent visitors, irritated by the complaints of high-ranking priests who disliked his free ways, his willingness to mingle, and his lack of decorum. How could he possibly explain to people how little any of these things mattered?

A few weeks after the spring equinox, on a day called the "day of purity and brightness," the sweet breeze swayed through the open doors of the meditation hall, and Dōgen gave a long lecture.

"When a nun who knows the truth and has the Dharma presents herself to the world, those who want the Dharma should listen. Anyone who wants to learn will submit to her teaching. Many people are so ignorant, they refuse to listen to women, even women who are teachers and are their elders. Any person who has got the Dharma is a true buddha. When that person sees us, we meet in a new place. When we see that person, this can only be called mutual study, because both people stop being limited to themselves. They become free of all forms, past all limits. Yesterday is gone, and it has nothing to do with bodies, or anything but now."

There was a long silence, and a few people adjusted their posture, rustling quietly. Then he continued.

"Stupid people think women are the cause of sexual greed. What's wrong with women? What's so right about men? Do you think the Dharma depends on such things? And this idea of enclosed grounds, where women aren't allowed—whose crazy idea was that? What kind of temple has no women?" He began to raise his voice. "Idiots! I am besieged with idiots, like dogs afraid I'll steal the bone!"

A few of the women were trying not to laugh at that point, and a few of the men were sitting very still. After another silence so long they were sure he had finished, he roared.

"We should throw ourselves to the ground and honor the buddhas! Through their acts, they cover all living beings with glory! *All* beings! Our prostration is the very marrow of our knowledge of this."

Then all were quiet for a long, long time, thinking. *When that person sees us, we meet in a new place. When we see that person, this can only be called mutual study. It has nothing to do with bodies.*

After a few years by the Uji River, Dōgen was worn down by the constant struggles with the established sects. A governor in Echizen, north of Kyoto in the mountains near the sea, offered him land on which to build a rural temple. He announced one day that he was leaving.

In 1243, on the sixteenth day of the seventh month, Dōgen and his closest dozen disciples moved to the mountains near the sea. Ryōnen still loved crazy Kyoto, its busyness, the parks and hidden temples, the gradual rebuilding of the broken city. Part of her hated to leave. She was old, she was tired, her joints ached, her feet were often cold. But part of her never hesitated; she wouldn't let him go without her. And the sea! She would finally get to see the sea.

It was a very long way by foot and cart along the Sabakaidō, the Mackerel Road that fishermen followed to bring their catch to Kyoto. They went past the great lake called Biwa, through valleys and past rice fields, over hills, through more valleys, and then along the shore's rocky cliffs—where the sea was constantly moving yet always the same, exactly as she thought it would be.

They lived in rough quarters for quite a while. But with the help of the governor's money and the governor's peasants, they built a temple.

Dōgen eventually named it Eiheiji, "Eternal Peace Temple." The mountain gate nestled between tall cedars on a hill, where the snow began falling early in the year. All winter long drifts piled high against the shutters and along the raised walkways, hiding everything but the temple itself, shutting out the city, the world, the arguments, the complaints. The halls were dim and echoing in the twilight, the meditation hall a flickering world of shadow and candlelight. The summers were moist and green, and a stream poured out of the mountain, cascading under small arching bridges.

Ryōnen, Egi, and Shōtaku lived in their own quarters near the gate in tiny rooms just big enough for sleeping and changing clothes. There were only a dozen or so people at the temple, and everyone sat together in the meditation hall, ate together, worked together. There wasn't ever enough time or enough muscle to do what needed to be done. Ryōnen got chilblains on her feet, and she limped most of the time, but she was content.

After a few years the shogun Hōjō Tokiyori had heard enough of the irascible Zen priest building a temple in the mountains to want to meet him. He associated with Rinzai priests and, wanting to see the leader of this new sect, sent an order demanding that Dōgen present himself to the government in Kamakura.

It couldn't be avoided. Dōgen and Ejō began the long walk out of the mountains, down the valleys, past Kyoto, and way beyond to the other side of Japan, the other sea. They were gone for eight months, almost all of it spent walking. While they were gone, Ryōnen died.

When Dōgen finally made it back to Eiheiji, he discovered the grandmotherly woman he loved was gone. He wrote a poem for her, a quiet comment on the snow. He wasn't well himself, and once he got sick, he stayed sick, writing fiercely, praying for more time. Egi moved up from the women's building to nurse him, sleeping beside him so she could clean him up when he didn't make it to the pail in time.

A month before his death, Dōgen called the monks together. He had to make decisions. He appointed Ejō as his successor, but pointed out that Egi was Ejō's Dharma sister, the Dharma sister of all the men there.

On August 5, Dōgen left for Kyoto to see a physician and died there a few weeks later.

In the decades after Dōgen's death, a fight over the direction of his temple caused a long and painful split between his disciples. Egi stood serenely still in the midst of it. She believed utterly by then in the transcendent nature of the self, buried under delusion and habits but there to be found if one would only look.

For five generations, women practiced under Dōgen's descendants—five generations of awakened women in one line, unbroken, face to face, with students of their own. Their names are a poem, they can be sung: Shūne, Jōa, Shūe, Somyō, En'i, Shōzen, Ekan, Myōshō, Ekyū, Sonin, Ninkai, Shinmyō, Shinshō, Jōnin, Myōshin, Sōitsu, Soichi, Myōjun, Myōzen, Genshu, Honshō, Sōki, Zenshō, Ryōsō, Myōkō.

So many women practiced and were recognized as masters from this line that a group of them formed the Sōtō-shū Nisōdan in 1334, the Sōtō Nuns' Association. They hoped to create training monasteries for women in the specific tradition of Dōgen's Zen. There was little support for such a radical idea, and in the century that followed, in the midst of massive social and religious upheaval, the system failed. None of the women's lineages survived. Almost six hundred years passed before a true Sōtō training temple for women was created.

Things change, but not always as quickly or completely as one might hope. Eight hundred years later, with only rare and brief exceptions that have made the rule more profound, no woman is allowed to practice at the temple where Ryōnen died and Egi nursed the founder.

the bucket

Mugai Nyodai

(1223–1298)

The Adachis were known both as brutal warriors and discreet negotiators; they moved deftly in the inner circles of the shogunate, with its association with Rinzai Zen, and in the imperial court, with its Shinto rites. The samurai served the clan lords, raising their children into clan loyalties. They believed that only constant practice could bring perfection in any skill and took intense pride in their families.

Shogunate women lived in the "great interior," where few men were allowed. When the men treated them roughly or disrespectfully, the women responded by forming ranks of their own. They trained in the use of the halberd, a long sword knife, as well as management, finances, singing, and the classic arts. Adachi Yasumori also made sure his daughter Chiyono studied poetry in its many precise and ordered forms, learned to play music, read the classics and the scriptures, and learned to read and speak Chinese. Chiyono was raised in a world where the teachings of Buddhism and Zen had been twisted to fit the violence and power struggles of politics and war.

Chiyono's family lived on a large estate at the edge of Kamakura, and her room looked out on the endless fields and steep green hills. The muddy roads were forever churned up by carts and oxen. Adachi Yasumori rode out in the mornings to practice archery, swordplay, and falconry in the fields with other samurai. His daughter learned some of the same things: archery, the history of the clans, the philosophy of the warrior's way. The women around her had a share in most things, helped with the decisions of the clan, kept the books, and had authority over their vassals, the many dependents who served the family in a hundred ways. It was a world lit by sudden flashes of sun across the gold crest of a helmet.

Chiyono married into the Kanezawa clan, which was known for scholarship instead of fighting. She had a daughter, lifted her kimonos above the muddy roads, watched the herons swooping over the rice shoots in the spring. She wrote poems tinged, as was a lot of the literature of the time, with *aware,* the poignant melancholy one feels in the midst of change and beauty. She wrote about snow and cherry blossoms, dew and youth—the perishable, the passing, the strange mixture of feelings evoked by the early days of spring that go by so quickly, like the tender pain of watching one's child begin to walk.

She was twenty years old, and then she was thirty years old, and it was as though the time had gone by as she had turned the corner from one room into the next.

Chiyono loved her husband, who was different from her father and his brusque samurai friends. Kamakura had changed completely from the small town her grandmother used to tell her about, a little sleepy town where cows wandered in the alleys and shopkeepers built their stalls wherever they wanted. When the shogunate moved to town, they made new rules—zoning for building, a curfew, limits on who could carry weapons—and people who didn't like them were invited to leave. Kamakura quickly grew into a small, well-regulated city.

Chiyono helped with the books, wrote long letters, and just like that, she was forty. Her daughter married and moved away, her beloved mother died, and then she was forty-five years old, and more. Chiyono began to visit the Rinzai monasteries, walking miles through the rough and busy streets, taking a horse when the mud was deep. She wondered what the real truth of Zen might be, out of the warriors' hands. Unmarried women of samurai families who wanted Zen training were allowed in the temples, and new temples were being built all the time. Whole neighborhoods echoed with complex drumbeats, rumbling chants, the deep ringing of the gongs rolling out across the hills in waves like water. Though she was married, she was clearly samurai, and when she came to a temple's gates, she would ring politely, ask for an audience with the teacher, and sometimes leave with copies of scriptures or sermons to read. Usually she left with more questions than she'd had when she arrived.

Sometimes she found herself on the edge of town, where the riffraff had been pushed, in busy rough streets. Once she and two of her maids rode their horses all the way to Hase many miles away to see the Daibutsu, a giant statue of bluish-green copper that had been built years earlier near the shore. Doves cooed coarsely in the trees around the temple. A priest, tiny below the Buddha's giant crossed legs, performed a service for Chiyono, but she had to hide her mouth when she saw him solemnly intoning a sutra in front of the statue. He was smaller than the Buddha's toe and looked like a beetle under its placid gaze.

One's life belonged to one's lord in those days. Scholarly or not, it was terrible loyalty that killed her husband. In 1277 he traveled to Kyoto with messages in spite of a bad cough and early wet weather. He never came back. Chiyono was fifty-four. As a widow, she should have returned to care for her aging father, but instead she kept walking every day, visiting temples, knocking on gates, until she met Wu-hsüeh.

A few years earlier, Kublai Khan's Mongol army had invaded to the south. Only a sudden storm had quelled the invasion. The berserkers came again not much later. That time, all the country's temples prayed, chanted, and made offerings, day and night, until a divine wind rose—the kamikaze, a great typhoon that destroyed the Mongol fleet.

The Eighth Regent, Hōjō Tokimune, who was married to Chiyono's aunt, ordered a temple called Engakuji to be built in honor of the dead. He invited a Chinese master called Wu-hsüeh Tsuyüan to lead it. Wu-hsüeh arrived in 1281 and began to give sermons in Chinese. They were translated into Japanese, then copied and passed out.

Chiyono read one of his sermons and went to Engakuji to meet him, climbing the long hill slowly and with decorous steps. Intensely polite but completely unwilling to be turned away, she passed through layer after layer of hesitant monks until she reached the abbot's door. She was wholly qualified by then—an unmarried woman of a samurai family, who wanted Zen training, though she was by then a plump woman with her hair going gray. Wu-hsüeh was almost exactly her age, but he looked much older, a very short man with white hair. He waved away the young monks and met her as his peer, bowing calmly.

In the conventions in which he had been raised in China, he could have been criticized for speaking to a woman alone. To do so violated the rules of monastic discipline. But the bodhisattva Precepts demanded that he give Dharma to anyone who asked. It was a common enough conflict for the Chinese priests. He didn't hesitate about which rule to follow and invited Chiyono to his small room. Outside the window she could see the twigs of a tiny juniper sapling he'd grown from seeds he had brought from across the sea. She gathered her kimono underneath her and sat at a small table while he prepared a bowl of his favored Chinese green tea.

From the hallway beyond the half-closed rice-paper door she heard the clatter of a work crew, monks repairing a shed. The grassy scent of tatami mingled with a small cloud of incense from the tiny altar in a corner. The master's room was cluttered with pens and scrolls.

"How can I help you?" he finally asked, giving her a cup.

"What is Zen?" she asked, sipping the tea. She asked this at every temple.

Wu-hsüeh answered, holding her eyes with his, "Zen is the heart of the one who asks, not someone else's words."

She smiled. "So why does the teacher give sermons that are recorded?"

Wu-hsüeh smiled back. "With a deaf man, you show him the moon by pointing. With a blind man, you show him the gate by knocking on it."

After a long pause, almost as an afterthought, he added, "When I was awakened, it was like a bird escaping a cage."

Chiyono visited Wu-hsüeh again the next week for tea, and then again, and then every day. She attended his public lectures in the evening, following the flickering lanterns along the covered walks. They spoke together in Chinese, but though he knew little of it, Wu-hsüeh encouraged her to find Japanese words for herself.

Chiyono was an unusual sight inside the monastery, with her thick layers of clothes and piled-up hair. He showed her the altars—the elaborate one in the ceremony hall, with its great Buddha, and the many dim and hidden altars in corners. She came to know the little grotto where the deer hid from hunters and the small pond filled with frogs. Filled with *aware:* the whole of the grounds of Engakuji felt melancholy to her, because she was filled with melancholy. She felt very alone. Her long grief, from losing her parents, her husband, her youth, had grown as precious as the elegant garden framed in Wu-hsüeh's window. But it was grief without meaning or purpose. She thought she'd known about love, wisdom, and death when she was a young woman. That had been a long time before; she knew a lot less now.

Women convicted of certain crimes had their heads shaved in punishment. Without hair, one's sex disappeared, as did one's status, clan identity, class, even age. Chiyono dressed, put up her hair properly, and came to the temple every day and left every evening. Then one day she dismissed her maid, cut off her hair, and arrived in a plain under-robe. Wu-hsüeh welcomed her with a small smile, unsurprised.

He found her a small room in a far corner, not far from the great bell on the side of the hill. Everything at Engakuji was up or down from something else, the buildings nestled among cypress and cedars and hydrangeas that lay bare and damp all winter, then bloomed white and pink and sky-blue in the early summer weeks. Spiders wove big webs across the path every evening, and Chiyono had to break through them every morning on her way down before dawn.

Ordained, she became Mugai Nyodai. Along with the monks, she rose before dawn every day for hours of silent meditation in the dark zendo. The stars whirled halfway round the sky between the night's meditation and the one at dawn. The moon waxed and waned with the season, the way her cold breath in winter formed brief clouds, there and gone. In the dark meditation hall they sat as still as stones and statues, eyes cast gently down. Sometimes the long silences were broken by the shouts of a monk in Wu-hsüeh's room, struggling to shatter his view of reality—to slice through the boundary of the perceived, the way the samurai sliced off an enemy's hand. The sutras, recited over and over again, sank into her marrow—sank past the sting of unattended ego and the lance of loss. Each morning they ate breakfast where they sat in the zendo—small plops of rice or gruel served by the ladleful into small black bowls.

Nyodai watched the snow fall on the garden and cover the tapestry of empty branches with an emptiness of its own. She mopped, swept, and washed, her bare head hidden by a cloth. She was no longer a plump, older woman of the ruling class, but a plump, older novice nun, expected to be silent and graceful and do as she was told. The monk in charge of work gave her an old lacquer bucket and told her to fetch water from the river. It was good novice work, an hour's walk each way, guaranteeing she would be gone from his presence for much of every day.

Each day after breakfast she picked up her bucket. Its bamboo braces were weak and loose, and it often leaked. She spent hours trying to repair the braces, because the bucket leaked like her life leaked, dripping out. Day by day she wrapped the bucket with new strips of bamboo, patiently tightening the staves the way she patiently hoped to fix her broken life. She knelt by the stream and watched the bucket fill, drop by drop, each drop part of the ocean, part of the rain, the puddles, the mist, her breath. Snow and fog, icicles, steam from the baths, mist caught in the high branches of the trees, frost on the stones of the path—all the same water as the water in her bucket. She knew this; she knew the world vibrated with life, and she longed for the immensity of being to touch her. But all she felt was hollowness in the midst of small things.

Which drop fills the bucket? All of them. Which leak empties the bucket? All of them. Which one matters the most? All of them.

Though she was a novice, she was also the abbot's friend and still took tea with him. One day she was sitting with Wu-hsüeh when they heard a deer cry in nearby Hakugendo forest. Wu-hsüeh said, "Where is that deer? Do you know who hears it?" Then he shouted—a deep, inarticulate roar that seemed to pierce Nyodai's heart. She fell into deep reflection, and taking up her bucket, walked to the stream.

That night she saw the moon reflected in the water. In the stream, it burbled and broke; in her bucket, it glowed in stillness. The same moon—different moons—no moon at all. She looked around her familiar woods and saw the icy glow of moonlight shining equally on everything, the whole moon reflected in a single still drop hanging from a leaf.

She carried the water back, gave it to the cook, bowed, and went to her room, where she wrote a poem:

The bucket took the stream water and held it,
and the reflection of the moon through the pines lodged there in purity.

The next day, when she showed the poem to Wu-hsüeh, he said to her, "A good start. Go away now and read the *Heart Sutra.*"

Whatever is form, that is emptiness; whatever is emptiness, that is form. Each day she carried water. She had stopped wishing to work in the kitchen or expecting to be appointed to clean the altar or sew robes or climb the steep hill to the west to ring the great bell with a log as long as her room. She was the water bearer; bearing water was her life. The bucket, the water, the moon, the steps to and from the stream, the humid air of summer, the chafing on her hands in winter, the soup she ate for supper, became one act, the act of going on. She stopped wishing not to grieve. She stopped longing to understand.

Summer came again with its stinging caterpillars, flies, flowers, soft mud, and the cool stream. One hot evening, when the moon was full, Nyodai walked dreamily along the path. She was alone with the crickets and could smell the night-blooming jasmine hidden in the trees, in the green, green hills. When she bent to scoop water into her bucket, its bottom fell out.

Gone at once was all that had bound her small, false self. Without a bottom, a bucket is not a bucket anymore. Without the boundary of ego, a self is no more separate from the world than a drop of rain is separate from the ocean. Nyodai's water spilled over the ground; it disappeared into the soil, melted into the grass, invisible and vast. Who hears the deer, carries the water? Who grieves, who learns?

The next morning Wu-hsüeh passed her in the hall and, seeing her face lit like a moon in the shadows, asked her to come to his room. There she stood and recited her new poem:

So many ways I fixed the bucket,
Its braces weak and soon to break—
Until one day the bottom fell out.
Then there was no water in the bucket,
No moon shining in the water.

He tested her with the classical koan of "Three Gates of Oryu," and she was able to meet every question clearly. He tried obscure phrases, dense and confusing scripture, his own poems of understanding. The words flowed around her like a stone; she flowed around the words like the stream, in a trickle, in a flood.

For a few days Nyodai didn't care about the plants or the soup and didn't fetch any water. At the abbot's signal, the work leader left her alone, gazing at a small hydrangea near the pond. But even enlightenment is like water, dripping everywhere, disappearing into the ground. Even disappearing disappears. She found another bucket and went back to the stream and the life she'd led before.

One day, as though giving her a cup of tea, Wu-hsüeh gave her a priest's robe of gold and white brocade with a ring of tortoise shell, a set of bowls, and a picture of himself. She was the first female Zen master in Japan.

The world was changing; people died. One day a messenger brought word to the temple. The entire Adachi family, her family, had been killed, massacred in yet another spasm of power between clans.

Her uncle Tokimune, the regent, took sick and begged Wu-hsüeh for ordination and training. He entered the monastery but died soon after, leaving Nyodai's aunt, the Lady Horiuchi, as a widow at the age of thirty-one. Horiuchi was much younger than Nyodai, and the older woman felt great sympathy for her; they were almost the only survivors left from their clan. A year later Horiuchi shaved her head, became a nun, and turned her fortune to the building of a convent across the valley from Engakuji.

As Nyodai watched the convent walls go up, she realized it was time to find the next place for her own life. She was well known by then, this aristocratic widow who had become a Zen master. The Uesugi family of Kyoto invited her to be the teacher at a temple they built there. It meant leaving Engakuji, leaving Wu-hsüeh. As this was her life flowing as freely as the stream, she accepted without regrets and left for the city. She and her teacher continued to write a great many letters back and forth until he died in 1286. When he died, it was like a bird flying free of a cage. He left her relics, a tiny box of his fingernail clippings, with the request that she build a reliquary for them.

Eventually Mugai Nyodai left the Uesugi temple to found one of her own. She called it Keiaiji and dedicated it to the memory of her dead family. She built a chapel there for the relics and called it Shmyaku-an, the Hermitage of the True Lineage. She met each person who came to her gate the same way, without bias, and made them tea and answered questions.

The time would come when Musō Soseki, the disciple of a monk she'd known at Engakuji, became abbot of several of the big monasteries in Kamakura, one after the other. He had never approved of Mugai Nyodai's transmission and refused to accept her as a true lineage holder. The day came when Soseki took over Shmyaku-an, moved the hermitage to a far corner, and built a male monastery on the site.

When she was quite old, she woke up one day and found she couldn't walk on her right leg or lift anything with her right hand. Her cheek sagged. But her mind was clear, and she kept teaching. Eventually Keiaiji became the head temple of the female Five Mountains system of Rinzai monasteries. Mugai Nyodai's poems became teaching koans, and the story of the bucket with no bottom became famous throughout all of Zen.

the knife

Kakuzan Shidō

1252–1306

The nun who would be known as Shidō was born in Kamakura in 1252, in the powerful Adachi family, and grew up in the same household as her cousin, Hōjō Tokimune. When she was ten and he was eleven, they were married, and she became Lady Horiuchi. Before Tokimune had turned eighteen, he became regent to the shogun and the most powerful man in the country. The lady learned the samurai ways, and from a young age she always carried a ten-inch-long knife, like all women of the warrior class.

Horiuchi and Tokimune were patrons of Zen. In 1282, to honor the dead after the abortive Mongol invasion, he built the great monastery Engakuji. A few years later, when he became seriously ill, he went there for training—for hope—but he died shortly after, when he was only thirty-three. The Lady Horiuchi waited a year and then shaved her head and became Kakuzan Shidō in 1285.

That same year, most of the Adachi family was killed. Shidō was ready to renounce the world entirely and decided to spend her family's wealth to build a temple on the hill across from Engakuji.

She called the temple Tōkeiji, and she trained at Engakuji, under Tōkei, the fourth teacher there. During the Rōhatsu sesshin in 1304, he gave her inka, authority to be an independent teacher. The head monk didn't like this. Shidō took the seat in front of the altar to answer challenges from the monks, to test her skill. When it was his turn, the head monk asked, "In our lineage, anyone who gets inka must give a discourse on the *Rinzai-roku.* Can you really handle that seat?"

Shidō stepped down from the platform and stood directly in front of him. So fast he couldn't see her do it, she pulled out her knife and held it a few inches in front of his face.

"Every Zen teacher in the lineage of our Master should go to the seat and preach on the scriptures," she said in a low voice. "But I am a warrior and I speak the Dharma face to face, using a sword. Why do I need a book?"

He really wanted to back up, away from the blade under his eye, but he knew everyone was watching. He kept his composure long enough to ask, "Before your parents are born, how will you express the Truth?"

She closed her eyes for a while, then opened them and looked at him again. She said, "Do you understand?"

He answered mysteriously: "Here in the Peachtree Valley, a pitcher of wine has been tipped right up. Drunk, the eyes see miles of flowers."

Many decades earlier, when the Shogun Yoritomo had died, his widow, Hōjō Masako, became the de facto leader, ruling with all the draconian ruthlessness of the men, doing what the men did, to get the power the men had. She killed her enemies and took their estates, had her first son assassinated and installed her second, weak-willed son as the official shogun, had her father arrested, and then had her grandson killed, just in case. This brought her admirers as well as power, and she was called Ama-Shogun—the Nun Shogun.

The Nun Shogun had powerful visions. In one, the voice of a god spoke to her from a great mirror and told her of a coming rebellion. She was able to stop it because of this warning, and in gratitude the Hōjō regent, Yasutoki, had a mirror six feet in diameter made and installed it in the Shinto shrine for the god Hachiman.

Shidō, with her long knife and her long reach and her total lack of fear, waded through yet another disruption of the clans and stole that mirror. No one ever knew exactly how she'd done it, but the day came when she calmly installed the great mirror from the Hachiman shrine at Tōkeiji and called its new home the Mirror Hall.

She looked at the mirror every day as she walked to and from the meditation hall, and then one day she stopped and sat zazen right in front of it. After that, she moved her cushion into the Mirror Hall and did all her meditation there. It was curious. She had done a lot of zazen, she had inka and deep understanding, and she had at times felt as though everything was clear all the way through—clear, clear to the bottom.

But in front of the mirror her mind kept flitting, resting and flitting away like a moth in the garden, like the sparrow whose head is never still. She looked in the mirror and saw—what? Nothing. Everything. Her own face and body. She looked in the mirror and noticed her eyes flitting, her hands trembling a little, her posture shifting every few moments. She looked in the mirror and tried to be still, to hold the gaze of her own eyes perfectly still, unmoving, like a statue. She tried to be like a picture. She tried to sit like a tree, like a rock, like a dream. She knew how to hold herself still and bright and relaxed and upright and serene and strong all at once; she knew how, but in front of the mirror it was very difficult. Finally, with eyes open and seeing herself, she could hold herself utterly still and soft just for a moment. After that, her mind began to relax and move less, flit less often and less quickly. She began to see through the reflection, through the skin and the eyes and the face and the reflection, to see nothing. Empty. Full. The mirror was clear, clear as water clear as air clear as the sky clear as the Truth. No dust could alight.

Shidō wrote this poem to express her understanding:

If the mind never rests on a single thing,
nothing can be clouded.
No need to speak of polishing.

Shidō especially loved and celebrated Wesak, the festival of the Buddha's birth in the early spring. Tōkeiji had beautiful flowers, and the azaleas by the little pond always bloomed in time for the festival. One week, just before Wesak, Shidō gave a sermon to the small group of nuns who had joined her there. It was April, one of the most beautiful months of the year, and the camellias and iris had already begun to open. Wrens chattered madly each morning in the eaves of the small meditation hall, like tiny bells to keep them awake during zazen.

That day Shidō stood on the floor in front of the altar platform, barefoot on the polished wood floor. She asked: "The Buddha born today—where does he come from?"

Runkai, her personal attendant who had been with her from the first day, stepped out of the group and pointed to the sky with one hand and with the other to the earth.

Shidō smiled and then asked: "When the Buddha who has been born hasn't yet died, where is he?" Runkai again pointed with one hand to heaven and with the other to earth.

For many years nuns at Tōkeiji sat meditation in front of mirrors at least once a day. The practice was called Tōkeiji Mirror Zen. Eventually that particular mirror disappeared during a clan battle that crashed through the walls, but it was replaced with another mirror, and then another. Many wrote poems about the realizations they experienced this way. Runkai, who would succeed Shidō as abbot, was one. She wrote:

Many the reflections
But the surface is clean.
It has always been free of clouds,
This mirror.

family

Ekan Daishi, Myōshō Enkan, Kontō Ekyū, and Mokufu Sonin

(late 1200s to mid-1300s)

Ekan Daishi was separated from her mother, Myōchi, at the age of eighteen. Several years later Daishi went to the Kiyomizu Temple in Kyoto to pray for help in finding her. The temple's waters are magically healing; they course out of the steep hillside into pools, and faithful people come to drink every day. For a week she went to the temple each morning and prayed and drank the water. On the sixth day she saw the carved head of a Kannon on the ground, lying in the mud. It was small and finely done. Finding it there seemed auspicious and strange to Daishi, and she put her palms together and made a vow.

"If you have pity for me," she said to the bodhisattva's head, "help me. Help me find my mother. If you do, I will have a body carved for you and honor you the rest of my life." Then she carefully picked up the head, took it home, and washed it clean.

The next day, the last day of her prayers, she met a woman on the road who put out her hand to stop Daishi. The woman smiled, and then told her where to find her mother. Daishi took the wooden Kannon head to a craftsman and commissioned a body made to fit. Only then did she go to a nearby town to be reunited with her mother, who had been Dōgen's lay disciple when she was young.

Many years later, when Ekan Daishi was thirty-seven years old, she had a dream. She swallowed the morning light, warm and as soft as silk, and it filled her entire body. A few days later she realized she was pregnant. Then she prayed, as she had often prayed, to the beloved statue of Kannon: "May this child be a spiritual leader, a benefit to all, and please, may the delivery be easy."

For the next seven months, she bowed 1,333 times each day and recited the *Kannon Sutra.*

The baby was born on the property of the Kannon Temple in the province of Echizen, without pain. A short while later Daishi took vows as a nun, and the baby's grandmother, Myōchi, helped raise him.

When Daishi could, she took the baby to her favorite temple in Kyoto, the Sanjusangendo, temple of thirty-three thousand Kannons—a thousand and one Kannons with multiple heads and arms. It was a place of gold and shadow. The sculptures filled her eyes, her mind—endless, sparkling, and strange. She wanted the images and spirit of Kannon to fill the baby's mind, the baby destined to be a great leader.

Since Dōgen's death many decades before, the second sect of Zen—Caodong in Chinese, and known in Japanese as Sōtō—had become firmly established, with Eiheiji as its headquarters. When he was eight years old, Ekan Daishi sent her son to Eiheiji, where he was called Keizan. He trained for many years under Gikai, one of Dōgen's successors. His mother eventually founded a Sōtō convent named Jōjūji, becoming its abbot around 1309. Men left, women stayed behind—this was the way of Buddhism. In Keizan's case, his mother left him first. But in some way, they never really left each other at all. They visited often; he relied on her advice, and she prayed for him, from before his birth until the day of her own death.

Keizan founded the temple of Daijoji in the city of Kanazawa and began to write the great collection of ancestral stories called the *Denkoroku.* While still living at Daijoji, Keizan met Mokufu Sonin. Her name was subtle and intricate; it meant "ordered silence" and "enduring ancestor" and many other things. Sonin had married Shigen Nobunao when she was thirteen. In 1312 she donated a large amount of land in a place called Tōkoku and asked Keizan to build a temple there. There was no money for building until Sonin's brother died. After that, she had the family home dismantled and rebuilt it on the land.

In 1317 Keizan entered this building formally as the abbot of Yōkōji. It was a long way in more than miles from Kyoto to Yōkōji. One traveled north, and a little west, up toward a peninsula jutting out into the cold, rough sea, with range after range of mountains covered in evergreen and broken by emerald rice paddies in the lowlands, where white egrets bobbed their heads among the silvery shoots. At this time it was still wild land, with pigs, bears, and snakes loose on the hills and only a few farmers for neighbors in most places. The weather was difficult—typhoons in the summer, blizzards in the winter, rain the rest of the time.

Nevertheless, the land was beautiful, azure and rich, thick with bamboo and cypress, grasses and ferns and wild flowers, cedars and misty fogs and always a gray sea, sharp rocks jutting out of breaking waves like the old ink washes of the Chinese painters. The clouds were thick and low and close at times, knocking into the hills and trees, the sky constantly shattering and being remade, dark, blue, implacable, alive.

Yōkōji quarters were very rough. The snow was deep in the winter, and the stream below ran hard. The residents were so poor they had to make tea from pine needles, but all the geomancy was correct. Like his mother, Keizan had many prophetic dreams that divided his life into clear segments and led him toward his future. His dreams about Yōkōji were strong and good, filled with spirits and buddhas. Even the stars overhead, streaming slowly between the black branches of the pines, were correctly aligned. The hills were no more beautiful than other nearby hills, but he could see through these particular hills to the hidden hills beneath. He believed that he could see the true monastery already there, the one belonging to the other world—the world of protectors and guides. In this place, where the boundary between worlds was very thin, he would build the Monastery of the Eternal Light.

A year later Daishi died. Almost at the moment of her death she reached for her son's hand.

"I made a vow to Kannon," she said. "You must continue it. You must help all beings come to the Dharma. Especially, most especially, because you can, you must help all women of the three worlds and the ten directions.

"Take the little statue," she added, nodding toward the Kannon she had found all those years ago in the mud. "Take care of it forever."

In her memory, Keizan ordered that a Sōtō women's temple, Hōō-ji, be built in the province of Kaga.

One night Keizan dreamed that his grandmother had come to him and asked to be ordained. The next day Sonin, who was still very young, invited Keizan to engage in "Dharma combat" with her, the spirited, metaphor-laden interview testing a student's understanding.

Keizan asked Sonin, "This year is almost gone, and another new year will come. So how about your religious life?"

Sonin answered, "In the branches of the tree without shadow, is there any kind of time?"

"Excellent!" Keizan was pleased. Here was a person with a deep and earnest mind, with the flavor of the Dharma in her words. Already he trusted her; already they were like master and disciple as well as friends. When she asked him to ordain her, he could not have been happier. Because of his dream, he believed from then on that Sonin was his grandmother reborn. Her wish wasn't fulfilled then, however; she remained in lay life, a married woman of property and a patron, as well as his friend.

In 1321 the Buddha Hall was built. That season a nun named Kontō Ekyū arrived and immediately made herself at home, as though she had always lived there. Since she couldn't read Chinese well, Keizan rewrote Dōgen's discussion of the Precepts in Japanese for her. She began to organize the nuns and manage their work. Month by month, season by season, more buildings and more altars were built and more people came, until dozens of monks and almost thirty nuns lived in the community.

The men and women sat together for morning services, then separated to do their work and study. The residents studied seven particular texts, especially the *Lotus Sutra,* the *Bonmōkyo,* and the *Yuikyōgyō.* Keizan gave them Dōgen's rules for the daily life of a monastery—rules for how to behave in the zendo, with each other, and during meals, how to use the library, how to wash and use the toilet with proper rites, and how juniors and seniors should behave toward each other.

The main purpose of the temple, as Keizan conceived it, was to perform ceremonies to save the souls of lay donors and patrons and their parents. This purpose was cyclical: many of the buildings, altars, bells, and statues were donated by laypeople with specific requests for such saving rites, and in return more saving rites were done. The men and women conducted these ceremonies together, and the seniors sat together in the public rites without regard to sex.

In 1319 a woman named En'i, a member of a powerful local family, donated a large amount of rice paddy land to Yōkōji. It was enough to ease the temple's poverty and make it secure. That same year Keizan ordained Sonin on the sixth day of the eighth month. Because of the original donation of land, Keizan fondly called Sonin the Fundamental Overlord of the Mountain after that.

In 1322 Keizan and the nuns founded Enzūin, the Temple of Perfect Penetration, across the stream from the mountain gate, hidden in the trees. Enzūin was dedicated to the well-being of women forever, and it was most especially meant as an honor to his grandmother. It was a tiny place up a narrow, winding path, held closely by big cedars on every side. The trees were old, with peeling, fragrant bark, and the floor of the forest was as soft as a futon made of their needles. It smelled green all the time in there, and the trees covered the little building in black shadow. At night the path was tricky because not even a single star could be seen through their canopy. In winter, when the temple was under snow, Enzūin was a cozy, shadowy, mysterious place.

At the dedication, the statue of Kanzeon, with its eleven serene faces, was installed as the main image. It had come to seem like an animate thing, hearing and acting on the prayers of its bearers. In its base Keizan placed a lock of his own baby hair and his umbilical cord, which his mother had preserved. In this way, he gave his own life to this women's hermitage in the trees.

Sonin was the first abbot there. Enzūin was forbidden to men, as parts of the main building were forbidden to women. But Keizan remembered the vow he'd inherited, and he lectured to the women, sometimes meeting privately with them to guide their studies. For years they lived there in quiet intimacy.

Sonin's mother was married to a leader in the Nakagawa area of Sakai, near Yōkōji. After her daughter had married and then been ordained, and after her son died, and later her husband, Sonin's mother began studying under Keizan. Soon she made a large donation of many rice paddies, and this was enough to make the temple prosperous. Keizan gave her the Precepts in 1323 and the name Shōzen, which means "meditation on nature." He wrote a poem for her and offered her a small hut hidden in a fold of the hills above the temple, called Zōkeian, to use as a hermitage. After that, he called her a priest and said sutras and offertories should be read forever in her honor.

On a day in early spring, a perfect day, the one day each spring that promises so many more such days to come—on that day Keizan bowed to Kontō Ekyū after the morning service and asked her to come to his reception room for tea. Ekyū folded her formal robes and put them away, spoke briefly with the other nuns about the work projects for the day, and then walked slowly along the wooden cloister. The dark floors, shiny with polishing, were cold beneath her feet. The early light came in strongly under the eaves, and little wrens chattered in the tall pines outside the walls.

Keizan's rooms were behind sliding rice-paper doors. She knocked once, and he called her in, as always. He knelt on one side of a low wide table. She entered, bowed, and knelt on the other side. They were such good friends by then, and she was so comfortably his student and he so comfortably her confidant, that nothing needed to be said while he whisked and poured the tea.

She looked beyond him into the tiny courtyard between this room and the next, where a small green tree stood in a gravel and moss garden. A plant was beginning to spread its wide green leaves beneath the tree. One of the nuns had carefully raked the gravel into a curving line to resemble a stream. She could see past it to the rooms beyond, over the roof to the leaning top of a maple glinting red in the morning light, and beyond it to the dark wall of evergreen trees and the corner of a dark, tiled roof.

Keizan poured the tea and watched her while she tasted it. On the side wall a scroll hung above a shelf with a tiny incense burner and a single willow stem in a vase. Now and then it knocked a bit in the breeze, unevenly, like a small hollow drum being struck. In the breeze was a whisper of the moist ground, the stream, the new plants, the earth.

He said, "I'm giving you this. Here." He handed her a scroll, a document of succession that declared her his Dharma heir. She received it gravely, but he could see the smile in her dark eyes. Then he gave her a self-portrait with a little calligraphy, a line or two of scripture, for her personal keeping. They finished their tea, and she rose, bowed, and went to work, the first Japanese woman to receive full Sōtō transmission.[7]

Another day, a fall day of gray light and misty rain that wet the turning leaves in fine spray, Keizan invited Sonin to his room for tea. A crow called as she walked—"caw, caw, caw"—fell off into silence, and began calling her again—"caw, caw." The air hung heavy under the leaden sky, close and warm.

As he had with Ekyū, he gave Sonin a portrait and a little calligraphy, and then something else. He had written in careful lines a document pairing their descendants in a kind of marriage agreement—Keizan's descendants and Sonin's descendants, bound in the future. Then he gave her back some of the land she had donated, land he had very carefully insisted be his alone forever. Now Whirling Water Peak and Grain Growing Plain were hers again, and all of it was theirs together, because she was his heir. Later Keizan wrote that he and Sonin were inseparable in this and many lives, as closely bound as a magnet and iron.

Keizan's cousin was ordained not long after that; she was called Myōshō Enkan. Her name meant "bright whole vision." She and Sonin became close friends, and Myōshō proved to be quite adept at Zen. It wasn't long before Sonin recognized her capacity and gave her the authority to ordain others.

Keizan decided to test Myōshō's understanding. "Do you understand the story about Linji and how he raised up his whisk?" Keizan asked.

Myōshō looked at him and remained silent.

He was pleased with this. As she turned to leave, he said, "Your words are difficult to contain in ink."

When Shōzen died in 1325, Keizan declared that monks and nuns at the monastery must do monthly memorials and one annual service in her honor. He began to prepare for his own death, parceling out temples to his disciples. Hōō-ji remained a convent, with Sonin the appointed abbot, and she lived there until she died at the age of eighty.

Even now in Yōkōji there is a scroll of Ekan Daishi and Mokufu Sonin as abbots of Enzūin, sitting side by side. On a steep hill at the end of a long staircase, its stone steps softened by the endless damp of deep trees and the tramp of many, many feet, are the memorials—Keizan's grave, a repository of Dharma treasures, and funerary tablets, including ones for Ekan Daishi, Sonin, and Myōchi.

the paper sword

Shōtaku

(mid-1300s)

From the time she was small, Sawa trained herself to increase her energy, her qi, through breath and body practices and the centering of her mind. The energy refreshed her, kept her balanced and calm. As she improved, the energy was more and more available whenever she needed it, until she could control the Field of Elixir in the Sea of Life, the kikai tanden where all of one's life energy is centered, below the navel. By the time she was grown, Sawa was a powerful person.

Sawa married Sakurada Sadakuni, a major retainer of the Hōjō family, but he was killed in 1331 during one of the many wars between the clans. His was just one of many deaths; bands of rogue warriors roamed the countryside, and no place was safe. Sawa cut off her hair, entered Tōkeiji, and became the nun Shōtaku. She was devout and practiced for many years under Daisen, the seventeenth abbot at Engakuji. Eventually she became the third abbot at the convent.

Tōkeiji had become an important temple in the center of political power. Located on a major highway, it was wealthy and large, with five subtemples, but its inner grounds were deeply cloistered. Except for certain rare ceremonies, only women were allowed in the inner area. Tōkeiji was sometimes called the Kakekomi-dera, the "Run-Into Convent," because it offered sanctuary and divorce to any woman who stayed for three years. Some of the women who came there were fleeing unfaithful or abusive husbands; others were unfaithful themselves and wanted the freedom to marry a lover. Now and then a woman simply wanted to be alone and able to control her life and property independently. It was said of Tōkeiji that it was "the place where men are deprived of their pride."

The most solemn and intense retreat of the year was held in early December in honor of the Buddha's enlightenment experience. During this retreat the nuns from Tōkeiji, even the abbot, had daily interviews with the abbot at Engakuji. They had to leave the convent, walk down one hill, cross a narrow ravine, and climb up another hill. After their interviews, they then left the monastery, walking back down the hill, across the ravine, and up the other side into the convent for the night. The wind off the sea was sometimes bitterly cold.

One night Shōtaku was returning to Tōkeiji very late. The sky was soft and black and filled with stars, the white splash of the Milky Way staining the vault of sky. The Japanese called it Ame no Gawa, the "river of heaven." In her sleeve she carried a piece of paper on which the abbot of Engakuji had written a short verse for her contemplation.

Poets spoke of *yūgen,* the mysterious quality one seems to glance out of the corner of the eye, a bare and profound sensation that strokes the heart, leaving a person almost painfully aware of transience—all that is hidden, remote, impossible to explain, the subtle and easily missed, the poignancy of a wisp of cloud crossing a winter sky, the tender grace in the call of an unseen bird. Shōtaku knew yūgen, she knew it often, and she was feeling it right then in the way her robe swished along the stone path in silence, so late at night.

It was so cold Shōtaku could hear tiny twigs in the trees cracking as they rubbed against each other. But she walked slowly, enjoying the peace and the swish of her robe, the sharp stimulant of the cold, the black sky. All at once a man jumped out from the dark woods onto the narrow path in front of her. He had on old samurai clothing that was unkempt and soiled, with a strange expression on his face. His long sword was drawn, and he pointed it at Shōtaku.

"On the ground, nun!" he shouted. "I'll take my turn now."

Qi is fluid, flexible; it forms matter, creates space—nonmaterial, but almost material. Qi makes matter, it makes space; it holds things together, allowing things to change. Qi made this elixir that kept Shōtaku firm and strong, until both matter and space were as much a part of her as her skin and blood.

Shōtaku took out the piece of paper the abbot had given her and rolled it into a tube. The bandit was a little taken aback; he didn't know what she was doing. Then she thrust it at him like a sword, shouting a great cry, a cry that seemed to shatter his bones. When she struck him with the paper, he fell down, dropping his sword. In terror, he left it behind and scrambled away into the trees.

Shōtaku walked back to Tōkeiji to study the poem.

the hidden flowers

Yōdō

(d. 1396)

Engakuji had closed its gate to women students. Only a woman who could prove she had high attainment was allowed to enter its halls. If a woman climbed the steps up to the mountain gate, she was stopped by a monk who would test her understanding with koans and bar her way if he didn't like her answers.

(One question often used went like this: "What is the gate through which the buddhas enter the world?" A monk asked this of Ninpō, who was abbot at Tōkeiji at the time. She grabbed the monk's head and stuck it between her legs.)

The closing of the monastery door was of a piece with events in the rest of the world. Nuns, like all women, were losing power. Confucian ideals were officially in place again, and their promoters disliked the idea of women entering spiritual life. Women should not even visit large temples until they were over forty years of age and past childbearing age, wrote one scholar. "They should concentrate on performing human duties," he added. "They must not divert their attention to invisible spiritual beings."

Men controlled much of a family's finances and property. Flower arranging and the tea ceremony had become a man's arts. Theater, painting, even calligraphy were increasingly kept from women. Tōkeiji's divorce business was handled by men, officials who lived with their families in detached houses below the main grounds. The men managed the budget and screened the women applying for refuge and were the chief mediators in the negotiations.

For a time, women were forbidden to ordain as nuns until they were past childbearing age. There was one exception to this rule, and that concerned an emperor's daughter. At least one was required to be ordained, a custom that helped reduce the imperial birth rate. Such women usually became the abbot of an imperial convent.

Many welcomed the opportunity—the convents offered a life freer in many ways than marriage. Imperial nuns weren't cloistered; they came and went from court and family rather freely.

The fifth abbot of Tōkeiji was Emperor Go-Daigo's daughter, but she had never been anyone but Yōdō almost as far back as she could remember.

More women came to Tōkeiji every year seeking refuge; almost five hundred eventually did so. They usually went to a local inn first and petitioned the temple for refuge through a hired intermediary. Then they were invited to the temple for an interview, which took place in a room facing a peaceful garden.

Tōkeiji had become a great flower temple, its grounds filled with blooms in every season. There were always butterflies nearby, and the trees and shrubs were always filled with birds, twittering from dawn until dark, filling the nuns' meditation with song. Behind the buildings rose a steep hill of cypress and ginkgo trees thickly woven with vines, forming shelter. The nuns had built many tiny gardens in hidden corners, planted with buttercups, narcissus, apricots, peony, and lilac. They put lilies along the walks and against the surrounding walls and filled a damp hollow with purple and white iris.

Once women entered the temple, couriers took official divorce papers to the husband and the shogunate authorities. The husband, sometimes with neighbors, family, and local authorities in support, could come and plead the case against divorce, so there were guards at the gates and wall. The refuge women paid fees for room and board. They were required to cut their hair to shoulder length and then were placed in ranks, depending on the size of their fee and their social status. They were assigned jobs according to rank, from cleaning and weeding to arranging flowers and greeting visitors. Otherwise, for the three years of their stay they lived like the nuns, with no contact with their parents, friends, or children. They rarely left the grounds during their three-year stay, and then only with a nun and wearing a name tag. Even if their divorce was granted before the end of their term, they were required to stay for three years, and now and then one decided to stay longer than that.

Uneducated women were educated at Tōkeiji; women without skills to survive learned those skills. Life could be hard there, under the strict schedule, in the plain rooms, and it could be lovely too. Now and then a family sent an unruly or unhealthy daughter to Tōkeiji for training and discipline or to recuperate from illness.

The gardens were a reason to live there all by themselves. The shaded places were lavishly painted with lichen and moss. On the hillside were terraces for graves, many of which had little altars with incense often burning. A small natural cave had been turned into a shrine that was always a little damp and smelling of soil. Wind poured through the endless leaves with the sound of the sea rolling over small rocks, fluttering the azaleas and camellias, the rusty maples, and the big drapes of spiderweb between branches. The fall shone with color, and then the snow would fall, covering everything, softening sound, correcting every flaw.

Yōdō, who had a big square head and small black eyes like stones, loved the flowers. She had arthritis and was stiff all the time—stiff getting up and down from the cushion, stiff climbing stairs. The hilly grounds were hard for her, but day after day she climbed the path up from the meditation hall into the little corners nestled against the hillside, admiring each day's changes—the first appearance of the tiniest buds, the growth of stems, the unfolding leaves, the color appearing like a ghost's touch overnight.

Best of all, she loved Wesak, the festival celebrating the birth of the Buddha held every year in early spring. Flowers would be gathered in great quantity and piled around the altars. She wrote many poems about it.

Adorn the heart of those who behold the Buddha,
Because the Buddha of these flowered halls
Is found right there.

When Engakuji was built, the workers had discovered a beautiful mirror buried on its land. Its discovery was considered a good omen, and it had a place of importance in the temple. In 1374 Engakuji burned, a conflagration lasting for days. With help from the staff below the gate, the young nuns, and a few of the imperial soldiers of Yōdō's father, the Engakuji mirror disappeared during the chaos of firefighting. Only the nuns at Tōkeiji knew where their new mirror had come from.

Yōdō's poems became used as teaching verses and koans for many future generations of women, beginning with the sanctuary residents. Because they were concerned with ordinary things and everyday questions, her poems were considered to be especially useful for people who had little literary background.

Off and on throughout the 1300s, the imperial court and the shogunate were at war with each other. Yōdō's father, the emperor, was at the center of it, trying to restore the emperor's power, facing exile, the last emperor for centuries to challenge the samurai rule. When he died in 1339, her brother, who was only twelve years old, became emperor. There were victories on both sides and a great deal of backstabbing, and in the many decades of Yōdō's life entire families were destroyed, Kyoto was devastated, and the entire country's economy was brought close to ruin.

Yōdō wrote:

Heart unclouded, heart clouded;
Rising and falling are yet the same body.

the irresistible one

Eshun

(1362–approx. 1430)

To Eshun, the whole world was kindling—peasants rebelling against harsh conditions only to be tortured and executed, constant battles between samurai bands, a broken court, endless poverty and endless greed.

Eshun's older brother, Ryōan Emyō, was a well-known monk. He had been a disciple of Tsugen Jakurei's at Yōtakuji, and then founded Saijōji. Eshun never married, refusing to even consider it. When she was past thirty, she went to Saijōji and asked her brother to ordain her. He refused.

"If I ordained you or other women, the monks would be corrupted by your presence," he said. Eshun was a beautiful woman; he didn't have much faith in the men he trained.

"This life is only for the daijobu ones," he added. Daijobu means the same as ta-cheng-fu—heroic, noble, grand. Manly.

Eshun went home and cut off her hair. Then she picked up a hot poker from the kitchen fire and scarred her face in several places. She put on plain clothes and returned to the monastery to see her brother. When he saw her this way, he relented and allowed her to practice there.

Eshun was single-minded and strong, else she would have been married long before. She beat many of the monks in debates, sometimes humiliating them badly by the subtlety of her answers. But they couldn't keep from harassing her with their attentions. Even with her scarred face and bald head, even in plain monk's clothing, she was irresistible. The men couldn't control themselves around her, and several had to be expelled for their behavior.

Engakuji housed more than a thousand monks by then and had a fierce reputation. Many people feared going there because of stories about how badly visitors were treated. When a special congress was held at Engakuji, none of the monks from Saijōji were willing to go. Finally, her brother appointed Eshun as his representative. She was well known in Zen circles by then, and when the Engakuji monks heard she was coming, they decided to frighten her with a trick.

The day of the congress she climbed the long, wide steps and walked through the great gate. A monk jumped out from behind a rock, threw his robes open, and exposed himself, shouting, "My monk's thing is three feet long! How about taking it on?"

Eshun immediately threw open her nun's robes and answered, "This nun's thing has no bottom." All the monks watching from their hiding places were embarrassed and skulked away.

Even the abbot at Engakuji mistreated her. He invited her to his room for tea and then served it to her in his washing bowl. She merely handed the tea back to him, saying, "No, honored abbot, you must use your own bowl."

One young monk at Saijōji fell madly in love with Eshun and constantly sent her love letters, slipping them under her meditation cushion and into the sleeves of her robes. Finally she sent him a note saying that their meeting would have to be secret because they were under vows of celibacy. When she passed him in the hall that afternoon, she whispered, "I'll fix a time and place, and tell you." She passed quickly on before he could answer.

A few days later the entire community was gathered in the meditation hall for a Dharma talk. Eshun came in last, completely naked. All the monks watched her in stupefaction while she walked calmly down the center aisle until she reached her admirer.

"Well?" she asked, in a loud voice. "If you really love me, take me now! It's nothing to be ashamed of, is it?" He leaped from his seat, ashamed, and ran away from the monastery forever. After that, Eshun was mostly left alone.

When Eshun was old and getting close to death, she asked several monks to make a woodpile for a bonfire in her yard. To their shock, she then sat down in the center and set fire to it.

Her brother rushed out of his room and up to the edge of the flames, but they were too intense. Through the blinding hot light, he could see her sitting in perfect stillness.

"My sister!" he shouted. She turned her head slowly. The skin on her face and hands was beginning to bubble and split.

"Is it hot in there?" he said, and they both knew what he meant. She was going to a place where nothing is hot or cold.

"For one living in the Way," she answered, her voice just carrying over the crackle of flames and popping wood, "hot and cold are nothing to fear. There is no need to ask that question."

And then she burned to death, following her beauty into emptiness.

skin
Daitsū Bunchi
(1619–1697)

For centuries spasms of war crossed and split Japan. The Ōnin War began in 1467 and lasted for ten years, devastating Kyoto. One by one the provincial lords broke away, no loyalty left for either shogun or court. A few shipwrecked Portuguese sailors traded their guns for freedom in 1543, and soon the Japanese armorers couldn't make enough guns. The feudal lords built stone castles now. Then the Jesuit missionaries appeared, then Spanish sailors, and then the Dutch, each with seductive gifts: potatoes and corn, velvet and pumpkins, eyeglasses, tobacco. The shogunate collapsed in a series of coup d'états, the shoguns unable to withstand the growing power of their own vassals. Meanwhile, the peasants had nothing more to lose and formed armies, marauding in the countryside and attacking in the cities, until the country was in fragments. The emperor and court were impoverished and ignored.

A few powerful warlords, savage and charismatic, climbed over the rest to the top. With terror and intimidation, Oda Nobunaga slowly brought Japan back together. In 1571 he decided to finally break the huge Buddhist strongholds. He set fire to the woods of Mount Hiei and burned down the entire temple complex, more than three thousand buildings. Those who escaped the fire were killed by his soldiers—tens of thousands of people, entire families. Then he overwhelmed Mount Koya as well, and finally he smashed the peasant groups.

When Nobunaga was assassinated, his trusted general Toyotomi Hideyoshi took over. Hideyoshi was sophisticated: he rebuilt the temples and supported the arts, helping to fashion a kind of military monarchy. To pay for it he taxed villages at half their crop, and the punishment for evasion was the death of everyone in the village. He destroyed one lord's family and cowed the other lords into a vow of obedience. He was eventually made regent and as the government's representative began the "sword hunt" to forcibly disarm the public, collecting every weapon that could be found. When Hideyoshi decided to disinherit his nephew, it was by ordering his ritual suicide and the torture and public execution of his wife and children. When aristocrats began wearing Christian symbols as fashion, the missionaries were warned off, and when they didn't leave, twenty-six Christians were tortured and executed in Kyoto.

After Hideyoshi died, Tokugawa Ieyasu became the most powerful man in the country, the first in the line of Tokugawa shoguns. The provincial lords served at the shogun's pleasure now, their families held hostage. An edict was issued dividing the country into four permanent classes. Samurai had to stay samurai and could not return to their villages. Peasants could follow no profession but farming, craftsmen could ply only the craft they already knew, and merchants, the lowest of all, could do nothing but buy and sell. The temples were strictly supervised, and all citizens had to register at a Buddhist temple.

In the early 1600s foreign trade was restricted to two ports. Another 120 missionaries and converts were executed and the missionaries expelled—followed by the Spaniards and the Portuguese. Then Japan closed its doors.

There was a kind of suffocating quiet at last.

Princess Ume no Miya was Emperor Gomizuno'o's first child, by a consort named Yotsutsuji Yotsuko. When arrangements were made for Gomizuno'o to marry Kazuko, the thirteen-year-old daughter of the shogun, his romantic dalliances almost ended things. It was an important match to the weak court; the wedding would unify the court and shogunate literally. Ume, a stark, intense, square-faced girl of frail health who rarely smiled, and her mother had no place in these plans. They retired to their own quarters.

When she was herself thirteen, Ume was married to her first cousin, Takatsugasa Norihira, who was ten years older than she and a court attendant. She had no taste for married life, and after three years she left her husband and returned to the palace. By this time she and the empress, known as Tōfukumon'in, were more contemporaries than rivals and became friends. Both the emperor and empress were devout Buddhists, and Ume began to study with her father's Zen teacher.

The aristocracy was gradually abandoning Buddhism for a Confucian revival—a return to reverence for history and education, propriety and morals, to concern with the everyday world instead of a mystical one. It was also a return to very old beliefs dividing the culture and country into separate realms: high and low, inferior and superior, male and female. A woman's place was the family and the home, not the world outside, not the spiritual world, with the exception of imperial nuns.

Because imperial nuns had been well educated in court, these convents became sanctuaries of art and poetry, places of beauty and exquisite craft called the "nuns' palaces." Each newly ordained woman brought with her many precious things, like a dowry—exquisite kimonos, decorated screens, pale-green vases of celadon, finely painted plates, and elaborate lacquer boxes and jewelry and toys and books. The nuns painted, did embroidery, played games, copied sutras, and enjoyed the illicit foreign import called tobacco, an excellent stimulant.

When Ume was a young woman, the tentative military peace bound the country more closely. Japanese people were prohibited from leaving the country, and foreigners were thrown out. When the last—the pesky Portuguese—were expelled, Japan was officially sakoku—"the closed country." That same year, 1638, her mother died.

In 1640, when she was twenty-two, Ume was ordained and went to a hermitage in Kyoto called Enshōji. She was genuinely devoted to the Dharma by then and studied with a Rinzai teacher named Isshi Bunshu. Isshi gave her the same *bun* as in his own name, which means "literary, " combined with *chi*, "wisdom," and called her Daitsu Bunchi. Isshi taught her many things and gave her a small scroll on which he had written a few lines in his own blood.

"The discourses on the *Wisdom Sutras* tell us to do this," he told her. "They say that if one truly loves the Dharma, one should use one's own skin as paper, one's own bones for a brush, and one's own blood for ink." He gazed at her a moment, measuring. "The blood should be mixed with glue from boiled skin and bones," he added, "if you can get some." She found this last more disquieting than the needle.

"Here," he demonstrated, showing her the tiny scars all along his ear. "This is the best place to prick."

When Isshi Bunshu died six years after her ordination, Bunchi began to study esoteric practices with Shingon priests. She had a dream in which a voice told her that she would only find peace if she lived nearer the Shinto shrines of Kasuga, Hachiman, and Ise, in the country south of Kyoto.

One of her uncles, an imperial prince, had become a priest, and he helped her obtain land near Hashima, far enough from Nara to be away from the constant distractions and duties of court. She was a mature nun now. Her friend the empress gently pressed upon the shogun Ietsuna until he also donated enough land to support a shogun's vassal, enough to ensure the new temple's future, and the empress gave some of her own money. The buildings were eventually moved to Yamamura, further south, near a friend she'd known since her days with Isshi, a priest named Jōin. The new temple was also called Enshōji, and she moved in 1669.

Here Bunchi found herself among farmers and peasants in a country of rice fields and hills and storms from the sea. Extended families lived in houses with steep, peaked straw-thatch roofs and slept on futons with wooden block pillows. The farmer class was only allowed to wear hemp and cotton clothing, and since cotton was a hard crop to raise, they used little of it. They made rain coats and hats of straw and wore wooden shoes, and their lives were rough and often short.

Families grew many crops to sell: millet and buckwheat, sweet potatoes, tobacco, plums, oranges, apricots, grapes, and persimmons, giant daikon radishes and lotus roots, indigo for dye, and several kinds of beans. Most crops were fertilized with human sewage collected daily by hand from home latrines and carried in buckets to the fields, where it was diluted with water. They ate a much more spare diet than they raised and gathered wild mushrooms and forest greens as supplement.

Rice was the staple; it was central, it was constant, it was inescapable. Farmers sprouted the seedlings in a nursery while the fields were being plowed and then flooded through elaborate treadmills and long irrigation systems. Then the rice was planted by groups of young women in bright clothes, bent endlessly at the waist and walking backwards. They planted five or six strands of new rice at a time, thrusting the small bunch into the mud. Bunchi stood on a bank and watched under a gray spring sky, listening to their field songs, the rhythms designed to keep their steps even so the rows would be straight.

Enshōji was a nuns' palace of a kind, but it was also small and remote, and she kept the training there strict and plain. There was little fanciness, even after other educated women came to share it with her, leaving the rich and sickening luxuries of the city. Every day Bunchi made offerings to the Kasuga Shrine, a Shinto spirit of great power, and asked her disciples to do the same. They spent their days in devotion.

In the hidden worlds of women, unseen behind screens and guards, words aren't always enough. No one else is listening, and anyone who is has heard it all before. The urge to speak must find a way out; it slips through like rain finding the cracks in the screens. The women learned to speak with their bodies, with their hands and eyes, with their imaginations and dreams.

Bunchi felt the death of luxury in her, the death of the meaning of luxury, and its purpose. It was replaced by a simplicity, like a spreading lake slowly covering the land. She felt the suffering of those around her all at once, like a wound in her chest, acute and clear. For months she walked around bent over at the waist, huddled around it as though stemming blood. And then she began to walk with it, and then to dance. She walked between the fields, along the roads, watching the life of the people who gave their lives to the land, and became intimate with them, and with the suffering. It lightened and at the same time grew in her body, which had never been strong or at ease. All beings are Buddha Nature, she believed, and all bodies are as empty as the breath, rising and falling away. But all she had was the body and its dying, and she would make art of it. She began to fill her quiet hours with art, with the effort to say somehow, with or without words, this truth she felt.

Tōfukumon'in, who had become a great Buddhist patron, presented a rubbing of a Kannon image to the temple: Kannon holding a willow branch, a sign of luck and nobility, in her right hand, draping it into her open left palm. Bunchi copied the rubbing in ink on silk again and again in the long evenings. She worked until there were blisters on her fingers from the brush. One winter she spent making a detailed kami shrine with a tiny deer lying calmly below wisteria, silhouetted behind silk drapes; her eyes watered with the struggle to place each tiny leaf exactly. She copied Hakuin's scrolls and others, trying to find her own words, her own pictures, her own scroll.

Outside, the people pounded drums and bent over, moving through the fields, through the sun and the hard frosts, and she heard everything in her small room of three tatamis where she lived like a deer nestled in grass, in the scent of the grassy mats fading from green to yellow, the smells of toilets and cooking and incense leaking through with the sounds of lovemaking and resentment on the road nearby.

Bunchi had learned embroidery a long time before, when she was so young she couldn't remember not knowing it. Another season, she worked entirely in thread, embroidering Chinese characters in gold and purple, in satin stitch on red silk, then stretched the inscription carefully over a wooden frame.

When her father, the emperor, became ill, she traveled to Kyoto to stay for a time, and every week she collected his fingernail cuttings. When he died in 1689, she entered the forty-nine-day period of mourning. She used it to make a memorial shrine to him, with a wooden plaque inside a small gold lined case with double doors. With his trimmed fingernails, she carefully spelled out *Namu Amida Butsu* and the names of the bodhisattvas Dai Seishi Bosatsu and Kanzeon Bosatsu. After returning home to the country, she made a clay statue of the emperor wearing Buddhist robes and seated in meditation, using his own hair for the beard and eyebrows.

It wasn't enough. She was surrounded by endless labor—the labor of being alive, the inescapable labor of rice, which is the labor of food, of life. She watched the weeks of pulling weeds, the worries over the September typhoons, the relief when the weather cleared—and the farmer in his little boat at dawn, the hardness and the beauty of the hardness, the losses, the births, working all their lives, working to death, depending on the gods, who didn't seem to listen very often. She had begun to give away her own life, at first in small increments and then in bigger ones. How could she watch and not do everything she could do, which wasn't much after all? She would give it away until there was nothing else left to give.

One night she pricked her ear and wrote a line of the *Heart Sutra* with the blood. Again and then again, first pricking one ear, then the other, until they were scarred over. Then she discovered how easily she could get droplets from the ends of her fingers. When they began to thicken into calluses and hamper her writing, she turned to her toes.

Still not enough. A child carrying water to the workers on a blazing summer day fell into the rice fields and drowned. She heard the wailing of the mother who had no hope of anything but this day, this life, this loss. As she sat in her grassy cell, Bunchi took up a carving knife used for making shrines and sliced a portion of skin off her forearm. It was slow work to cut just beneath the first layers and the thin fat without injuring the muscles she needed for the writing itself. A few days later, when the skin had dried and begun to yellow, she pricked her fourth toe on the right and squeezed droplets of blood onto her ink stone and used the skin as paper. On it she wrote a few dozen characters of the *Kai-kanromon Sutra,* chanted for the dead: "If you want to know the buddhas of the past, present, and future, you must see that the world of phenomena is born from the mind."

A few weeks later, when her left arm had begun to heal, she took up the knife and cut a larger piece of skin from her thigh. This time it bled badly, and she collected a good bit in a bowl before binding the wound tightly. By then it was dusk, and she could hear the crickets beginning to chirp and the call of men to their homes as they slowly returned from work. She reached over to light the lamp so she could write, and suddenly stopped. Carefully, she opened the lantern and poured a little oil into her palm. Lighting this, burning her body with the light, with her love, she began to write.

firewood

Ryōnen Gensō

(1646–1711)

Once again Kyoto was a great city, one of the three great cities of Japan. Osaka was the center of commerce and trade. Edo, once a small fishing settlement near marshlands, was the capital, a place of castles, politics, and theater. Kyoto was the oldest, home of the imperial court, a center of fashion and luxury and art. Many people in Japan could read and write, and schools had spread throughout the country. Foreigners were forbidden, but a few intelligent people realized there was knowledge in the outside world they might put to use. The children of the aristocracy had access to "Dutch" schools, carefully controlled arenas for teaching foreign subjects like European medicine, science, and economics.

Fusa was born into two noble families near the gates of the imperial temple, Sen'yu-ji, in eastern Kyoto. Her father, Tamehisa, was from the Katsurayama clan, famous for its warriors. He was an art expert known for his skill in calligraphy and tea, and a student of Rinzai Zen. Fusa's mother was of the Konoe family and had been lady-in-waiting to Empress Tōfukomon'in.

Fusa's grandmother had been in the imperial court as well, wet nurse to the Emperor Gomizuno'o. The entire imperial family knew Fusa, so when the Empress Tōfukomon'in's granddaughter, Yoshi, was orphaned, it was easy for the empress to invite Fusa to enter court life as the child's companion. Fusa was seven and Yoshi was nine, and they had similar temperaments. Together, Fusa and Yoshi studied art and poetry of different traditions, Confucianism and the Chinese classics, calligraphy and music. Fusa loved Yoshi but was interested in Buddhism more than anything else. From the time she was young, she told people that she wanted to be a nun.

Both of her younger brothers had been ordained as small children. Daizui Genki had become a Rinzai student, and Umpō Genchu eventually entered the new sect called Ōbaku, a new form of Zen imported from China. The school was Chinese in its customs, and Chinese in its aesthetic. The services were chanted in Chinese, and even the head temple, Mampuku-ji, was named after a mountain in China. It combined traditional koan study with the nembutsu, repeating the name of Amida Buddha, and other esoteric practices. Great stress was placed on monastic rules. Ōbaku had vitality; it was exotic and serious, and several of its leading teachers were extraordinarily accomplished in calligraphy and ink painting. Ōbaku had brought new types of Chinese medicine to Japan, including a treatment for the deadly smallpox.

Fusa quizzed her brothers whenever they were near, harrying them for detail and direction. They loved their sister, with her delicate features and quick mind, and cheerfully answered her questions. But they didn't take her too seriously and after a while would send her on her way to play with Yoshi.

When they were young women, Yoshi married, and so did Fusa. She had been a lovely child; she grew up to be a beautiful woman. Her face was finely sculpted, her skin pale and clear, her black eyes large and penetrating. Her father arranged an alliance with Matsuda Bansui, a doctor and Confucian scholar who was sixteen years older than she was. Matsuda had several children by his mistresses already. Fusa agreed to the marriage on one stark condition. She would produce an heir to please her father and mother and the world, and then Matsuda would let her go.

Fusa and Matsuda had a male child, and when Fusa was twenty-six years old, she called in their contract. First she looked around and carefully chose a new companion for her husband, another woman of aristocratic family and good education. When she was sure the arrangement was settled, she left her husband. Yoshi had left hers as well, and Fusa became her court companion again.

When Fusa's mother died, the two women were even more like each other. They were motherless, but contented in each other's company, in their studies and art. Fusa, who had become a skilled calligrapher and poet, spent many hours each day composing Buddhist poems and recording them in a style all her own. Her hand was confident and rhythmic, with rich, strong strokes balancing dark and light in a way that seemed completely natural. She was sad, she was happy. She lived with her dearest friend and every day was in the presence of her empress, but she longed for something else at times.

One fine spring day Yoshi started to cough, and before Fusa could imagine the possibility, before she could allow herself to dream of it, Yoshi died. She was thirty-three.

Fusa had long known impermanence—how could one not know this in their world? She saw the world coalesce and collapse in a thousand ways every year; change and loss were a part of life. But when Yoshi died, Fusa had a profound experience, a realization of utter evanescence and of how little time there was to understand this thing.

The emperor's daughter, a princess Fusa had known since she was a small child, had become abbot of Hōkyō-ji, a Rinzai monastery. Her Buddhist name was Richū, and she was devoted to the memory of Mugai Nyodai, the widow of a samurai who had founded the entire system of women's Rinzai temples. When the beloved temple of Keiaji burned down, what remained of its treasures was taken to Hōkyō-ji under Richū's care.

Fusa had said all her life that she wanted to be a nun, and now there was nothing in the way. She had no duty, no family needs, no contracts, no responsibility, no love, no companions. It was natural that she would turn to Richū and the long tradition of imperial nuns. In 1672 Richū ordained Fusa and gave her the name Ryōnen Gensō, which means "to realize clearly."

Two years later, while Ryōnen and the former princess lived behind the walls without their hair, the empress died. They mourned her deeply, this woman who had married the emperor as a young girl and become a great patron of the temples and the Dharma. She was Ryōnen's last connection to the court, to the world of her birth, to her former life. Ryōnen wanted something she couldn't get from Richū. In 1678, when she was thirty-four, she left for Edo.

The road from Kyoto to Edo was called the Tōkaidō, and it was never quiet, never still. Pilgrims, couriers, traveling musicians, priests, merchants, and soldiers passed between the cities without cease. Travel along the road was pleasant in many ways. It was just wide enough for two horses to pass, and rows of trees lined many of its miles—cedars and pines planted partly to give travelers shelter and partly to make sure they stayed on the road where they belonged. When the road came to a river, there were ferries and sometimes porters who would carry people across.

In the small towns and way stations along the way, there were inns and bathhouses and restaurants, and most were social places, filled with entertainment. The road was heavily secured, and the slow, steady pace of travel kept the shogunate happy. There were many checkpoints. At each one Ryōnen had to show her pass, her letter of identification, and the letter of authorization to travel required for women. Hairstyles were important as part of one's identity papers; hers distinguished her as ama, a nun, a category separate from laywomen, attendants, religious pilgrims, and so on.

Most people traveled, like Ryōnen, on foot. Powerful people rode in chairs carried by men who ran in a stiff-legged gait, a method that was faster, higher in status, and very uncomfortable. Ox-drawn carriages were reserved for the imperial family. There were so few wheels used that the roads had no ruts. Express messengers could get from Edo to Kyoto in ten days. They sometimes traveled with an escort who carried a lantern bearing the word goyō, "official business," allowing them priority at all ferries and passages.

The lords who owned and managed the land of the provinces were not allowed to travel freely by the shogunate anymore. They were too widely spread out, too easily out of control. So the government required them to carry passes and reservations and to leave their wives under guard in Edo when they went home to the provinces. But when they traveled, they often did so with hundreds of servants and vassals, many horses, beautiful lacquer palanquins, and flags and banners and halberds. At each village the headman had to make sure the road was swept and flattened or sanded out and that enough porters and supplies were available, including refreshments.

The trip was fascinating to Ryōnen, but she was anxious to be done with it. After nineteen days of walking, she arrived in Edo, with its million people, its crowded and noisy streets, its humid, smelly summer air.

Without waiting even a day, Ryōnen went to Kōfuku-ji, the temple of the Ōbaku priest Tetsugyū Dōki. Her brother was Ōbaku, a sect that revered calligraphy and art and honored discipline, ritual, and charity. Dōki was the highest-ranking Ōbaku priest in Edo. He was active and well known, helped with many projects for the poor, and had hundreds of students. Ryōnen knocked on the gate with every expectation of being accepted. When a monk came to see what she wanted, she asked to be admitted; he led her to the abbot.

"I wish to study here with you," she said, head bowed modestly, letting him see only the fine stubble on her scalp.

But he was already shaking his head. "We can't have that," he said. "We can't have women here. The young monks would not be able to control themselves. They would be distracted from their studies." He signaled his attendant. "Have some tea before you go."

She left right away, leaving the tea behind, and walked to Daikyūan, the hermitage of Hakuō Dōtai, another Ōbaku master. There was no gate, and no monk to answer one if there had been.

"I would like to study here with you," she told Hakuō in her simple way.

He looked at her for a long time, then said, "I see without a doubt how sincere you are. I see how much you want this. But think of me. You're a beautiful woman. If you stayed here, people would gossip about us. It would hurt my reputation, and my students might not understand."

Ryōnen bowed graciously and left. Hakuō was a little sorry to see her go; he felt there was something special about her, a force, something his other students didn't have.

She found her way to an inn and rented a room. The servant girl came and laid out the futon and made a fire in the brazier under the low table so Ryōnen could warm her feet while she had tea. After the girl left, she pulled the table away and stirred the coals with the poker. She was careful with her hands; she needed her fingers for writing, for devotion, for calligraphy, for turning the pages of the sutras. But she didn't need her face, and so she picked up a coal in the tongs and laid it on her skin.

She was alone, and the pain was breathtaking; it was like being plunged into a pool of ice. With her eyes closed, hand shaking, she moved the coal from her cheek after a moment and placed it on her forehead, then her chin, her nose, her other cheek. She was trembling all over, searing herself, wrapped in the smoky scent of cooking skin. In her mind, she could see a bodhisattva sitting in flames. Her face was disappearing, like her mother disappeared, her empress, her dearest friend, her dream of studying the Dharma. She did this difficult thing, this very difficult thing, and her pain turned to smoke and rose and disappeared too. Her ignorance would disappear, she knew. Her need would vanish, her sorrow evaporate and vanish, because all is change, all is movement, all is nothing, because this shifting of ephemeral form itself is ceaselessness, this itself is eternity. She was gone.

Some time later, when she awakened to the room again, her face throbbing and wet, she quietly opened her bag and pulled out the pens and scroll she carried. It had taken her many years to learn to mix ink correctly, and she did it now without hardly a thought, even though her entire body was shaking.

First Ryōnen wrote in formal Chinese, the language of the court.

When I was a girl, we played in court, burning incense.
Now I burn my face, to study Zen.
Each season flows easily into the other, and
I do not know who writes this in a world of change.

Then she took a different brush and wrote in the familiar Japanese, the language of home.

This is the living world,
but my face has been burned away.

I would be a sorry thing if I didn't know
it is the firewood that burns up my delusion.

She put on her outdoor clothing again and walked back to Hakūo's temple, ignoring the cries and whispers that followed her along the street. She came to his room and opened the door. "I would like to study here with you," she told him in her simple way, once again, while blood-tinged fluid dripped off her face.

He could not speak for quite some time. Then he agreed, and found her a place to sleep. She stayed four years. They took tea together every day, but she was careful not to compromise him and was always decorous and polite around his other students.

Ryōnen became Hakūo's leading disciple. The poems she'd written about burning her face became well known. She made many copies as gifts, in her thick, powerful calligraphy, diagonal lines barely bringing each character to the next, flowing from one stroke of the brush into the next stroke, inevitably. Sometimes she dipped her brush between each character, sometimes after two or even four characters, and so every character was unique. The eye couldn't predict the heaviness to come, the lightness to follow, and the effect was entrancing, satisfying, new.

The burning of her face became a tale told in taverns and salons. A woodblock of the scene, showing a shocked servant girl rushing to stop Ryōnen's act, was published in pamphlets and books of the time, including the *Guide to Famous Places in Edo.*[8] Her poems were collected in a book called *Wakamurasaki* (*Light Purple*), and her calligraphy has been reproduced many times, in many books.

Just before he died in 1682, Hakūo certified her enlightenment. After his death, she managed the little temple, concentrating on good deeds, like building bridges and making a school for local children. Ryōnen worked for years to get imperial permission to build a new temple in Hakūo's honor. At this time it was very hard to start a new Buddhist temple; all she could hope for was permission to restore an abandoned one. After eleven years of applications, in 1693 she was given permission to use a ruined temple called Renjōin, just outside the city limits of Edo. When it was finally rebuilt, she named it Taiunji—Serene Cloud

Temple—and called Hakūo the founder and herself the second abbot.

Tetsugyū Dōki, who had refused to allow her entrance to his monastery, visited her there and wrote a poem in her honor.

Toward the end of her life she wrote a poem called "Seeking the Beauty of the Spring Moon, After the Style of an Autumn Poem":

As I grow old, I tend to be melancholy when the seasons pass.
But I live on, and see the flowers fall.
Leaving, I know it is hard to know when we meet again,
So I must be comforted by travel, facing the end of spring.

Ryōnen was famous by then, but in a way, she always had been. She had been privileged even among the privileged, beautiful even amid beauty. It hadn't given her satisfaction, and it hadn't saved her from pain. Finally, she found her freedom. Love gone, face gone, alone in a rough, hard city amid the clang of constant building and the shouts of constant change, she was free. She found joy in the great blessing of a cool breeze, the crunch of stones under foot, a giant bee in fragrant flowers, a night-black butterfly darting by, the trickle of water, the incense lightly rising above the white cloister walls.

In 1711, just before she died, she wrote this poem.

I am sixty-six years old, it is autumn, I have lived a long life.
Moonlight shines strongly on my face.
We don't need to discuss the koans.
Just listen to the wind in the cedars outside.

After she died, Taiunji was taken over by men and gradually dwindled away into disrepair. Its treasures were scattered about. A hundred years after she died, in the great Edo fire of 1811, it was destroyed, along with her diary, many of her poems and paintings, and portraits of her. Everything burned.

Her grave was relocated to Tetsugyū's former temple. She was admitted at last, completely firewood.

the lonely one

Teijitsu

(1700s)

The buildings of Eiheiji lay between towering trees, connected to each other by covered walkways. On the hillside below where the trees were thinner, a village grew, with carpenters and sake brewers, coopers and roofers, blacksmiths and lacquer makers, tilers and paper makers, pastry cooks and silk dyers. Each was born into a profession and a position and lived in it and died in it, serving the monastery and each other. They did fine work; in the airless peace of the Tokugawa years, the crafts and arts of Japan were refined, perfected, and finally became transcendent.

After Dōgen's death, his temple of eternal peace had been split by conflict, dissent, and arguments over its direction and purpose. For generations the abbots of Eiheiji lacked clear support from their own monks, who would retire and then return when the power shifted, start new temples, change ways, then return to Dōgen's way again. Caught between fire and warlords, Eiheiji declined. Ultimately five different lines of Zen were born from his single one. Sōtō Zen in Japan was much more the product of Keizan's line at Sojiji, with its many subtemples, than of the far fewer subtemples belonging to the source, Eiheiji. Eventually, Eiheiji and Sojiji were officially declared to be equal head temples, together the head of all other Sōtō temples, but their leaders didn't stop jockeying for position, shoving each other aside like players intent on winning.

Women remained outside such troubles. After Dōgen's time, after the explosion of masterful women in his generation and for generations afterward, after his sermons of oneness and equality, the nuns were shut out again. It was as though a spring blossom, full in summer, had died, locked up, frozen. Women were forbidden to practice at Eiheiji and allowed to enter only at certain times. They couldn't teach independently anymore, ordain their own students, or live inside the main temples, even if the temples were empty. They were forbidden to lead important ceremonies like funerals, a major source of income for priests. Many nuns washed monks' robes for their meals and themselves wore only the black robes of a novice their entire lives. Their voices stopped calling, stopped talking, and finally even stopped whispering, until nuns disappeared from the records, like ghosts.

In the early 1700s, under a disciple of the Eiheiji abbot Shōten Sokuchi, a nunnery called Hakujuan was built in Daiku village, a few miles from Eiheiji. Eventually it was moved to the outskirts of the temple, but for a long time it was far enough from the great monastery and its bustling village that many people didn't even know it was there. The nuns sometimes hosted guests who were traveling to the monastery, but for the most part they simply lived their lives in a bare quietude in the mountains. It was a plain wooden temple without decoration or luxury.

Shōten was the first official head of Hakujuan, and Teijitsu was its second. It is said she was a disciple of Menzan Zuihō. She was a perfectly ordinary woman, born with a bad hip into anonymity, living in anonymity, dying eventually in the same anonymous realm.

Teijitsu was often in pain, and she found sitting on the floor difficult—though sitting on the floor was what she had done all her life. Her world was almost completely unadorned, without softness or comforts. It was ache, cramp, and spasm; it was humid, and it was cold; it was hungry sometimes; it was dull; it was hard. She made up poultices in the evenings and rose earlier than the other nuns so she could stumble away her morning stiffness alone.

The fact is that ordinary life for ordinary people usually is hard. Teijitsu, like a million million people, made of her life what she could, where she found herself. It was only after many years of practice and devotion that her heart began to grow and fill with it. She hated her life at times—the long winter nights were cold, so cold, cold beyond comment, and she would lie in the dark all through them, waiting for the throb in her hip to soften enough for her to sleep. The long summer days were sticky and damp and hummed with biting insects. Sometimes she had to part curtains of self-pity and resentment just to rise from her bed, but she didn't tell anyone, she didn't let it show. She wanted to be warm, just simply warm—not cold, not hot—and be warm in a soft bed, well rested, without pain, and this couldn't be.

With time, with the repetition of these waves of emotion like breaking seas, she began to know them for what they were. She watched the paper maker, his hands chafed and sore from the hours of wet rolling, hours that became days and months and years. She saw the blacksmith, broad across his bare back, swinging, swinging, endlessly swinging his hammer, without choice. Teijitsu began to see that everyone was bound up in the small tight places of their days, that these dark spaces of the human realm are tunnels through which each person must crawl alone. The monks in the beautiful buildings above her, nestled in the trees, seen and honored and served, must have had the same dark places. She crawled through the small dark places because there was nothing else to do.

Sometimes the quiet of Hakujuan, which was one of its only virtues, was broken by the noise of guests, and often they were given to complaint—whining about conditions, gossiping about the temples and their struggles, being angry in a world designed to cure anger. She would listen, but as the years passed she found herself strangely dreaming sometimes. The waves of feeling would roll past, and she could feel life rising and falling like the deck of a ship—as though her own body were rolling through the waves of time. Arising, abiding, and falling away—this is all the Blessed One taught. *This is all it is,* she thought, *this is it.* All things arise, abide, and fall away, and we suffer only because we hold to what we are bound to lose. Pain is a given, but suffering—that we make. *This is all he taught,* she reminded herself, walking through the rooms of the nunnery as though rowing a raft through the tide—up, down, up again.

This is all he taught, she thought, until it was a mantra, until it was breath: everything rises and falls away, the trees and her hip, the way the sun fell across her lap in a moment of repose, the bit of sweet fruit she loved for supper—all would disappear. The trees would die, the buildings would burn, the people would die, the kingdom itself would rise and fade like the endless line of emperors and lords. The great rivers pouring off the snowy peaks would rise and fall from spring to autumn. For all she knew, the sky itself simply arose each morning with the sun and died in the twilight with the day—everything, her ignorance, her understanding, her enlightenment, her loneliness, her Buddha Nature, would arise and abide and fall away.

Standing on the small porch of Hakujuan, she saw the shadow of a little wren cross the footpath, followed by the shadow of a hungry crow, and she saw that the little wren arose, abided, and fell away. And then she saw that arising arose, abided, and fell away—and that abiding arose, abided, and fell away—and that falling away arose, abided, and fell away. She saw that knowing this arose, abided, and fell away. Then she knew there was nothing more than this, no ground, nothing to lean on stronger than the cane she held, nothing to lean upon at all, and no one leaning, and she opened the clenched fist in her mind and let go and fell into the midst of everything.

the worker

Ohashi

(1700s)

Most people lived their lives on the edge of poverty—sometimes above, sometimes below. One paid taxes whether the crops grew or not, and moneylenders charged high interest. Almost anyone could fall on hard times and end up in unmanageable debt. When food was scarce, women resorted to abortion, which was dangerous, and sometimes, with regret, they "thinned out" the newborn girls, who would never be the strong workers their brothers might become. There were laws against "body selling," but it was inevitable. To make it through the worst years, people indentured themselves, their wives, or their children.

Ohashi's father was a samurai. When his lord died, he lost his job. The market for unemployed samurais wasn't strong, and besides, he hadn't been a very good samurai in the first place. He took to drinking, and the family began to starve.

Ohashi, the eldest and a pretty girl, quickly saw the path ahead of her. One of the more lucrative practices for many householders was to place the wife or a daughter in a brothel for a time. Such arrangements usually lasted only a few years, and she knew several women who had worked as prostitutes for a while. They returned home experienced and worldly women, debts paid, and often as not with several marriage proposals. When she was fifteen, Ohashi signed a contract with a madam in a nearby village and moved into the rooms over the tavern. She found the work to be both tedious and unpleasant a good part of the time. That it was less tedious than working the rice fields and more pleasant than laboring in a silk factory was one of her only consolations; the other was that it wouldn't last for long.

After a few years, her father was still out of work, and still drinking. Her mother became ill, and Ohashi's younger brothers and sisters did their best to find food and keep the family from being evicted. Only Ohashi had regular income. She began to despair of her future, wondering if she would ever be able to quit and go home to a different kind of life.

One day she was mulling this over with one of her regular customers, a monk from a nearby temple.

"You can find the Buddha in every circumstance," he murmured, drawing circles around her small breast with his finger. "Any circumstance," he added, pausing for a moment, distracted. "Hmmm."

"How?" she asked, pulling up his head, insistent. "How do I find the Buddha here?"

"Just do what you are doing with complete attention," he said, as though it was obvious, and then climbed back on her again.

After that, Ohashi meditated vigilantly every day.

For work she wore her hair in an elaborate bun and painted her skin white and her lips dark red. But in her off hours she wore the plain kimonos of the working class and sat in the tavern, playing dice games and talking to the other customers.

There she met another monk, a strange man named Hakuin who told her his own complicated story over tubs of rice beer. He seemed like a regular fellow in many ways, rough and easy in his manners in spite of poor health. He spoke to men and women, people of high and low birth, the same way. He didn't visit the girls upstairs, preferring to talk and joke with the tavern-goers instead. Ohashi didn't know much about Buddhism or Zen or koans, but she understood Hakuin when he talked about trying to find meaning in the world.

Hakuin came and went in his travels. He was determined to teach Zen to laypeople—"all *kinds* of people!" he announced one night, swirling in cheerful excitement in the center of the tavern—and he was happy to teach her when she asked. One night he recited the Emmei jikku Kannon gyō and suggested that she employ it now and then when her faith waned.

"Remember," he said, pointing emphatically, "you only need three things. You need great faith. You need great doubt. You need great determination!" He jumped up. "And we need more beer!"

She liked him, missed him when he was gone, made sure to keep him company when he appeared. One evening after a long week—a party of samurai had been visiting and kept the girls working double shifts—Ohashi began to cry and told Hakuin that she didn't know how long she could keep doing this work. She was grateful for the job, but it wasn't the work she wanted to be doing. She missed her brothers and sisters; she felt unfulfilled. She was bored at times; she was tired; she found the customers dull. More and more, it was a strain to smile and bow in welcome when they arrived. Her duty to her family was unavoidable, but she had begun to fear growing old in the room above the tavern.

She began to cry, telling Hakuin all this.

"I want to study Zen!" she finally wailed at last.

When her tears were spent, Hakuin said, "What else are you going to do?" And Ohashi cried some more then.

Finally, he patted her hand and said a little more.

"You must never say that the world or business keeps you away from studying Zen. Don't say that daily life is too pressured or confusing for meditation. Just concentrate in the midst of things, right in the middle of all your worries and fears."

He could see she didn't believe this was possible, but Hakuin had found for himself it was one of the best ways to understanding—painful, but efficient. He had many women as students, formally and otherwise, and knew the constriction of their lives in the world.

"Dear, you can find stillness anywhere, and it's best to find it in noise and action. Then it's real, then you know it utterly. Koans and sitting meditation are meaningless without work. So just do your work. Eventually, you will just do what you are doing and not know the difference between meditation and anything else.

"Ask yourself, every day, who is it that does this work?"

After that conversation, Ohashi's attitude improved. The madam noticed, the other girls noticed, and the customers noticed as well. That her serenity made her even more popular became a small joke to her. She would practice as a slave or prisoner practiced, as a baby practiced, as the working ox out in the field practiced. What else was she going to do? Things were constrained; life was constrainment, bound by bodies and time and forces far out of reach. So it would be.

Ohashi was not a fearful person, but she had always been terrified of thunder. One summer night during a violent storm she made herself sit on the veranda in the dark. Such challenges broke the monotony of her days. All around her the building shook with the pounding of the clouds, and the rain slashed sideways, soaking her kimono against her skin. Suddenly a bolt of lightning struck the ground a few feet away, and she collapsed, unconscious.

When she awakened a few minutes later, the darkness seemed to glow, the veranda beneath her cheek felt like velvet, and the barriers in her mind had disappeared.

A few weeks later Hakuin returned, and before he left he gave her a scroll with a verse certifying her awakening.

One story about Ohashi tells us that one of her richest patrons, who was a student of Hakuin himself, eventually ransomed her from the madam and married her. Another says that she became a nun with her husband's permission. In either case, Ohashi was a woman with few choices who learned to make a free choice every day. Who did her work? Who awakened in the dark, wet and new?

AFTERWORD
THE NEW ANCESTORS

In a way, we do all the wrong things with our ancestors. We elevate them for the wrong reasons—because they were stronger than we think we are, more accomplished, more subtle and expressive of a truth we intuit more than understand. We elevate specific people from our past because they are the ones who stand out—the ones known by emperors, the ones who attracted famous students. We do this with men and with women both, in part because these are simply the people whose lives are recorded, whose names we still recall today.

What is it that we should honor in other persons? Part of it is any person's ability, any man, any woman, to step outside the prison of their form. That means people who can pass outside the realm of layperson and monk, male or female, at least for a time—those who can express the Dharma in such a way that they become it, that their lives are it. Such people are often forgotten for this very reason—they pass through the world very quietly, not disturbing things or leaving a trace.

To separate ourselves from each other in *any* way is delusion—but how many of us can transcend this tendency? All of us for a moment or two; a few of us for longer. Those who can—those few—they are the real heroes. What I want to honor and remember in other people is their ability to inhabit all forms with all forms, to be whatever is needed, to be whatever they are.

Still, we feel a deep desire to express honor and respect, and so we choose particular people whose names have survived, whose stories have become archetypes and lessons, and we recite them with gratitude. When I recite this list of names, my traditional list of ancestors, or a list any other person considers worthy of respect, I try to remember that it is only a drop representing an ocean. And that, as the entire ocean is contained in a single drop, our lineages contain us all.

After the Meiji Restoration in the middle of the nineteenth century, Japan rapidly became a technologically modern country while retaining its deeply embedded culture, arts, and beliefs. Buddhism also went through rapid change after that time. The few women described briefly here were instrumental in reopening Zen Buddhism in Japan to women, in helping to restore the nuns' training temples and educational system, and in bringing Buddhism to the West, and the West to Japanese Buddhism. Because the lives of these women are well documented—some of them are still remembered today by living people—I've chosen not to make stories but simply to share a few highlights. Many books are available for more details; among others, I recommend the books by Paula Arai, Sandy Boucher, Marianne Dresser, and Lenore Friedman listed in the bibliography. Sallie King discusses Nagasawa Sozen in *Buddhism in Practice,* edited by Donald Lopez.

Tenmyō Jōrin
(late 1800s to 1900s)

When the military government began to dissolve in the mid-1800s, it was common practice for Buddhist temples to run schools. Almost half of all men were literate, but only 15 percent of women were. Nuns were strictly limited in their practice. They had no official training temples, and the subtemples were not allowed to grant degrees; neither were nuns allowed to study anywhere else. Nuns were also denied higher forms of Buddhist education at the university level; because of this, they were allowed only to wear black robes, the color of novices, their entire lives. Caught in the same logistical trap that Princess Seishi had experienced, nuns were then denied positions of authority for lack of education, and without authority, they couldn't rise in rank and thus change the policies that had such a great impact on their lives.

On April 25, 1872, the Meiji government issued new rules allowing monks to grow their hair, wear lay clothing, eat meat, and get married. On January 23, 1873, they issued the same rules for nuns, except that nuns would not be allowed to wear lay clothing. Around this time nuns began starting new schools to train novices; they were allowed to teach, but not allowed to grant degrees. While the inner lives of nuns had begun to modernize, they were still strictly limited by the laws.

Tenmyō Jōrin was born to an upper-class family of the name of Mizuno in 1848. She asked permission to be a nun at the age of nine and began training immediately, while still living at home. The next year she left for a temple called Yōrin-an in Kyoto, with her teacher, Kankō-ni. In 1884 Tenmyō became the twelfth abbot of Yōrin-an, which had been in existence since the 1500s. In 1890 she became the Dharma heir of a male teacher named U Hata. It was very unusual at this time for women to practice with men at all. After this, she was received by the abbot of Eiheiji and given the title Ni-oshō, which means "female teacher." (The title oshō was not normally given to women.)

In 1902 Tenmyō became the national leader of nuns. That year she met three other nuns: Hori Taian Mitsujō, Yamaguchi Daishin Kokan, and Andō Jissan Dōkai; all had been nuns from a young age. That year the Sōtō Zen establishment lifted the restrictions against women's training and educational facilities. On May 8, 1903, Tenmyō Jōrin, along with the other three women, established the Aichi-ken Soto-shu Nisō Gakurin, or Nigakurin, a training system for Buddhist nuns. They spent the rest of their adult lives striving to create new monasteries for women during decades of tremendous cultural and political upheaval.

Tenmyō also revived the ceremony of reciting the Anan Koshiki, the old text thanking Ananda for intervening with the Buddha and allowing women to ordain. For decades the nuns at the women's temple did this ceremony monthly, in private. Tenmyō became blind in her old age and died at the age of eighty in 1927.

Ruth Eryu Jokei Fuller Sasaki
(1893–1967)

Ruth Fuller was born in Chicago to wealthy parents and was able to pursue her interest in Asian languages and religion at an early age. In 1930 she met D. T. Suzuki, and a few years later she traveled to Japan to study Zen at Empukuji, south of Kyoto, and Nanzenji in Kyoto. Ruth Fuller was one of the first Westerners to do traditional Zen training in Japan. In 1938 she moved to New York and began studying under Shigetsu Sasaki. He gave her the Dharma name Eryu ("wisdom dragon"). She and Sasaki were teacher and student, cooperative translators, and just before his death in 1944 they were married.

After his death, Fuller returned to Japan to build a training center specifically for Americans and to invite a Japanese Zen teacher to come to the United States. She worked tirelessly as a translator of Hakuin and other masters. Beginning in 1956, and using her own money, Fuller restored the temple where she was staying, Ryosenan, a subtemple of the Rinzai temple Daitokuji. There she received a second Dharma name, Jokei, which means "transmission of the Sixth Patriarch's Dharma." Then she served there as the first American woman priest at a temple in Japan. Ryosenan became the headquarters of the First Zen Institute of America in Japan and is still an active temple today. Ruth Fuller lived to be seventy-four years old, dying in 1967.

Nagasawa Sozen
(dates uncertain)

Nagasawa Sozen was the disciple of Harada Daiun Sogaku, and studied both Sōtō and Rinzai methods in the first half of the twentieth century. Sozen, whose name means "Zen ancestor," was abbot of the Tokyo Nuns' Practice Center and had many disciples of her own, both nuns and laywomen. Though her teacher was Sōtō, he taught her the koan method as well. She developed a reputation for being tough and abrupt with her students, assaulting them verbally and frequently ringing a student out of the interview room without warning. She was also fond of the kyosaku stick during retreats, which she conducted with severity. For all this ferociousness with her students in the beginning of their practice, she was known to be loving and kind after they had a breakthrough—it was said she had no mercy before, nothing but mercy after.

In her time she was one of the only women running a Zen practice center and leading retreats without the supervision of a male Zen master. Some of her students led lives of considerable difficulty owing to the war, including women who had lost children and husbands and whose daily lives were marked by deprivation. Her students revered her and showered her with love. "For the trouble taken by my teacher I have truly deep gratitude, which I can only express with hands palm to palm," wrote one lay student of Sozen. "I bow to you." In 1956, after her death, they collected their experiences of her in a book called *A Collection of Meditation Experiences.*

Nagasawa Sozen was head nun of Kannonji, one of the most important Japanese convents, and during the 1930s and 1940s she became a national leader for Japanese Buddhist women. She was in charge of the second Sōtō Sect National Meeting of Nuns in the 1930s.

Kendō Kojima
(1898–1994)

Kendō Kojima was born in 1898 and lived into the 1990s; she was a great leader for Buddhist women. Time after time she created opportunities to do things Sōtō Zen nuns had either not done for centuries or never done before. She was the first leader of the Pan-Japanese Buddhist Nun Association and executive director of the Japanese Federation of Buddhist Women; she was the only Japanese person at both the third and fourth international Buddhist conferences.

At the time of the war, Sōtō nuns were given only a fraction of the money allotted to men, their education was limited, transmissions were not officially recognized, and they couldn't be part of the administration's highest level. In spite of the immense cultural and political chaos surrounding her, Kojima risked everything in her life to insist on these things being changed. Her story is well told in detail by Paula Arai.

Yoshida Eshun
(1907–1982)

Yoshida Eshun was born near the beginning of the twentieth century. She was a student of Eko Hashimoto Roshi's, who taught at Eiheiji for many years and in other temples. He was abbot of Ungoji Zen temple. Her parents had forbidden her from becoming a nun, but one night in her early teen years, she hid under her futon and cut off all her hair, and they relented. She became abbot of Kaizenji in Tsushima City, and founded a convent there, which was explicitly open to laypeople as well as ordained.

When she was sixty-three years old, in 1970, she came to the United States and taught many people how to sew traditional robes, okesas and rakusu, in *nyohō* (the way of the Dharma). Most of us still sew our robes the way she taught, except for changes due to measuring systems. She encouraged Shunryu Suzuki and Dainin Katagiri to do Jukai more often and make people sew their own robes. She trained both Blanche Zenkei Hartman and Tomoe Katagiri. Tomoe recalls her as a strict teacher, with "big ears, like Dumbo's."

Houn Jiyu Kennett
(1924–1996)

Peggy Kennett was born in England and served in the Royal Navy during World War II. She then studied medieval music, specializing in the organ. At the same time she began studying Theravada Buddhism and eventually joined the London Buddhist Society. At a meeting there in 1960 she met Keido Chisan, the abbot of Sojiji, one of the two head temples of the Sōtō Zen church. Kennett first traveled to Malaysia, where she was ordained by Sek Kim Seng, and then to Japan, where she became Keido Chisan's disciple. She received transmission from him in 1963. He eventually gave her inka, the authority to teach independently. For a time she served as the abbot of a small temple in Japan.

Houn Jiyu Kennett was the first Western woman to practice at Sojiji. After Keido Chisan's death, she found her position in Japan more difficult and moved in 1969 to San Francisco. There she founded the Zen Mission Society (now known as the Order of Buddhist Contemplatives). In 1971 the group bought land in northern California, near Mount Shasta, where Kennett founded Shasta Abbey, Shasta Zen Chisanji. She envisioned it as a traditional residential Sōtō training temple that would accept men and women equally; as many as fifty monks lived there at a time in a strictly monastic setting. She set the traditional daily chanted liturgy to a Gregorian style of plainsong; the result was similar to traditional Pali and Sanskrit scriptural music. She wrote several books and translated portions of Dōgen's work and other scriptures into English.

Kennett had more than one hundred disciples, many of whom are teaching in the United States today. She died on November 6, 1996, at the age of seventy-two, from complications of diabetes.

Maurine Myo-on Stuart
(1922–1990)

Maurine Myo-on Stuart was Canadian, born in Saskatchewan in the central plains, and trained as a concert pianist. She married and had a career as a musician while raising three children. She started Buddhist practice in her forties, saying that her many years of intensive practice as a pianist prepared her for the sitting practice of a Zen student. For many years she was involved in the Zen Studies Society in New York City, practicing with Eido Shimano, while raising her kids. Eventually her family moved to Boston.

She was ordained by Eido Shimano and led the Cambridge Buddhist Association for eleven years. She was a student of Yasutani as well. At the Dai Bosatsu in New York in 1982, Soen Nakagawa gave her the title of "roshi" in a private conversation; she was never officially made his Dharma heir.

She had many students of her own, mostly women, and led sesshins for women only. She was a refuge for many women who felt they had oppressive or abusive relationships with a male teacher, and she was able to lead such women to a new experience of Zen. She was considered "full of warmth and spontaneity and willingness to invent" and presented her traditional Zen practice in a modern and American style. She never shaved her head, saying, "That would have been an affectation for me. I'm a person in the world." At times she would massage the students' shoulders instead of using a kyosaku during zazen. Occasionally she would play a piece by Bach instead of speaking for teisho. One of her students who was also a pianist played Bach fugues and preludes as her koan study, with Maurine giving her instruction on her playing as her guidance and teaching. "I presented my koan and she directed a few words at the essence of what was coming *through* my playing," said Deborah Polikoff in the book *Turning the Wheel.*

Maureen died on February 26, 1990, of cancer, a few days short of the age of sixty-eight. She had no formal Dharma heirs of her own, but her students have continued to practice and offer the Dharma to others in a variety of ways.

Gesshin Myoko Prabhasa Dharma Cheney
(1931–1999)

She was born as Gisela Midwer and spent her childhood in wartime and postwar Germany, a place of fear and deprivation. On seeing her grandmother's body in a coffin, she had the first of many awakening experiences in her life.

After marrying an American, she moved to the United States in the 1950s. She was a painter. After a powerful experience of awakening that happened without warning, she separated from her husband and began to paint intensively, living alone. After a time she had another unmistakable and life-changing experience of connection to all beings, without obstacles in time and space. Eventually, in 1967, she found her way to the Zen master Joshu Kyozan Denkyo-Shitsu Sasaki and was ordained as a nun. Her name, Gesshin Myoko, means "moon heart, brilliant light."

Gesshin helped Sasaki to develop Cimarron Zen Center in Los Angeles. They trained together intimately for years and did sanzen twice daily as Gesshin mastered the traditional koans. Gesshin supervised the founding and construction of the Mount Baldy Zen Center, a monastery.

She became a teacher in 1972, then went to train in Japan at Tenruiji with the master Hirata, also studying Japanese and traditional calligraphy. After that, she was head teacher of Cimarron.

In 1980 Gesshin began traveling throughout the United States and Europe. She developed a style of sesshin that was more accessible to older students and even to families. She set the schedule only after meeting the participants. Often this meant shorter periods of zazen and more frequent and longer periods of walking meditation, both fast and slow. She incorporated yoga as well. Sometimes she began sesshin with "gentle" days to get people started or offered a "free-form" day without a schedule in the midst of the retreat. "You go with the nature of things," she said.

Over time, she became convinced that Rinzai Zen had limitations and studied other methods. She became involved with the Vietnamese Buddhist community in Los Angeles and trained with the head of the United Vietnamese Buddhist Churches of America, Venerable Dr. Thich Man Giac, who named her a Dharma heir, the forty-fifth generation in the lineage of Vietnamese Rinzai Zen. He gave her the name Thich Minh Phap, or Prabhasa Dharma, which means "wondrous light." After that, she often went by this name. In 1983 she founded the International Zen Institute, which has several branches in the United States and Europe, and published her poetry.

After she was diagnosed with ovarian cancer in 1991, Gesshin began working with cancer patients as well. She died May 24, 1999.

Chant and Dedication

LINE OF WOMEN DHARMA ANCESTORS

Chant leader alone—
We offer the merit of this recitation of _______ in gratitude, to:

All together—
▲ Prajna Paramita Dai·oshō
▲ Maha Māyā Dai·oshō
▲ Ratna·vati Dai·oshō
▲ Shrī·mālā Dai·oshō
▲ Nāga Deva Dai·oshō
▲ Pra·bhūtā Dai·oshō

▲ Maha Pajāpatī Dai·oshō
▲ Khe·ma Dai·oshō
Punnika Dai·oshō
Pata·chara Dai·oshō
Bhad·da Dai·oshō
Dhamma·dinnā Dai·oshō
Su·manā Dai·oshō
Kisa·go·tami Dai·oshō
Su·bhā Dai·oshō
Dhammā Dai·oshō

Suk·kā Dai·oshō
Up·pala·vannā Dai·oshō

▲ Zongchi Dai·oshō
(Tsung Ch'ih)
Shi·ji Dai·oshō
(Shih-chi)
Ling Xing·po Dai·oshō
(Ling Hsing-p'o)
Ling·zhao Dai·oshō
(Ling-chao)
Liu Tie·mo Dai·oshō
(Liu Tiemo)
▲ Mo·shan Liaoran Dai·oshō
(Mo-shan Liao-jan)
Miao·xin Dai·oshō
(Miao-hsin)
Hui·guang Dai·oshō
(Hui-kuang)
Hui·wen Dai·oshō
(Hui-wen)
Fadeng Dai·oshō
(Fa-teng)
Kong·shi Dao·ren Dai·oshō
(K'ung-shih Tao-jen)
Wen·zhao Dai·oshō
(Wen-chao)
Yu Dau·po Dai·oshō
(Yu Tao-p'o)
Miao·dao Dai·oshō
(Miao-tao)

▲ Zen·shin Dai·oshō
Kō·myō Dai·oshō

Sei·shi Dai·oshō
Ryō·nen Dai·oshō
Shō·gaku Dai·oshō
Egi Dai·oshō
Mugai Nyo·dai Dai·oshō
Kaku·zan Shidō Dai·oshō
E·kan Dai·shi Dai·oshō
Myō·shō En·kan Dai·oshō
Kon·tō Ekyū Dai·oshō
Moku·fu So·nin Dai·oshō
Shō·taku Dai·oshō
Yō·dō Dai·oshō
E·shun Dai·oshō
Dai·tsu Bun·chi Dai·oshō
Ryō·nen Gensō Dai·oshō
Tei·jitsu Dai·oshō
Ohashi Dai·oshō
▲ Ten·myō Jōr·in Dai·oshō
Naga·sawa So·zen Dai·oshō
▲ Ken·dō Koji·ma Dai·oshō
Yo·shida E·shun Dai·oshō

E·ryu Jo·kei Dai·oshō
(Ruth Fuller Sasaki)
Myo·on Dai·oshō
(Maurine Stuart)
Ges·shin Myo·ko Dai·oshō
(Prabhasa Dharma Cheney)
▲ Ho·un Jiyu Dai·oshō

Chant leader alone—

We also offer the merit to Nyogen Senzaki, (*additional names may be chanted here*), to teachers in all lineages no longer extant, and to all teachers who died without dharma heirs.

We pray that we may be able to show our gratitude to all women of the dharma in all directions and in the three worlds. May we live our lives in such a way that we honor all those beings, women and men, known and unknown, who gave their lives to the dharma for our present benefit. May the merit of this awaken the heart of compassion and understanding all over the world, and thereby relieve suffering and ignorance. We pray that all beings may prosper and all misfortune cease.

All together—
● All buddhas throughout space and time,
● All honored ones, bodhisattvas, mahasattvas,
● Wisdom beyond wisdom, maha prajna paramita.

This is laid out for ease in chanting. The dot between syllables is to separate sounds. Underlined syllables are held slightly longer for emphasis. The black triangles (▲) indicate a muffled strike on the edge of the gong, used to note particularly significant names. The dark circles (●) indicate a full ring of the gong.

EPILOGUE

the womb

Prajnaparamita

She lies down calmly, and gives birth to Perfect Wisdom. In that moment of release, all women are the same woman, all babies are the same baby. A mother reaches for her child without regard to its individual nature, and any wish she might have had about its form vanishes. The baby is perfect just as it is. Prajnaparamita gives birth to all beings and all things with equal love, seeing the unique perfection of each one. She gives birth to Mahayana Buddhism, to Nagarjuna and to Zen, to Bodhidharma and Dōgen, to Aryadeva and Tsong Khapa Lo Sang Drakpa, and to you, and me.

Vast and deep and endless; a single, brief sound. She is short and long, fine and broad, a matrix, a womb, a nest, a web, a loom, a vessel, the ocean, the seed.

She is everything the baby needs.

Prajnaparamita comforts, guides, encourages us to explore. Like all good parents, she reveals and explains things when the child asks, and only as far as the child can understand. She waits patiently, never tired, never afraid—fierce and protective, but not indulgent. She doesn't spare us mistakes; we are transparent to her. She will always precede us.

Prajnaparamita gives us doubt, that great gift. Eye, ear, nose, tongue, body, and mind—disappearing into no eye, no ear, no nose, no tongue, no body, and no mind. Then *no* disappears, and there is only *yes.* Birth and death disappear, until there is only life. Pursuit and hunger, disappearing, until there is nothing to pursue, no need. Until there is no I, no you, no path, no end to the path, no beginning. With such great doubt, we can awaken to possibility. She shows us space without obstacles. She shows us how to live in objectless totality with intimacy so close there is no gap.

She is the Tathāgatagarbha, the Womb, the Great Mother of All the Buddhas—including you, including me. She sings a lullaby to help us rest, words beyond words:

going, going, always going on beyond, always becoming—always being—always birthing and being born Buddha—gate, gate, para gate, para sam gate, bodhi svaha

NOTES

INTRODUCTION

1. See two commentaries on the *Lotus Sutra,* the *Miao-fa lien-hua ching wen-chü* and the *Fa-hua i-shu,* and two commentaries on Queen Śhrīmālā and gender: *Sheng-man i-su pen-i* and *Sheng-man pao-k'u.* Shakyamuni's vow 138 in the *Karuṇā-puṇḍrika-sūtra,* also called the Hige-kyo, is quoted in Dōgen's fascicle *Shukke Kudoku.*

INDIAN ANCESTORS

1. This version of Yaśodharā's and Rāhula's life is unusual. It is recorded in the book *Sacred Biography in the Buddhist Traditions of South and Southeast Asia.* It ends with her attempting suicide by leaping off the palace roof. She is saved when her husband miraculously catches her. After this, she is ordained.

CHINESE ANCESTORS

1. Huiguang, Huiwen, Fadeng, and Wenzhao are included in a thirteenth-century collection called the *Jia tai pudeng lu.* This long record has never been translated into English as a whole, so these women who were famous in their time are almost unknown today. I am deeply indebted to Judith Boltz, whose translation of the sermons of these women is used here, and to Ding-hwa Evelyn Hsieh for guidance and help with the translation.

JAPANESE ANCESTORS

1. The *Cambridge History of Japan* makes a convincing case for the 538 date instead of the more commonly accepted 552.

2. The ancient chronicles of Japan (*Nihon Shoki*) state that she was 11 years old in 584, and I take her birth date from there. (Japanese birth dates differ from Western style and this could be either 11 or 12 years of age.) If she was 12 in 584, when she ordained, she would have been 16 when traveling to Korea.

3. Hōryūji, and Shitennoji, Chuguji, Koryuji, Tachibanadera, Wada-hai-dera, and possibly other temples were established at this time.

4. The *Sutra of the Sovereign Kings of the Golden Light Ray* (*Konkō myō saishō ō gyō*) is a story of the Buddha visiting the deva kings. Its importance to a new government is clear in passages such as this, cited by Tsunoda: "In this way the nations of the world shall live in peace and prosperity, the people shall flourish, the earth shall be fertile, the climate temperate, and the seasons shall follow in the proper order. The sun, moon, and the constellations of stars shall continue their regular progress unhindered. The wind and rain shall come in good season. All treasures shall be abundant. No meanness shall be found in human hearts."

5. The statue is made of 490 tons of copper mixed with seven and a half tons of lead and tin in an alloy, with 990 pounds of gold dissolved in mercury for the gilding.

6. Nara Museum records and Todaiji archives and priests do not state when Todaiji was officially closed, only that "customarily" women did not enter the Buddha halls and that this custom began not long after the temple was finished.

7. The form of transmission at this time is veiled in secrecy, and few records exist describing it. William Bodiford writes, "It is extremely difficult if not impossible to determine the degree to which current practices compare to those of historical times." This imagined scene takes place in a real room, facing a real garden in the modern Yōkōji complex, and envisions a settled intimacy between student and teacher that many of us know today. As for its historical truth, the Yōkōji records describe the meaning of the transmission of Shozen, Sonin and Kontō Ekyū in vague and subtle language; one part refers to "shoshi," which is not a complete transmission. Bodiford states that Ekyū was fully transmitted. Whether or not Sonin and Kontō Ekyū could be considered Dharma heirs is partly a matter of interpretation. Some Japanese sources say that Sonin was Keizan's Dharma heir.

8. The woodblock shows Ryōnen kneeling by a fire. Her poem states that she "picked up an iron." Does this mean a clothes iron, a fire iron, or a piece of iron? Barbara Ruch believes that she stopped at an outdoor place where women were ironing with flat containers filled with charcoal and used one of these tools. I prefer the image of her choosing a private place.

MALE CHINESE NAMES*

Pinyin	**Wade-Giles**
Huike	Ta-tsu Hui-k'o
Daoyu	Tao-yu
Daofu	Tao-fu
Jinhua Juzhi	Chin-hua Chü-chih
Dayi Daoxin	Ta-i Tao-hsin
Nanquan	Nan-ch'üan P'u-yüan
Chengyi	Ch'eng-i
Zhaozhou Congshen	Chao-chou Ts'ung-shĕn
Pang Yun	P'ang Yün
Shitou Xiqian	Shih-t'ou Hsi-ch'ien
Mazu Daoyi	Ma-tsu Tao-i
Danxia Tianran	Tan-hsia T'ien-jan
Zihu	Tsü-hu
Baizhang	Pai-chang
Guishan Lingyou	Kuei-shan Ling-yu
Gaoan Dayu	Kao-an Ta-yü
Guanqi Zhixian	Kuan-chi Chih-hsian
Linji Yixuan	Lin-chi I-hsüan
Dongshan Liangjie	Tung-shan Liang-chieh
Xuefeng Yicun	Hsüeh-fĕng Yi-t'sun
Guifeng Zongmi	Kuei-fĕng Tsung-mi
Yangshan Huiji	Yang-shan Hui-chi
Hui neng (Dajian Huineng)	Ta-chien Hui-nĕng
Fan Zuyu	Fan Tsu-yū
Kumu Fazheng	K'u-mu Fa-chen
Foyan Qingyuan	Fo-yen Ch'ing-yüan

Yuanwu Keqin	Yüan-wu K'o-ch'in
Fayan Wen'i	Fa-yen Wen-yi
Ganlu Zhongxuan	Kan-lu Chung-hsūan
Fan Xun	Fan Hsün
Sixin Wuxin	Ssü-hsin Wu-hsin
Langye Yongqi	Lang-yeh Yung-ch'i
Deshan	Tě-shan
Huang Shang	Huang Shang
Dahui Zonggao	Ta-hui Tsung-kao

**Names are listed in order of appearance in text.*

CHINESE WOMEN ANCESTORS

Pinyin	**Wade-Giles**
Zongchi	Tsung Ch'ih
Shiji	Shih-chi
Ling Xingpo	Ling Hsing-p'o
Lingzhao	Ling-chao
Liu Tiemo	Liu Tiemo
Moshan Liaoran	Mo-shan Liao-jan
Miaoxin	Miao-hsin
Huiguang	Hui-kuang
Huiwen	Hui-wen
Fadeng	Fa-teng
Kongshi Daoren	K'ung·shih Tao-jen
Wenzhao	Wen-chao
Yu Daopo	Yu Tao-p'o
Miaodao	Miao-tao

BIBLIOGRAPHY

Addiss, Stephen. *The Art of Zen: Paintings and Calligraphy by Japanese Monks: 1600–1925* (New York: Henry N. Abrams, 1989).

Aitken, Robert, trans. *The Gateless Barrier: The Wu-men Kuan (Mumonkan)* (San Francisco: North Point Press, 1990).

Arai, Paula Kane Robinson. *Women Living Zen: Japanese Sōtō Buddhist Nuns* (Oxford: Oxford University Press, 1999).

Arnold, Sir Edwin. *The Light of Asia* (London: Trübner & Co., 1879).

Aston, W. G., trans. *Nihongi: Chronicles of Japan from the Earliest Times to A.D. 697* (London: George Allen & Unwin, 1956).

Auboyer, Jeannine. *Daily Life in Ancient India*, trans. Simon Watson Taylor (New York: Macmillan, 1965).

Azuma, Ryushin. "Keizan-zenji and Women" (January 1998). In Ryushin Azuma, *Zen and Women.*

Basham, A. L. *The Wonder That Was India* (New York: Grove Press, 1954).

Bodiford, William M. *Sōtō Zen in Medieval Japan* (Honolulu: University of Hawaii, 1993).

———. "The Role of Women in Medieval Sōtō Zen." Paper presented to the conference "The Culture of Convents in Japanese History," Columbia University, New York (November 21–22, 1998).

Boucher, Sandy. *Turning the Wheel: American Women Creating the New Buddhism* (San Francisco: Harper & Row, 1988).

Cabezon, José Ignacio, ed. *Buddhism, Sexuality, and Gender* (Albany: State University of New York Press, 1992).

Chang, Garma C. C. *The Buddhist Teaching of Totality: The Philosophy of Hwa Yen Buddhism* (University Park: Pennsylvania State University Press, 1971).

Chung, Priscilla Ching. *Palace Women in the Northern Sung: 960–1129* (Leiden: E. J. Brill, 1981).

Chung-yuan, Chang. *Original Teachings of Ch'an Buddhism* (New York: Vintage, 1971).

Cleary, Thomas, trans. *Sayings and Doings of Pai-chang: Ch'an Master of Great Wisdom* (Los Angeles: Center Publications, 1978).

———, trans. *The Book of Serenity: One Hundred Zen Dialogues* (Hudson, NY: Lindisfarne Press, 1990).

———, trans. *The Flower Ornament Scripture: A Translation of the* Avatamsaka Sutra (Boston: Shambhala, 1993).

Cleary, Thomas, and J. C. Cleary, trans. *The Blue Cliff Record* (Boston: Shambhala, 1992).

Cook, Francis Dogun. *How to Raise an Ox* (Los Angeles: Center Publications, 1978).

———. *Hua-yen Buddhism: The Jewel Net of Indra* (University Park: Pennsylvania State University Press, 1977).

Cranston, Edwin A., trans. and commentary. *A Waka Anthology* (Palo Alto, CA: Stanford University Press, 1993).

De Bary, William Theodore, Chang Wing-tsit, and Burton Watson. *Sources of Chinese Tradition* (New York: Columbia University Press, 1960).

Dresser, Marianne, ed. *Buddhist Women on the Edge: Contemporary Perspectives from the Western Frontier* (Berkeley, CA: North Atlantic Books, 1996).

Dumoulin, Heinrich. *A History of Zen Buddhism* (New York: Random House, 1963).

———. *Zen Buddhism: A History*, vols. 1 and 2, trans. James W. Heisig and Paul Knitter (New York: Macmillan, 1988).

Dunn, Charles J. *Everyday Life in Traditional Japan* (Tokyo: Tuttle, 1969).

Dutton, Anne. "Temple Divorce in Tokugawa Japan: A Survey of Documentation on Tōkeiji and Mantokuji." In *Engendering Faith: Women and Buddhism in Premodern Japan*, ed. Barbara Ruch (Ann Arbor, MI: Center for Japanese Studies, 2002).

Ebry, Patricia Buckley. *The Inner Quarters: Marriage and the Lives of Chinese Women in the Sung Period* (Berkeley: University of California Press, 1993).

———. *The Cambridge Illustrated History of China* (New York: Cambridge University Press, 1996).

Fa-hsien. *A Record of the Buddhist Countries* (Peking: Chinese Buddhist Association, 1957).

Faure, Bernard. "The Daruma-shu, Dōgen and Sōtō Zen." *Monumenta Nipponica* 42 (Spring 1987): 22–55.

———. *Visions of Power: Imagining Medieval Japanese Buddhism,* trans. Phyllis Brooks (Princeton, NJ: Princeton University Press, 1996).

———. *The Red Thread: Buddhist Approaches to Sexuality* (Princeton, NJ: Princeton University Press, 1998).

———. *The Power of Denial: Buddhism, Purity, and Gender* (Princeton, NJ: Princeton University Press, 2003).

Fenollosa, Ernest F. *Epochs of Chinese and Japanese Art,* vol. 1 (New York: Dover, 1913).

Ferguson, Andy. *Zen's Chinese Heritage: The Masters and Their Teachings* (Boston: Wisdom Publications, 2000).

Fister, Patricia. *Art by Buddhist Nuns: Treasures from the Imperial Convents of Japan* (New York: Institute for Medieval Japanese Studies, 2003).

Frédéric, Louis. *Japan: Art and Civilization* (New York: Harry N. Abrams, 1969).

Freese, Barbara. *Coal: A Human History* (Cambridge, MA: Perseus Publishing, 2003).

Friedman, Lenore. *Meetings with Remarkable Women: Buddhist Teachers in America* (Boston: Shambhala, 1987).

Heine, Steven. *The Zen Poetry of Dōgen: Verses from the Mountain of Eternal Peace* (Boston: Tuttle, 1997).

Heinrich, Amy V., ed. *Seasons of Sacred Celebration: Flowers and Poetry from an Imperial Convent* (New York: Institute for Medieval Japanese Studies, 1998).

Horner, I. B. *Women Under Primitive Buddhism: Laywomen and Almswomen* (New York: E. P. Dutton, 1930).

Hsieh, Ding-hwa E. "Images of Women in Ch'an Buddhist Literature of the Sung Period." In *Buddhism in the Sung,* ed. Peter N. Gregory and Daniel A. Getz Jr. (Honolulu: University of Hawaii Press, 1999).

Golas, Peter. "Rural China in the Song." *Journal of Asian Studies* 39, no. 2 (1980): 291–325.

Grant, Beata. *Daughters of Emptiness: Poems of Chinese Buddhist Nuns* (Somerville, MA: Wisdom Publications, 2003).

Groner, Paul. "Vicissitudes in the Ordination of Japanese 'Nuns' During the Eighth Through the Tenth Centuries." In *Engendering Faith: Women and Buddhism in Premodern Japan,* ed. Barbara Ruch (Ann Arbor, MI: Center for Japanese Studies, 2002).

Gross, Rita. *Buddhism After Patriarchy: A Feminist History, Analysis, and Reconstruction of Buddhism* (Albany: State University of New York Press, 1993).

Hall, John Whitney. *Japan from Prehistory to Modern Times* (New York: Dell, 1970).

Hall, John Whitney, Marius B. Jansen, Madoka Kanai, and Denis Twitchett. *The Cambridge History of Japan* (Cambridge: University of Cambridge Press, 1993).

Hoshin, Anzan. *Matrix of Suchness: The Lion's Roar Discourse of Queen Śrīmālā* (Ottawa: Great Matter Publications, 1995).

Idema, Wilt, and Beata Grant. *The Red Brush: Writing Women of Imperial China* (Cambridge, MA: Harvard University, Asia Center, 2004).

Kamens, Edward. *The Buddhist Poetry of the Great Kamo Priestess: Daisaiin Senshi and Hosshin Wakashū* (Ann Arbor, MI: Center for Japanese Studies, 1990).

Katsuura, Noriko. "Tonsure Forms for Nuns: Classification of Nuns According to Hairstyle." In *Engendering Faith: Women and Buddhism in Premodern Japan,* ed. Barbara Ruch (Ann Arbor, MI: Center for Japanese Studies, 2002).

Keene, Donald. *Travelers of a Hundred Ages: The Japanese as Revealed Through 1,000 Years of Diaries* (New York: Henry Holt, 1989).

King, Karen L., ed. *Women and Goddess Traditions in Antiquity and Today* (Minneapolis: Fortress Press, 1997).

King, Sallie. "Awakening Stories of Zen Buddhist Women." In *Buddhism in Practice,* ed. Donald S. Lopez Jr. (Princeton, NJ: Princeton University Press, 1995).

Kuitert, Wybe. *Themes in the History of Japanese Garden Art* (Honolulu: University of Hawaii Press, 2002).

Lazrove, Anne. "Mugai Nyodai and Muso Soseki's Revival of Shomyaku-an." Unpublished paper, Yale University (1997).

Leggett, Trevor. *Zen and the Ways* (Boulder, CO: Shambhala, 1978).

———. *Warrior Koans: Early Zen in Japan* (London: Arkana, 1985).

Leighton, Taigen Daniel. "Sacred Fools and Monastic Rules: Zen Rule-Bending and the Training for Pure Hearts." In *Purity of Heart and Contemplation: A Monastic Dialogue Between Christian and Asian Traditions,* ed. Bruno Barnhart and Joseph Wong (New York: Continuum, 2001).

Leighton, Taigen Daniel, and Shohaku Okumura, trans. *Dōgen's Pure Standards for the Zen Community: A Translation of the Eihei Shingi* (Albany: State University of New York Press, 1996).

Levering, Miriam. "Lin-chi (Rinzai) Ch'an and Gender: The Rhetoric of Equality and the Rhetoric of Heroism." In *Buddhism, Sexuality, and Gender,* ed. José Ignacio Cabezon (Albany: State University of New York Press, 1992).

———. "Stories of Enlightened Women in Ch'an and the Chinese Buddhist Female Bodhisattva/Goddess Tradition." In *Women and Goddess Traditions in Antiquity and Today,* ed. Karen L. King (Minneapolis: Fortress Press, 1997).

———. "Dōgen's *Raihaitokuzui* and Women Teaching in Sung Ch'an." *Journal of International Asian Buddhist Studies* 21, no. 1 (1998): 77–110.

———. "Lineage or Family Tree? The Implications for Women." In *Innovative Women in Buddhism: Swimming Against the Stream,* ed. Karma Lekshe Tsomo (Richmond, VA: Curzon Press, 2000).

Lillehoj, Elizabeth. "Princess, Nun, Artist, and Poet: Negotiated Identities of Two Seventeenth-Century Women." Unpublished paper, DePaul University (1997).

Mason, R. H. P., and J. G. Caiger. *A History of Japan* (Boston: Tuttle, 1997).

McCrae, John R. "The Antecedents of Encounter Dialogue in Chinese Ch'an Buddhism." Thesis, Indiana University.

Mikoshiba, Daisuke. "Empress Kōmyō's Buddhist Faith: Her Role in the Founding of the State Temple and Convent System." In *Engendering Faith: Women and Buddhism in Premodern Japan,* ed. Barbara Ruch (Ann Arbor, MI: Center for Japanese Studies, 2002).

Morris, Ivan, trans. *As I Crossed a Bridge of Dreams: Recollections of a Woman in Eleventh-Century Japan* (New York: Dial Press, 1971).

Murcott, Susan. *The First Buddhist Women: Translations and Commentary on the* Therīgāthā (Berkeley, CA: Parallax Press, 1991).

Nakai, Patti. "Women's Liberation in Buddhism." Available at: http://www.livingdharma.org/Living.Dharma.Articles/WomenLibInBuddhism-Nakai.html.

Nishijima, Gudo Wafu, and Chodo Cross. *Master Dogen's Shobogenzo* (Woking, Surrey, UK: WindBell, 1994).

O'Halloran, Maura. *Pure Heart, Enlightened Mind: The Zen Journal and Letters of Maura "Soshin" O'Halloran* (Boston: Tuttle, 1994).

Okumura, Shohaku, ed. *Dōgen Zen and Its Relevance for Our Time: An International Symposium Held in Celebration of the 800th Anniversary of the Birth of Dōgen-Zenji* (Palo Alto, CA: Stanford University, Sōtō Zen Education Center, 1999).

Okumura, Shohaku, and Taigen Daniel Leighton, trans. and commentary. *The Wholehearted Way: A Translation of Eihei Dōgen's Bendōwa with Commentary by Kōshō Uchiyama Roshi* (Boston: Tuttle, 1997).

Packard, Keiko Imai. *Old Tokyo* (New York: Oxford University Press, 2002).

Paul, Diana Y., ed. *Women in Buddhism: Images of the Feminine in the Mahayana Tradition* (Berkeley: University of California Press, 1979).

Price, A. F., and Wong Mou-Lam, trans. *The Sutra of Hui Neng* (Boston: Shambhala, 1969).

Ransom, G. B. *Japan: A Short Cultural History* (Rutland, VT: Tuttle, 1931).

Red Pine, trans. *Poems of the Masters: China's Classic Anthology of T'ang and Sun Dynasty Verse* (Port Townsend, WA: Copper Canyon Press, 2003).

Rexroth, Kenneth, trans. *One Hundred Poems from the Japanese* (New York: New Directions, 1964).

Rhys Davids, C. A. F., and K. R. Norman, trans. *Poems of Early Buddhist Nuns (Therīgāthā)* (Oxford: Pali Text Society, 1989).

Roberts, J. A. G. *The Complete History of China* (Gloucestershire, UK: Sutton, 2003).

Ruch, Barbara, ed. *Engendering Faith: Women and Buddhism in Premodern Japan* (Ann Arbor, MI: Center for Japanese Studies, 2002).

Sansom, G. B. *Japan: A Short Cultural History* (Tokyo: Tuttle, 1973).

Sasaki, Ruth Fuller, Yoshitaka Iriya, and Dana R. Fraser, trans. *The Recorded Sayings of Layman P'ang: A Ninth-Century Classic* (New York: Weatherhill, 1971).

Schober, Juliane, ed. *Sacred Biography in the Buddhist Traditions of South and Southeast Asia* (Honolulu: University of Hawaii Press, 1997).

Senzaki, Nyogen. *The Iron Flute: 100 Zen Koans* (Boston: Tuttle, 1964).

Sheng-yen, trans. and ed. *The Poetry of Enlightenment: Poems of Ancient Ch'an Masters* (Elmhurst, NY: Dharma Drum, 1987).

Shih, Heng-Ching. "Women in Zen Buddhism: Chinese Bhiksunis in the Ch'an Tradition." East Asian Libraries Cooperative (2002), available at: http://www.geocities.com/zennun12_8/chanwomen.html.

Sinclair, Kevin, *The Yellow River: A 5,000-Year Journey Through China* (Los Angeles: Knapp Press, 1987).

Singer, Kurt, ed. *The Life of Ancient Japan: Selected Contemporary Texts Illustrating Social Life and Ideals Before the Era of Seclusion* (Tokyo: Japan Library, 2002).

Snelling, John. *The Buddhist Handbook* (Rochester, VT: Inner Traditions, 1998).

Souyri, Pierre François. *The World Turned Upside Down: Medieval Japanese Society*, trans. Käthe Roth (New York: Columbia University Press, 2001).

Sponberg, Alan. "Attitudes Toward Women and the Feminine in Early Buddhism." In *Buddhism, Sexuality, and Gender*, ed. José Ignacio Cabezon (Albany: State University of New York Press, 1992).

Stevens, John. *Lust for Enlightenment: Buddhism and Sex* (Boston: Shambhala, 1990).

Tanahashi, Kazuaki, trans. *Moon in a Dewdrop: Writings of Zen Master Dōgen* (San Francisco: North Point Press, 1985).

Tsai, Kathryn Ann, trans. *Lives of the Nuns: Biographies of Chinese Buddhist Nuns from the Fourth to Sixth Centuries.* A translation of the *Pi-ch'iu-ni chuan*, compiled by Shih Pao-ch'ang (Honolulu: University of Hawaii Press, 1994).

Tsomo, Karma Lekshe, ed. *Sakyadhita: Daughters of the Buddha* (Ithaca, NY: Snow Lion, 1988).

Tsunoda, Ryūsaku, William Theodore de Bary, and Donald Keene. *Sources of Japanese Tradition* (New York: Columbia University Press, 1958).

Varley, H. Paul. *Japanese Culture* (Honolulu: University of Hawaii Press, 1984).

Waddell, Norman, trans. *Wild Ivy: The Spiritual Autobiography of Zen Master Hakuin* (Boston: Shambhala, 2001).

Warner, Jisho, Shōhaku Okumura, John McRae, and Taigen Daniel Leighton, eds. *Nothing Is Hidden: Essays on Zen Master Dōgen's "Instructions for the Cook"* (New York: Weatherhill, 2001).

Wayman, Alex, and Hideko Wayman, trans. *The Lion's Roar of Queen Śrīmālā: A Buddhist Scripture on the Tathāgatagarbha Theory* (New York: Columbia University Press, 1974).

Wertime, Theodore A. *The Coming of the Age of Steel* (Chicago: University of Chicago Press, 1962).

Wright, Arthur F. *Buddhism in Chinese History* (Palo Alto, CA: Stanford University Press, 1959).

Yamada, Kōun, trans. *Gateless Gate* (Los Angeles: Center Publications, 1979).

Yampolsky, Philip B., trans. *The Zen Master Hakuin: Selected Writings* (New York: Columbia University Press, 1971).

Yang Hsüan-chih. *A Record of Buddhist Monasteries in Lo-Yang*, trans. Yi-t'ung Wang (Princeton, NJ: Princeton University Press, 1984).

Yusa, Michiko. "The Lotus Sutra and Dōgen's Zen Hermeneutics." Paper presented to the international conference on the *Lotus Sutra* (2002).

Zongxu, Zou. *The Land Within the Passes: A History of Xian*, trans. Susan Whitfield (New York: Viking, 1991).

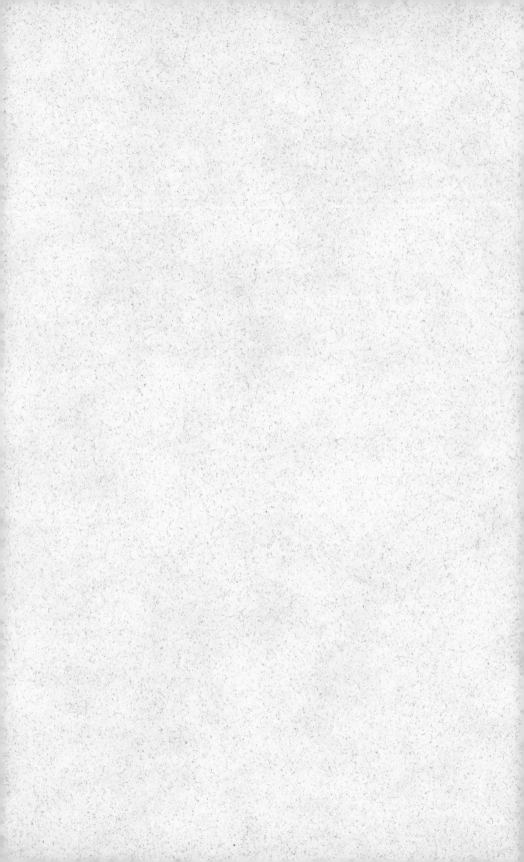